Rescue at the Top of the World

Shawn T. Shallow

Paradise Cay Publications, Inc.
Arcata, California

Cover design by Rob Johnson, www.robjohnsondesigns.com
Book design and editing by Linda Scantlebury, www.we-edit.com

All photographs from Tuttle, Captain Francis (1899). *R.C.S. Report of the cruise of the Revenue Cutter Bear and the overland expedition for the relief of whalers in the Arctic Ocean, from November 27, 1897, to September 13, 1898.* The journals of Lieutenant David Jarvis, Lieutenant Ellsworth Bertholf, and Surgeon Samuel Call. Treasury Department Doc. 2101, Division of Revenue Cutter Service. Washington, D.C.: Government Printing Office.

Printed in the United States of America
First Edition

ISBN 0-939837-65-X

Published by Paradise Cay Publications, Inc.
P. O. Box 29
Arcata, CA 95518-0029
800-736-4509
707-822-9163 Fax
paracay@humboldt1.com

To Margaret,
my loving wife

SPECIAL THANKS

Special thanks for research assistance to:
> Frank Larson, U.S. Bureau of Indian Affairs
> Laura Pereira, New Bedford Whaling Museum
> Captain Gene Davis (retired), Coast Guard Museum Northwest
> Kathleen Lopp Smith, author

Special thanks for editing to Linda Scantlebury. Linda took a rough stone and turned it into a gem.

Special thanks to Matt Morehouse for challenging me to create a book of significance.

Special thanks to Mike Han for saving my life to write this book.

Special thanks to Jason Griffin for making the process fun.

FOREWORD

Welcome to one of the greatest overland rescue expeditions of all time.

It was November of 1897. President McKinley had just received word that the bulk of the U.S. whaling fleet was icebound north of Alaska. This was devastating news. Just thirty years earlier the fleet had been similarly trapped and not a single crewman survived. Five years before that, the crews of thirty-two ships slowly starved to death and disappeared without a trace. The United States couldn't absorb another horrendous loss of this nature. They needed a miracle.

President McKinley summoned L. J. Gage, Secretary of the Treasury. The Revenue Cutter Service, under his control, seemed the only hope. But there were big problems: The only ship patrolling those waters, the *Bear*, had just returned from Alaska. Worse still, over 1,500 miles of pack ice now separated the closest landing point and the stranded men. Even if the Cutter Service could launch a rescue, dogsleds couldn't carry enough food to feed the three hundred men until spring. If the rescuers obtained food en route, they still probably couldn't survive four months of sub-zero temperatures, unstable ice, wolf packs, and mountain passes never before traveled in winter.

Unlike the participants in the later Shackleton Antarctic expedition, who anticipated danger as part of a grand undertaking, these Arctic rescuers suffered incredible hardship without any hope of glory. They had no crowds to cheer their return, or publicists to promote their memoirs. In fact, countless heroic acts by Eskimos, missionary guides, sailors of the Revenue Cutter Service, and the whalers themselves, were lost for a century.

Now we have them back. Shawn Shallow has worked with several researchers over a two-year period to assemble century-old journals of the actual participants, articles, ships' logs, congressional reports, and academic examinations. These materials he has meticulously pieced together and dramatized to recreate the event in vivid detail, adding dialogue to place you in the center of the action.

I hope you enjoy this journey into the annals of Coast Guard history played out during the Alaskan Gold Rush. You'll see that everyday people like the men and women of the U.S. Coast Guard can rise to become heroes in a national crisis. And you'll understand how the Coast Guard earned its motto, *Semper Paratus*—always ready.

Sincerely,

William F. Merlin
Rear Admiral
United States Coast Guard (retired)

Admiral Merlin's 34-year career included serving as Chief of Command, Control and Communications USCG; and Commander, Eighth Coast Guard District, where he was responsible for Coast Guard operations in eight states on and near the Gulf of Mexico. His sea duty included three trips to Point Barrow and the Arctic on an icebreaker. He is a Distinguished Graduate of the Industrial College of the Armed Forces, holds a Master of Science degree from the United States Navy Postgraduate School at Monterey, and is a graduate of the United States Coast Guard Academy.

PREFACE

In 1897 an unexpectedly early winter surprised a group of American whaling ships carrying three hundred men, trapping them in the Arctic ice, 1,500 miles from where navigable waters cease in winter, and triggering one of the greatest overland rescue missions in the world's history. Here was the milieu in which this rescue occurred:

1897 was a time of accelerating change in America. The Civil War had ended; Reconstruction was winding down. Industrial giants were emerging; immigrants were rushing to supply big business with cheap labor. Industrial strife and labor unions would soon follow.

Technology, too, was advancing. The electric light bulb, invented just twenty years earlier, was beginning to appear in cities across America. The steam engine was slowly appearing on sailing ships.

The telegraph was still the primary means of communication; five years hence the first message would be transmitted via a new transoceanic cable linking the United States and Europe. The Wright brothers would toil away for five more years before their strange contraption would fly.

Arthur Conan Doyle had begun publishing the first Sherlock Holmes mysteries. Charles Dickens not long before had written "A Christmas Carol." Herman Melville, author of the famous whaling story *Moby Dick*, had died just eight years earlier.

William McKinley had just been elected president of the United States. Victoria was queen of England and empress of India. The czar was still the supreme power in Russia, as European undercurrents ultimately leading to World War I were already beginning.

While the U.S. Army, Navy, and Marine Corps maintained full-time forces, the Air Force wouldn't be a separate entity for another fifty years. The Revenue Cutter Service had not yet joined with the Life Saving Service to form the U.S. Coast Guard. However, it was solely responsible for patrolling the new Alaskan territory acquired from Russia.

The Gold Rush of the Upper Yukon had just begun.

Traditional industries such as commercial whaling were in decline. While whale oil and parts were still needed for street lamps and industry, whale oil was no longer in high demand to light the American home, which was increasingly turning to electricity. Likewise, whales, which had once filled the oceans, were becoming harder to find: those whaling ships remaining in service were forced to hunt in Arctic waters for the elusive bowhead.

This was the bigger picture in 1897. But for the whalers trapped in the ice and those who struggled to rescue them, all that mattered was surviving that devastating Arctic winter.

Although this disaster was every bit as dramatic as the famous Sir Ernest Shackleton struggle in Antarctica years later, the Arctic plight of the whalers and their ultimate rescue would remain relatively unknown in the twentieth century. Shackleton's crew represented the best of British society; the crews of the eight American whaling ships included lowly laborers of every ethnicity. Without the benefit of fundraisers and publicists, the Americans' heroics were all but forgotten.

It is with great pleasure that we here bring you the story of these whalers and their rescuers, meticulously built from century-old diaries, obscure articles, ships' logs, and congressional reports. It is a story of ordinary people whom circumstance called to struggle, to endure, to sacrifice, and to triumph.

As you read this dramatized narrative, we invite you to refer to the notes section (pages 249 through 268) for additional information about these real people and their times.

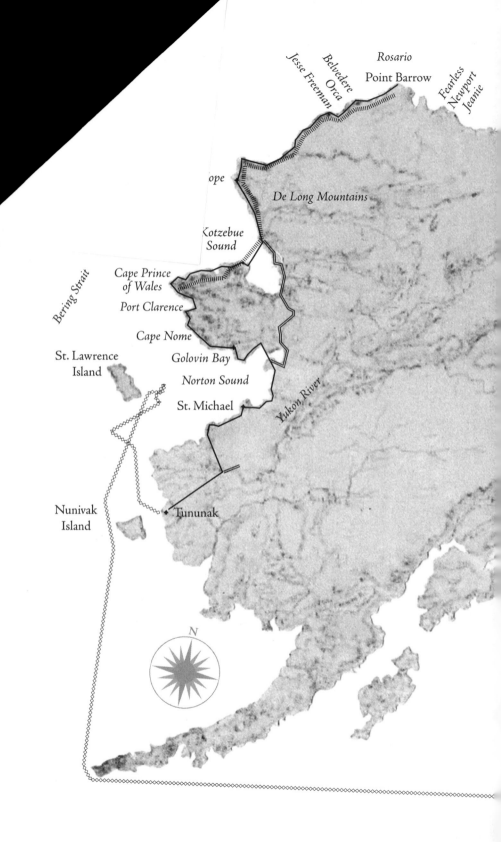

Rosario

Belvedere
Orca
Jesse Freeman

Point Barrow

Fearless
Newport
Jeanie

De Long Mountains

ope

Kotzebue
Sound

Cape Prince
of Wales

Bering Strait

Port Clarence

Cape Nome

Golovin Bay

St. Lawrence
Island

Norton Sound

St. Michael

Yukon River

Nunivak
Island

Tununak

N

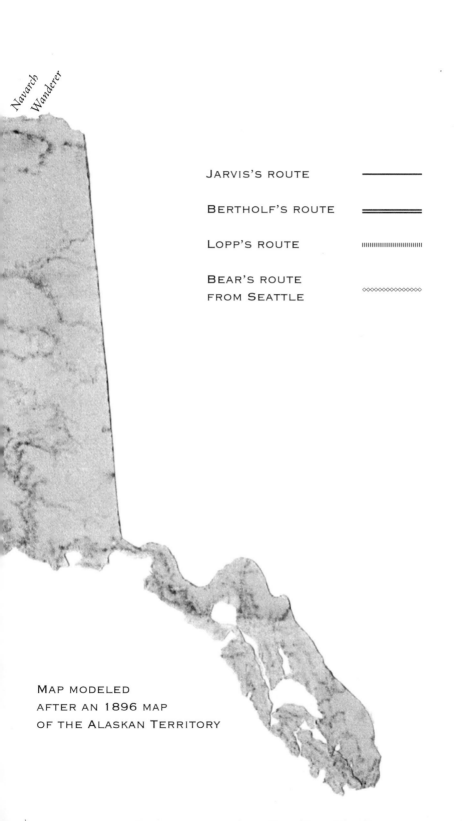

Navarch

Wanderer

JARVIS'S ROUTE ————————

BERTHOLF'S ROUTE ════════

LOPP'S ROUTE ⅢⅢⅢⅢⅢⅢⅢⅢ

BEAR'S ROUTE
FROM SEATTLE ◇◇◇◇◇◇◇◇◇◇◇◇

MAP MODELED
AFTER AN 1896 MAP
OF THE ALASKAN TERRITORY

Rescue
at the
Top of the World

Chapter One

Jim . . .   *It Begins*

Jim Lee could hear his heart racing. He paused and looked at his hands. They were shaking. It wasn't from the physical exertion—it had been at least twenty minutes since he stopped chopping a hole in the ice. No, it was from setting the keg of black powder and small lead balls.

Jim glanced over his shoulder at the ship's carpenter, who was staring his way. "Hurry up, ya bugger, I'm freezing!" the carpenter grumbled, his jagged teeth chattering.

Jim didn't answer. Instead, he just rubbed his hands together, pretending to be warming them. If for no other reason, he didn't want the men to see he was scared.

Turning back to his work, he gingerly set the last bottle of powder in a small crack in the ice. He reflected ironically that years earlier, gunpowder of this nature generally spelled death or dismemberment to a Civil War soldier. Now it meant life to the trapped whalers.

Rising, he adjusted his coat, brushed off his hands, and stepped back a dozen feet to grab the middle of a 25-foot-long, 2-inch-wide strip of wood holding a long fuse.

"This better work," said Zach, a lowly foremast hand like Jim, "or we're dead for sure."

Nobody bothered to answer. They all knew their fate if the explosion didn't clear the ship.

"All right then, let's do it," said the carpenter.

Jim winced as the carpenter lit the fuse. The smoking flame rapidly moved along the flexible arc of wood as the three men gently pushed it forward to the bottles in the ice. When it was clear that the pole was seated to bring the flame to the main concentration of powder in the bottles, the men set down the fuse pole and ran to the *Orca*, forty yards distant.

The *Orca* was a brig, a whaling ship from the east. Considered state of the art for 1897, she had three masts, a full complement of sail, a steam engine, and a tryworks in the middle for processing whale blubber. She was part of a larger fleet of eleven ships, most caught in the Arctic ice like themselves.

Jim scurried up *Orca*'s gangplank. At the top, he joined the rest of the crew looking on, fifteen men in all.

"Blow up, ya' bugger!" yelled the captain. Jim had never done this before and didn't know whether to cover his ears. He noticed that none of the other men moved, so he just stood in the back and watched. As the young hayseed on his first cruise, it seemed as if that's what he always did anyway, to stay out of trouble.

As the explosion sounded, every man covered his head with his hands. Small particles of frozen seawater shot in all directions as the ice pack suddenly inched open. It was not unlike lumberjacks setting off explosives in timbers clogging a river bottleneck as they attempted to float tree trunks downstream for processing.

A small channel opened as some of the broken ice began to flow southward. "Well, we might make Point Barrow after all," said the captain, pleased. Turning to the mate, he ordered, "Get us under way." One sentence, pleasantly delivered, was all any man had ever gotten out of the skipper during a day.

"Aye, aye, sir," returned the mate smartly. He knew to be quick when the captain gave an order.

"Come on, you lazy buzzards, tumble to it!" yelled the mate, imitating the style of the "old man." Hastily the men hauled up the gangplank and moved into their positions.

Whaling in this part of the world was tricky business. If a ship didn't time things exactly, she would run into disaster. The season began in the spring, when large schools of bowhead whales traveled north under and through cracks in the pack ice. Once the whales got toward the top of

Alaska, they turned east following the shore, where they eventually made their way to breeding grounds. There, in the northern waters of the polar rim, they mated until late fall. As the mating season closed, they turned southward, traveling to the southwest along the Siberian shore to the warmer waters of the Pacific.

Whaling ships like *Orca* waited until August when the ice had melted enough to create open sea channels. Then they sailed north through the Bering Strait between Alaska and Siberia to the whales congregating above. There they hunted whales in earnest until mid-September. By month's end, they knew to start sailing to the southwest along the Siberian shore, following the whales to avoid the onslaught of winter. If the whalers waited too long, they risked being trapped by the ice. Their ship would be crushed and they would be left to die. Their race started at the top of the world and didn't end until mid-October when they made it south through the Bering Strait.

But this year something was different. Nature had decided to change the timetable. In late August, frigid northerly winds blew pack ice onto the shore and began freezing the ocean much earlier than expected. New ice appeared and blocked the southward route. A handful of the fleet had had an unusually good season and began their southerly trek early, barely making it through the Bering Strait in time. The rest of the fleet, eight ships, were caught in the ice north of Point Barrow, the northernmost tip of North America.

With *Orca* caught fast in the ice, each of her crew knew the fate that awaited him. Thirty years earlier the fleet had been similarly trapped. Not a single man was ever heard from again. Five years before that, a larger fleet of thirty-two ships had met a similar fate. The list of sailors that became permanently part of the pack ice was extensive. Now *Orca* was stuck; she had to escape or perish.

Jim looked on as the wind, gusting out of the northwest, filled the sails and *Orca*'s hull began to break free.

"Is she going to make it?" the carpenter asked nobody in particular as he leaned over the side to scan for progress.

"Maybe," answered Joiner the sailmaker, an experienced Arctic hand.

3

Jim took it in; he often watched Joiner to figure out how to secure a line or other matters of seamanship. Whalers weren't much on formal training.

As Joiner spoke, cracks in the ice appeared. *Orca* began to move. She seemed to cry in pain, straining against her icy shackles, but she lurched ahead anyway. Each time the *Orca* made headway, she hit the ice, rose slightly, and staggered forward. Finally she was moving relatively unimpeded through the ice and slush.

"Well, at this rate we won't make it home," observed the carpenter, "but we might make Point Barrow."

"This old tub's *got* to make Point Barrow," declared Joiner, turning to the carpenter. "That's your job!"

The carpenter didn't answer; a wooden whaler was no match for millions of tons of pack ice. He simply turned and went back to his cabin amidships. He was only considered half a seaman by foremast hands who did the actual work of sailing the ship. They reminded him of that fact periodically with comments like the one just delivered.

Point Barrow, lying hundreds of miles to the south, had suddenly become the most important place on earth to the men of the *Orca*. Jim, listening, had been able to piece together its importance from earlier discussions in the forecastle. As the youngest member of the crew, he typically kept to himself rather than be derided for knowing nothing. But in this way, by observing and listening, he'd learned a lot about whaling and the life of a seaman. He'd learned that the Point Barrow station was built after the fleet had been similarly frozen in the ice a quarter century earlier, with all hands lost. To prevent that happening again, the U. S. government built the Point Barrow whaling station.

It sounded impressive. In reality it was just a handful of shacks near an Inupiat Eskimo village.

The foremast hands were bitter when they talked about it. Apparently the maintenance of a station for simple whalers like themselves, considered by many to be low-class ruffians, was too costly. So the government closed the station and sold the buildings to a private whaling company. The men knew there wouldn't be the food and facilities to house them should the ship be destroyed, but they headed for it anyway. At the top of the world, you didn't have many choices. The alternative was living on the ice for as long as they could––which wouldn't be long. At least the station would provide shelter.

Jim stood motionless for a moment watching the ship slowly grind her way through the ice. In all the excitement, he'd forgotten to protect his face. Now it stung from the Arctic wind that whistled off the pack ice, laden with small particles of frost and snow, as if fine glass had been shattered in the air. The relentless bite of a –45 degree wind chill stung like bees protecting their hive. At this temperature, with each wisp of Arctic cold your eyes ached as if freeze-dried. If you didn't cover your face and hands––not an easy task on a whaling ship––you'd lose parts of your nose and fingers to frostbite.

"Why yer standin' here?" asked Joiner. "Yer arms'll become part of the gunwale if yea ain't careful."

Jim turned toward the stout, weathered man. Standing there in a long wool coat, more patches than original cloth, Joiner was the prototypical whaler. With a dark complexion and a full black beard, Joiner looked as if he belonged at sea––that is, with the exception of his bright blue eyes and constant smile.

"I was just watching the *Belvedere* and *Freeman*," said Jim. The *Orca*, *Belvedere*, and *Jesse Freeman* had been traveling together. And like *Orca*, the other two ships, two miles distant, were now attempting to blow themselves free of the ice. Their explosions boomed and echoed across the icy wastes.

Unlike Joiner, Jim was making his first cruise aboard an Arctic whaler––or any whaler, for that matter. In fact, this was also Jim's first time away from home.

"You ought to be afore the mast wit' yer mates," said Joiner. The watch had changed, and many of the men of Jim's watch had gone to the warmth of the forecastle, in the bow of the ship. As a sailmaker, Joiner himself lived farther back toward the stern in a small cabin amidships, behind the tryworks, with the cook and carpenter. It was a foul place when the tryworks were fired up to cook the blubber of a recently captured whale. Cooking blubber was a dreadful, disgusting job for everyone on the ship,

5

but necessary for extraction of the whale's oil. And this oil was an integral part of their dreams to make their fortunes by selling the precious liquid for fuel lamps.

"The 'bergs make you scared?" asked Joiner with warmth, not malice in his voice. Joiner had watched the young landlubber be derided constantly for not knowing the basics of rigging a three-masted whaler, then be accused of laziness for taking the time to relieve his seasickness by throwing up over the side. After a month of watching Jim bear the abuse, Joiner had stepped in and befriended the young man.

"Yeah, it's a little scary," answered Jim. "I hear a lot of stories from my bunk." Unlike Joiner, who had a special job, Jim was a general seaman. This meant he lived in a room in the bow of the ship below the forecastle. The bunks were cramped and foul, but they were generally warm, one benefit of bodies being packed like sardines in a can. During the evening, men passed the time regaling each other with stories of other voyages in the Arctic. Many of the stories involved men who died trapped in the ice or who fell overboard into the frigid waters.

"Don't worry, kid, this old tub's built to take a beating," said Joiner, slapping the top of the rail as if patting an old cow that's given more than her share of milk.

Jim smiled warmly at Joiner. He understood that Joiner was out to make him feel better, as he always did. If it hadn't been for Joiner, Jim wouldn't have been as physically and mentally strong as he now was. Like many other hayseeds, Jim had been pretty seasick at first. Joiner took him aside after he had emptied his guts over the rail.

"You're well cleaned out, Jim; you need to give up your longshore swash and switch to hearty salt beef and sea bread. That'll fix you right up."

And Joiner had been right. Before Jim knew it, his ribs were well sheeted, like a vessel ready for the next gust of wind.

Now Jim lowered his smile to create a serious look of concern and signal Joiner that he needed a straight answer. Joiner gave him the truth.

"Well, I won't kid you," said Joiner, the smile wiped from his own face. "Whaling in these parts has more than its share of danger. Many a ship's been caught in the ice with no way to make it home. We got at least two months of food on board because that's what we needed to get to San Francisco. After that, we got to get some elsewhere. Maybe we can find help near Point Barrow. We'll stay on the ship as long as she lasts, maybe till spring if we get a safer anchorage."

"Can the ship last that long if we get to a better place by some islands?" asked Jim, trying to conceal his fear.

Joiner placed his arm around Jim's shoulder, as a grandfather would comfort a grandson who just lost a fish at their favorite fishing hole. "I don't rightly know, Jim."

Chapter Two

Jim . . .   Trapped

Jim was violently shaken awake in his bunk. Looking around the forward hold, he could barely make out the crew in various stages of undress. Some men were sitting up in their bunks, some were half in and half out of their berths, and others lay sprawled in shock on the floor. Obviously all were violently thrown by what had shaken the ship.

"What happened, did we run aground?" asked Jim.

"Don't be dumb," somebody shot back. "We're north of the straits."

"So what is it, then?" continued another hand. "A ship?"

The fourth mate, Charlie Walker, yelled down the scuttle. "All hands ahoy! Bear a hand up."

Jim hastily pulled on his pants and wool sweater. At first he thought to skip his outer coat and run up the ladder like most of his crewmates. But he was struck with an ominous premonition to take the extra time to get his coat, gloves, and hat. You never knew if you might be stuck on deck for a while.

"Tumble up there, men, tumble up," Walker yelled. The foremast crew sprang on deck at a run, and Jim scrambled quickly up the forecastle ladder. Arriving at the top, he saw two immense walls of ice at the stern, like mountainous teeth clutching the ship in a deadly grip.

The captain, first mate, and third mate were examining the pilothouse. It was badly damaged, almost as if it had been hit by a bomb.

"What happened?" Joiner queried the mate hurriedly scurrying about in the confusion.

"We almost made open water when we got caught between two ice floes. They ripped out the stern post and steering gear. And damn it all if the wheel didn't get blown clear into the pilothouse!"

Jim ran to the center of the main deck as the ship began to shudder. Her hull groaned as thousands of tons of pressure relentlessly squeezed the infrastructure. With each compression, the ship let out another cry.

A crack pierced the air and everyone froze, listening to the splitting and creaking of wood. Stunned, the men's eyes met in awful comprehension: The hull had breached and icy-cold sea water was flooding the ship.

The captain yelled, "Get your gear and prepare to abandon ship!"

The men hesitated in disbelief.

"Come on, get going!"

"Get your things, Jim," urged Joiner.

Each man quickly made his way to his respective compartment. Defying their urge to flee, the sailors continued with their tasks. They could perform any duty, despite the overwhelming urge to leave the ship. Such discipline was born of working on yardarms at heights upward of a hundred feet in a heavy gale. In those conditions, they were often seconds away from being thrown into a pitching sea and certain death. It was all part of the job.

As foremast hands, they had little in the way of extra clothes. Each man tossed his meager possessions—including his letters from home—in sea bags and climbed the ladder to the main deck.

"You there!" yelled the captain. "Help the cook grab any provisions we can carry."

Three men jumped into the cookhouse next to the tryworks. There wasn't much to grab. The main food stores were in the lower decks of the ship, but there wasn't time to retrieve them.

"All right, boys, abandon ship." These were probably the words most feared by any hand on a whaler or merchant ship.

Another loud crack boomed from below. "Damn," swore the carpenter. "She must have breached again. We're all dead if we stay."

Jim was barely aware of what was happening around him. His body shook in fear. As if in a bad dream, he felt himself being pulled over the gunwale as officers and men clambered over the side to escape.

Jim stared back at the doomed ship in shock. From where he stood, *Orca* looked fine, almost as if she were waiting to be unloaded. But he knew she was like a chick still in the egg, slowly being devoured by a large snake. The ship had no escape. She would slowly die a miserable death.

The men stood briefly in confusion on the ice.

"You!" growled the captain. "Lash those together," he said, pointing to the scattered provisions they had managed to get off the ship. Jolted into action, the men quickly lashed the supplies into three makeshift sleds to be pulled by two or three men each.

"What now, Captain?" asked Charlie.

"The *Belvedere* and *Freeman* will see we're in trouble. Just walk in their direction, toward that open water there, and pray to God they see us."

As Jim began to slog through the snow, boots crunching, he was struck by the irony of the backdrop. The combination of ice, snow, and sky was mesmerizing in its beauty. The sunlight bounced off the ice crushes as off a prism of glass. As far as the eye could see, the white of the ice merged with the blue of the sky, forming a tapestry of pure color. It would have made a beautiful painting. It was ironic that this scenery could also be the instrument of their death, like the poison of a beautiful flower.

Some say your life passes before your eyes at death. In this instance, Jim's life sputtered through his memory—not exactly his whole life, just the part that had brought him to the *Orca*.

Like many whalemen, Jim had gone to sea to make his fortune. He knew the wages were generally bad. But every once in a while, a ship hit it big. As a foremast hand, Jim would get a small take of the ship's revenue, about a 1/189th lay. It was a small take, but if the ship did well, Jim would take home a tidy sum.

Traditionally, whale ships sailed the southern waters in pursuit of their prize. The whales they killed would be sold for oil in lamps; baleen, or slats from the whale's upper palate, was used for whips and walking canes; whale bone found its way to the fashion industry for the construction of corsets.

Whaling got harder as whales became more and more scarce. But the north had something the south didn't: the bowhead. When bowhead whales were discovered swimming the northern waters of the Arctic, the whaling industry resurged, for each bowhead could generate up to 300 barrels of whale oil and 3,000 pounds of bone. That was triple the typical southern whale's yield. Bowheads became the winning lottery ticket. After a successful whaling run, a laborer like Jim could go home and buy a farm or set up a business.

So an Arctic whaler was the choice, but not an easy one. Chasing the elusive bowhead didn't come without a price. That price included the relentless bone-chilling cold of the Arctic and the possibility of being trapped in the advancing winter pack ice—and death. Jim's dreams of riches were replaced by the realization that he may have gotten a losing lottery ticket. His pursuit of riches had just been replaced by the pursuit of life.

As the crew of *Orca* trudged across the ice, they could see *Belvedere* and *Jesse Freeman* working their ways toward them. With steam as well as sail, *Belvedere* was the more powerful of the two. She had quickly taken the lead and was now only a mile distant.

"Come on," said Joiner, heading for the ships.

"Can they make it?" asked Jim, a quaver in his voice.

"I suspect so, but it's tricky business. If they get close enough to pick us up without getting caught between them floes, like *Orca* did, we still got us a problem. The ship bobs, the ice bobs. You can miss your footing and fall in the water."

Carefully, carefully Captain Milford guided *Belvedere* to the edge of the floe. Cautiously, cautiously *Orca*'s crew inched to the edge of the bobbing ship. Then within moments, the crew of *Orca* was snatched up the side onto the deck of *Belvedere*.

It had been a race against winter to save all the men and escape in the rapidly freezing water. But winter was winning. To the sailors on board *Belvedere*, it became clearer by the minute that a trip home would be impossible. Right now they had to just find a safer anchorage, where they could weather the crushing ice.

Chapter Three

Jim...   *Belvedere*

Jim huddled in the fetal position and tried to get warm. Just two days ago he and his fellow crewmen had escaped death on the ice by climbing aboard the *Belvedere* and *Jesse Freeman*. After rescuing the men, both ships turned to the northeast and fought their way through thickening ice in an attempt to reach Point Franklin, where they intended to seek refuge from the relentlessly advancing sea ice by holing up behind the Sea Horse Islands. There, the stable ground ice of the islands would stop the encroachment of sea ice, and possibly save the ships.

Unfortunately, only two hours after they set out for the islands, *Jesse Freeman* had been caught and crushed just as *Orca* had been. *Jesse Freeman*'s crew, in its turn, had escaped to the *Belvedere*. Three crews now crammed spaces intended for one.

As junior foremast hand, Jim was relocated to the forward steerage, a v-shaped hold that stowed lines and other gear of the ship. Although uncomfortable, the tight space provided warmth. Next to Jim crouched thirteen-year-old Jake. As the captain's cabin boy, he wasn't seen as part of the crew or as a real sailor. He had none of the duties typically assigned a foremast hand. Instead, his chores included cleaning the captain's cabin, then cleaning the officers' cabins, mending their clothes, and doing any necessary small chores. Since Jake normally slept in the forward steerage, he was right at home. Now he reached out to his guest.

"Jim?"

Startled, Jim turned. "Yes, Jake?"

"What's going to happen to us? I mean, how long will we be here?"

"Not too long."

"No?"

"There's not enough food. If we can't fish for it, or hunt it, we'll have to go somewhere else."

"Where else could we go?"

"The whaling station at Point Barrow."

"You mean where Captain Millard dropped off some food?"

"That's right."

At the beginning of September, Captain Millard, master of the *Belvedere*, had had a premonition about the early advance of winter. As a result, he put in at the Point Barrow whaling station and dropped off his excess provisions to help any ship caught in the ice. The next day the *Belvedere*, *Jesse Freeman*, and *Orca* moved quickly southward. Unfortunately, winter came earlier than even Captain Millard anticipated and trapped all three ships. Now *Belvedere* was left with only enough provisions for about a month. After that, they would have to find more food, or starve.

"How far is Point Barrow?"

"I'm not sure. Maybe two days or more over the ice." Two days over the ice was like an eternity to men ill-equipped for the trip. They could easily freeze to death in that amount of time.

Jake just sat and absorbed the information. He had already learned in the past week that a hold full of men had little patience for an inquisitive cabin boy. He'd avoided ill treatment by staying apart. But he trusted this new friend, a novice like himself.

Over the next few days, the men generally kept to themselves. With no shipboard duties and cramped space, time hung heavy. Besides cold and deprivation, boredom and loneliness were the biggest enemies. To fight off these silent killers, the foremast hands were generally quiet and purposeful in their daily routines.

Jim tried to compose a letter. He paused as he looked around the dimly lit forward hold. By the dwindling light he could still make out what each man did to pass the endless time.

"Damn!" grunted an older foremast hand, drawing Jim's eye.

Jim could see the man sitting cross-legged, carving on a whale tooth and trying to keep warm. His slow, purposeful scrimshaw etchings generally went on for hours at a time. Usually he made some exclamation of frustration every hour or so as he tried to avoid permanent mistakes.

Jim knew that the extensive time this hand spent on carving wasn't at all unusual. Many of the men passed the time making intricate gifts for loved ones. In a manner of speaking, this kept them connected to their families back home. It was amazing what could be produced from whale parts. They made yarn winders, pie crimpers, small boxes, and of course, hairpins. Each man took great pains to carve scenes of tearful reunions and even more tearful goodbyes. Somehow their day-to-day work on the carved objects strengthened their hope of survival and even evoked the spirits of their families for support.

Yet important as these crafts were, they were secondary to letters. Like Jim, each man guarded like gold the letters he had rescued from the ship. And why not? They had been harder to come by than the most precious gems, for the "saltwater mail system" was notoriously unreliable.

Under this ad hoc arrangement, ships outbound from home took on mail with their cargo. As they encountered another ship, they'd look through the satchel to see if any letters were intended for that crew. Letters often had little more than Jim Jones, Pacific Ocean as an address. Usually passing ships found one or two letters, at most, intended for their crew. These ships would then proceed to foreign ports and drop off their satchel in hopes that another visiting ship might trip upon letters bound for them.

This haphazard system often resulted in lost or destroyed mail. Most letters never found their intended recipient; likewise, letters sent by the crew seldom made it home. To increase the odds of mail delivery, the men would write multiple letters, hoping that even one would find its mark. Given the odds against its safe delivery, receiving a letter was a cause for great celebration.

Under these circumstances, a love letter affectionately written and rejoicingly received was dearly cherished. Most men had read and reread their letters so many times that they had them memorized. After learning one by heart, they'd sometimes sell it to a lonely shipmate for anything from money to two tins of tobacco. Even though there was profit involved in the trade, their action was often more out of friendship than anything else.

But on the *Belvedere* there was no trading. These letters were guarded like life itself.

As Jim brooded in the gloom, thoughts of his present situation brought more bitterness. Even if he survived, the whaling catch was lost and there were no wages to be paid. He'd be lucky to make it home a pauper. At the moment, the divine plan didn't seem to be in his favor.

Chapter Four

Jim. . .   Orca's Graveyard

Another day passed and the *Belvedere's* food supply was already feeling the strain. Something had to be done, or they'd all starve sooner rather than later.

As a first step, Captain Millard ordered the building of a small shack on shore about a mile from the ship. On land the food would be safe from any cracks that might form in the ice. *Belvedere* had made the Sea Horse Islands, but now, stuck in their congealing waters, she could still fall prey to the advancing ice mass.

Dutifully the crew transferred food from the ship to the shack for protection, stretching a line of guide rope the full mile between the shack and the *Belvedere* in case someone had to walk to the building in a storm or under cover of darkness. At the shack holding their precious provisions, the crew placed a 24-hour guard to protect the stores. Whether animal or man were to get inside, the trespasser's fate would instantly be sealed.

But it still wasn't enough; they had to find more food. After much consideration, they determined that George Tilton, third mate of the *Belvedere*, would lead a small party back to the *Orca* to search for food. Captain Millard selected a number of men for the duty, Jim among them.

Officers Tilton and Walker led the small group several miles through the gloom to the ice-embedded *Orca*. By the dim, flickering light of their seal oil lamps, she looked like a ghostly mass rising in the shadows. Jim shuddered to see her crumpled hulk, its masts and spars now splayed in all directions, like a man run over by a wagon, his bones reaching for help as he was slowly crushed.

16

Looking at the broken ship, Jim felt a surge of guilt. As ice had pushed upon itself and *Orca*, large boulders of ice had broken off and risen above the surface, like teeth being pushed out of line by molars coming in. It reminded him wryly of the carpenter's jumbled mouth. The sailors, awed, stood for a moment, peering silently at the ghastly scene, dreading to speak lest they wake the demons they feared lurked below.

Finally Tilton spoke. "You've gawked enough," he barked. "Walk around her now. Find us a good boarding point." Obedient, subdued, Jim joined the reconnoiter, his boots crunching on the snow.

To their surprise, the vessel had not been entirely swallowed up. The deck still remained mostly intact. That meant that they could climb aboard and look down the hatches for any openings to the area below, which was probably filled with sea water.

"Well, where do we board?" asked Tilton in a hushed voice as the group now came full circle. He too was feeling the effects of the eerie scene.

"We can span the gap with a quick jump from an ice crush at the stern to the fantail," responded Jim. Since it was a question not requiring seafaring experience, he felt comfortable giving an answer without fear of derision.

"Aye, that looks like the best. Unfurl the line and let's make a quick business of it." The group brought several lines for the boarding party to hold onto, reasoning that if a man went through the ice or the decking collapsed, those who would remain behind to catch the offloaded cargo could grab on and hopefully pull the victim to safety.

"All right then, let's be going now," commanded Tilton. The men slowly took their positions. Nobody was in a hurry to board that ship. It was like visiting a rotting corpse in a deep crypt in a graveyard.

Jim watched as the carpenter went first, his tools clanging as he jumped from the ice to *Orca's* sunken stern. Jim went next. He jumped and managed to land his left foot on the gunwale to slow his descent onto the deck. Sliding forward, he caught himself on the wheelhouse. The rest of the men followed, with two staying on the ice, holding the rope to help with any escape. In the event the boarding crew found and tossed to safety any provisions that had survived the shipwreck, these two would also catch the items and stack them a safe distance from the *Orca*.

They crept cautiously toward the hatches, not wanting to raise the spirits they feared lurked below. Jim peered down the hold from which he'd emerged weeks earlier. It had a new floor of frozen water halfway up to the level of the ice lining the outside of the hull. Though the *Orca* had sunk no farther in the ice, yet the ice within reached too far to the top; they couldn't descend into the space.

"This one's no good," whispered the carpenter.

"All right, go forward."

Carefully the men crept to the forward cargo hatch. It took some effort to break its icy seal. Jim held the lamp over the opening and peered below. Though this hatch had frost on the walls, it wasn't filled with ice as the first had been. Jim was almost disappointed; it meant they had to climb down into the hull.

"All right, all right, the sooner we get going, the sooner we can leave," said Mate Tilton.

Jim handed the lantern to the carpenter and began to descend the ladder. It was slippery and even colder than the surface had been. Reaching up, he received the lantern. If Jim had felt eerie before, it was nothing compared to how he felt now. It was like being in the dark jaws of a huge monster about to bite down and swallow its prey.

There was a loud crack.

Jim spun around into the darkness, expecting to see a ghost. "Who's there?"

He paused, breathless. No one answered. As before, the ship's beams, straining against the pressure of the ice, had cried out from the constant beating.

The carpenter came next, followed by the cook. Since the cook knew the location of the stored food better than anyone, he had been a likely choice to make the trip, despite his round body and protestations to the contrary. Now, eyes wide in his dark face, he scanned the black corners as if to spot the specters hiding there.

"Is this food here?" asked Jim, touching a barrel and addressing the cook.

18

"Is this food?" repeated the carpenter, irritated. He was losing his patience with the food preparer.

Startled, the cook answered. "Dem's potatoes, and dat be flour."

Jim and the carpenter broke the barrels from the lower deck's frozen grasp. Heaving with all their might, they passed the barrels one by one up the ladder. Searching further, they found canned meat and 400 sacks of flour; it took several hours to pack it all out.

Suddenly a loud crack pierced the air. There had been other cracks, but this one was different—louder, more ominous. The splitting wood creaked, as if something were beating it.

"Let's go!" yelled the carpenter.

Despite his round body, the cook sprung up the ladder, followed closely by Jim and the carpenter. The knowledge that the ice could crush the remainder of *Orca's* hull acted like a tailwind to a sprinter. Nevertheless, Jim struggled up the ladder, his hands numbed by the icy wood.

"Damn you, move!" yelled Walker, grabbing Jim's collar from above and dragging him up the ladder.

Orca shuddered as the ice breached her hull and the little ship quickly lost her form. Just in time, the men scrambled over the side to the waiting supplies. As they watched, *Orca's* mizzenmasts began to move, then collapse. The hull slowly began a roll over in the clamping jaw of the ice.

Within minutes, *Orca* was gone.

"That's it, then," said Walker bitterly. As *Orca's* fourth mate, he had just watched an old friend die of a devastating disease.

But there was no time to linger; they had to get back to the *Belvedere* or freeze. The men moving supplies off the ship had already rigged lines around the supplies to haul them over the ice. Now each grabbed a line and began to pull.

Jim looked back, his stomach in knots. Though he was relieved at having made it off the ship in time, he had just seen his dreams of wealth officially vanish for good. He blinked and shook his head to rid himself of the image. It would be a long walk back.

Chapter Five

Jim . . .   *Time to Leave*

"You men of the *Orca* and *Freeman*," a voice yelled through a hatch. "Turn to and collect your gear."

Now that Jim was back on the *Belvedere*, he and his young friend Jake quickly gathered their possessions. During the past two weeks' stay, they had begun a good friendship.

"What's going on?" asked Jim as they reached the main weather deck.

"Point Barrow," was the short reply.

So it was true. For days the men had heard various scuttlebutt ranging from plans for a walk to Point Barrow to going to Cape Smyth. Both schemes had been dismissed out of hand because of the amount of ice travel required. Instead, most of the crew speculated that they'd remain aboard the *Belvedere* and try to support their meager food supply by hunting and fishing. Apparently the crew was wrong.

The three captains stood together on the quarterdeck, a small area not frequented by the crew but designated for official or ceremonial functions. "Let's form it up into ranks," said Captain Millard of the *Belvedere*. He was a fair man, liked by his men.

"Come on, *Orca*, let's go," interjected the chief mate. The men quickly shuffled into three equidistant lines, out of habit standing next to mates from their own respective ships. The officers assembled in a separate line adjoining but perpendicular to the formation. From the men came random coughs occasioned by the cold, but no talking.

After the men were settled and equally spaced, the captain spoke once again.

"Men, as you know, we're in a right tough spot. While we'd like to keep you aboard the *Belvedere*, we can't. We'll all starve if you remain here. The station at Point Barrow should be holding more food and a spare bay. It's still not enough, but it's more than here." He paused and regarded the men. Fear plainly showed on their faces. Point Barrow lay more than sixty miles away—over the ice.

At this point the chief mate spoke up. "So boys, that means we walk."

A groan escaped from two of the crew.

"Here, here," he yelled, "You ain't released yet." He might have been referring to the fact that the formation wasn't released from standing at attention or that even though their ships were gone, they were still part of his command. The men fell silent once again. "You men of the *Orca* and *Freeman*. Grab your gear and prepare to move out. Dismissed!" the chief mate barked, executing the captain's orders.

Jim had mixed feelings about the change. On one hand, the *Belvedere* was a relatively safe place to be. Its anchorage kept some of the ice from piling up and crushing the ship. It had food, as meager as it was. But it also had mind-numbing boredom. The men had been given menial tasks to keep them from scuffling. But the fact that they were idle, under stress, and cramped into a small space meant they were at each other's throats. Maybe walking to Point Barrow was really the lesser of two evils.

The crewmen went below and pulled together their belongings. Jim went down with them, even though he had nothing more below decks.

"Is this good, Jim?" asked young Jake tremulously.

"I think so," fibbed Jim. The truth was, he really didn't know.

"Grab your gear and get topside," interjected a bearded foremast hand. Jim eyed the man. He really didn't like the hand's attitude, but the man was right: they couldn't linger.

Mustering loosely on deck, the crew grabbed some provisions for the walk. They had enough for half rations each for three days. If it took longer, they'd be in worse shape than now. When the men with their foodstuffs were pulled together, they went over the side to begin the trek over the ice. Jim looked back and saw the crew of the *Belvedere* watching them leave.

They had all gone on deck as a sign of respect for the departing crews. He wondered what they were thinking. They were probably happy that they didn't have to make the march to Point Barrow. On the other hand, they didn't have enough food for spring and may have been wishing they'd gone, too. The future looked bleak no matter what you did.

For the remainder of the day, the men of *Orca* and *Freeman* walked in a rag-tag formation to insulate themselves as best they could against the cold. Nobody spoke. Tired and scared, each man preferred to trudge along with his own thoughts.

They took turns pulling the improvised sled bearing the provisions. Intermittently they stopped and ate. They were weak, but said nothing. They knew this was their last hope. As the Arctic fall's early dusk came on they stopped to rest; the men huddled together around seal oil lamps, their knees drawn up to their chests.

"How much farther, Jim?" asked Jake, inching closer for warmth.

"Another day, I guess."

"What do you think it will be like when we get there?"

The carpenter shot an annoyed glance back at Jim. "Pipe down," he snapped. "Can't you see some of us is tryin' to sleep? Hard enough to do sittin' up, wit'out you jawin' away."

Jim went on in a whisper. "There should be a building with a big fire. They'll have some warm food and maybe even some meat."

Jake smiled, but Jim didn't want to continue the conversation. If he got many more questions, he was bound to get into trouble. He'd either have to tell Jake how bad it truly was or else lie outright to lessen the lad's anxiety.

Jim patted the boy's arm. "You get some sleep, Jake, you'll need it," he said in a fatherly tone. Jake smiled warmly and dutifully closed his eyes. Jim did the same.

In the morning they began again. It was still dark at this latitude; the sun would not appear until after 9:00 A.M. Legs aching, desperately needing food, Jim was now staggering. They all were.

Luckily their frigid trek was almost over. In the distance the exhausted men could make out three, maybe four of what could loosely be called buildings—in reality, little more than large shacks. Drawing closer, the men saw what appeared to be a main shack flanked by two side shacks. On the outside of one of these a sign read The Pacific Steam Whaling Company. Another bore the legend The Cape Smyth Whaling and Trading Company. Surprisingly, in front of the shacks stood a small cluster of men, maybe six in all.

At first, no one moved in their direction. Then one of the men separated from the group and walked toward them. As he approached, they noticed he wore a seaman's wool coat, but the furred reindeer-skin pants and boots of an Eskimo. It was as if he belonged to both worlds.

"Hi, Charlie," said Captain Sherman of the *Orca*. All the whaling captains knew Charlie Brower, manager in charge of the Point Barrow Station. Charlie was known to be fair, capable, and good with the Eskimos. His only fault lay in a general arrogance. But years of survival in the Arctic gave a man confidence.

"We knew you were coming," said Brower. "We've been dealing with provisioning the rest of the fleet."

"The *rest* of the fleet?" returned the captain.

"Yes. There are seven ships trapped besides your group. The *Wanderer* and *Mary Hume* are trapped the farthest northeast near Herschel Island. *Newport, Rosario, Fearless,* and *Jeanie* are trapped to their west near Smith Bay. The *Navarch's* gone.

"My God!"

"Yes, and I almost went out with the *Navarch* myself. I was visiting aboard when she got trapped northeast of here. Thirty-one of her crew and I tried to go southwest in hopes of being spotted by another ship. But after a week on the pack ice, I convinced them all we'd be better off on the water. So we climbed onto a piece of ice about twenty feet square and drifted southward.

"After four days, we were spotted by the *Thrasher*. From a distance, they thought we were a walrus," he guffawed. "Only sixteen of us survived that mess," he continued grimly. "Now I'm back here a month later, just in time to deal with *your* life and death struggle."

Captain Sherman's lips tightened.

Brower went on. "We've made small preparations for your arrival. I'm sorry it wasn't more. We didn't know your number exactly. But Fred Hobson, Tom Gordon, and I have been working hard to put something together. We've started preparing berths, and we've collected food from Eskimos as best we've been able. But we've got a long way to go if you're all going to survive until spring."

"I'm sure you've done your best, Charlie," said Captain Sherman.

"Well, come and look it over, then," rejoined Brower.

As the crews of *Orca* and *Freeman* drew near the men clustered by the Point Barrow Station, Jim felt a wave of uneasiness, for he recognized on the faces of the others a look of distaste. It was not the reception Jim had anticipated. From society in general, he'd come to expect disgust, for the public saw whalers as dirty and odorous, perhaps because of the burned whale-oil smell that often permeated their clothes, perhaps because the oil left stains, making them look unclean. Since many whalers came to shore and inevitably got drunk, whalers in general were labeled drunkards. Many Quakers and the like saw their lifestyles away from their families and children as unnatural. They surmised that anyone wanting to stay away from his home was up to something unfamily-like.

Jim had heard that when whalers came ashore in exotic locations such as Tahiti and Hawaii, they were routinely met by missionaries who attempted to curtail their drinking habits. These same missionaries lobbied to enact local laws to stop the whalers from carousing on their one day off the ship. The whalers in their turn saw the missionaries as busybodies, living a life of luxury and leisure at the expense of hard-working churchgoers, many of whom were tithing whalers themselves.

Given these stereotypes, Jim was used to being on the receiving end of a reproachful gaze. But receiving that gaze at a whaling station was totally unexpected. Here he had expected some measure of warmth and congratulations on having made it this far.

Yet Jim's disappointment was about to be compounded. As the crewmen watched, the fifteen officers were waved congenially into one of the larger buildings. The crewmen themselves were brought to a much smaller building, partially opened to the weather, into which berths measuring 22 by 55 inches had been constructed three deep. There was barely room enough to stand between sleeping spaces for eighty men. In the center of this hovel squatted a small cook stove. As Jim peered around the dank shed, he wondered why the majority of the men were being squeezed into this smaller space.

"Well, boys," said Brower, as the men filed into the room shoulder to shoulder, trying to make it inside, "welcome to the Old Kelley House."

"This shack's smaller then a forecastle," complained a bearded crewman, thereby emerging as the group's spokesman. "Why can't we stay in the bigger building?"

"You can't stay in the Refuge Station," responded Brower, "because that's where Edward McIlhenny's conducting his work. He collects wildlife and such for a university back home." McIlhenny was funded by his Louisiana family's fortune acquired producing the highly lucrative condiment Tabasco. This backing allowed him to pursue his interests as a naturalist and collector, interests that had brought him to Point Barrow, the top of the world.

"But that's what the government built it for—I mean, for the refuge of stranded sailors." It was a valid point requiring a response. It was true; before leasing the Refuge Station to the Pacific Steam Whaling Company, the U.S. Government had designed the building to house sailors stranded by an emergency.

Charlie Brower was in the hot seat. "I'm sorry, men. You're right; that building was created to house a hundred men in an emergency, but it's presently lived in by Mr. McIlhenny and his three assistants. He's only agreed to allow the fifteen officers to stay there."

Angry grumbles began among the crewmen. "You mean to tell me," interjected the bearded spokesman, "that we's got to squeeze into a collapsed, rotten shack filled with snow and open to the cold 'cuz this McIlhenny would rather let us freeze than see us stay in the building the government built for us?" The room was hushed. While Brower was the messenger, it was obvious that he wasn't the culprit.

Brower nervously scanned the room. "Listen, McIlhenny's been working just like the rest of us to get food to give you a chance at living.

25

But he ain't going to give up his work, and he paid to rent the place. If he says he'll only take the officers, then he'll only take the officers. Now pick a bunk and settle in."

With that, Brower left. It was clear that he had a temper and was not to be pushed too far.

"Those stinking officers don't care if we freeze," snarled a foremast hand.

"We've got rights," the carpenter snapped.

"Well, boys," said Joiner, "We can stand here and waste time complaining about our lot as sailors, or we can start fixing our quarters. What will it be?"

Again the room fell silent. Everyone knew the answer. The relationship between the officers and crew of a ship had been the same for hundreds of years. It was a two-class system, the haves and the have-nots.

Chapter Six

Jim... Life in the Old Kelley House

Jim lay in his berth, cold and wet, shivering in the fetal position. He thought about stretching out—his body ached from being rolled in a ball for so long—but stretching released trapped body heat. Jim couldn't believe they had six months of this to go—that is, if they survived that long. Only a week ago they had moved into the Old Kelley House, but already it seemed like a lifetime in purgatory. Though the men had enclosed their own sleeping areas and had helped board up the shack's open wall, the complete lack of insulation made it an impossibly cold environment. Snow on the outside and patchwork within stopped air circulation. With no ventilation, and with eighty men cramped into the space, the air was foul, damp, and cold. All the condensation from their breath just stayed in the room. The moisture moved to the walls, where it froze, creating ice three inches thick at the base.

The only source of heat was the small cook stove in the center of the shack. Its iron surface saw frequent use, cooking meat or boiling water for tea and coffee. There wasn't much of either commodity, but it was something. Steam from cooking joined with the moisture of their breath to contribute to the ice forming on walls. When this vapor wasn't freezing, it was condensing and dripping on the men. Jim's own bunk looked and felt like a slightly damp sponge. To add to the grim conditions, body waste was accumulating inside the shack. Things couldn't get much worse.

Earlier, two men had been sent to tell the outside world of the stranded whalers' plight. Charlie Walker, fourth mate of the *Orca*, went by way of Herschel Island. George Tilton, third mate of the *Belvedere*, went down

27

the west coast to the Pacific Ocean. Their routes were to take them over 1,700 miles through the Arctic winter. There was a reasonable chance they wouldn't survive.

But Charlie Brower, in his characteristic way, felt that he had the situation under control. The messengers, at least in his mind, were to tell the world that things were serious, but sustainable. Unfortunately, from the vantage point of the men in the Kelley house, things were anything but sustainable.

The men were on half rations; wood and heating oil were running out. Many of the men had closed in their berths like cracker boxes, using driftwood and anything else they could find, hoping this would help retain heat and shield them from the stench of the shack. In addition, some men had brought small whale-oil lamps from the ship. Their smoke and soot mixed with the foul air and made things even worse. When the men emerged for their food ration, they were covered in oily soot. It was the worst imaginable environment, virtually a cold, dark, wet cave accumulating filth like a septic tank.

In these conditions, the men were becoming hard to control; conflict became a daily occurrence. Rumors flew. Some said it was the fault of the captain who had delayed departure to await the arrival of a boat that was to return his Eskimo paramour to her home. Some said it was because all three captains had spent two vital days in drunken revelry. One thing was certain: the powder keg was about to explode.

Jim suddenly sat upright in his berth. Someone outside was screaming.

"I'll kill you!" yelled the captain.

"Killing me now would be better than a slow death at your incompetent hands," yelled back Joiner.

"I'm still the captain and you'll obey my orders!"

"We don't recognize your orders. Not since you wrecked the ship and abandoned us in this hell hole," screamed Joiner. "Two days you wasted, drinkin' and jawin' with them other captains. Two days could have got us all out of this ice trap!"

"Wrecked the ship?" screamed the captain, swinging his walking cane in a rage. Joiner dodged; two of his officers restrained the captain. Joiner's crewmates had now come outside to watch the fracas.

"You abandoned us to survive in a sewer, while you live it up in that building with tea and crumpets. It's unlawful for a captain to abandon his men and have no care to whether they freeze or starve, while you enjoy the good life," spat Joiner. There was truth in what he said. By maritime law, a captain was obligated to feed and house his seamen. He wasn't allowed to neglect their living conditions. Any maritime court would have considered the conditions the men themselves found to be intolerable.

"It's not my fault we're stuck here," said the captain, now calming under his officers' restraint.

Behind the seaman stood the men of the shack, now virtually empty. Beside the captain the officers clustered, in a tense standoff.

"It don't matter, you still ain't taking any mind to our condition," Joiner snarled, glaring. "We have to fend for ourselves for food. We live in a collapsed shack while you live it up in the building built for our refuge. You, sir, ain't fit for command!"

Enraged, the captain shook against the hold of his officers in an attempt to get at his antagonist. Finding no escape, he finally settled down. Then he smiled wryly as an idea occurred to him.

"All right," the captain said, "I'm only fit for command while there's a ship. If there's no ship, there's no crew."

The crewmen, perplexed at the argument, stood in silence looking at each other, their tension mounting.

The wily captain continued. "If there's no ship and there's no crew, then there's no wages to be paid and no food to be given you. You're no longer bound to the ship."

With that, the men's fear and frustration erupted into shouts. To be released from the ship meant that, for all practical purposes, they were really abandoned. Any food provided would have to be paid for, along with housing and heat. It was as if they had been dropped off in port and left to find a flat as a civilian.

"You can't do that, you yellow good-for-nothing," bellowed a crewman.

"That's against the law!" screamed another.

"This ain't a proper port. We can't be released unless it's a proper port," shouted a third, jaw thrust forward.

Finally, Brower and McIlhenny stepped in. "Hold off!" yelled Brower, "Hold off, now!" Brower repeated his calls for reason; the crewmen surged forward, yelling accusations at the officers and captain. For two tense minutes an attack seemed imminent. Finally the crowd quieted.

As the noise subsided, Brower addressed the crowd of seamen. "What's the problem?" he asked. The gesture underscored how far things had degenerated, for it was a violation of protocol for him to ask the seamen rather than the officers. His act implied that he himself didn't recognize the officers because of their neglect of the men.

"We're starving and freezing in there without a word of care or help from them. The only food and help we get is from you, Brower. Since we can't turn a profit for them, they've abandoned us. And they have the gall to come out here and order us to tend to their comfort!" With that, the men yelled scattered insults at the captain, and a conflict once again erupted. After many words from Brower, the group finally quieted.

"What's your side?" Brower asked the captain, who was red-faced and still shaking from anger.

"I don't have to stand here and answer your inquiries like a common seaman. I'm the captain," he stormed. With those words, he stomped off into the officers' quarters. The rest of the officers were left staring at the angry mob.

"Well," said Brower, "what do we do?" It was an honest question to the group. It appeared that the captain would no longer be involved in governing the men or taking the responsibility for their survival.

Finally, the chief mate from the *Freeman* spoke from the group of officers. "Mr. Brower, it appears that without a ship, nor the means of acquiring food for the men, we're entirely at your mercy for survival. You have access to the Eskimos for any hunting and fishing. You alone have the means for our welfare." It was true; Brower had stepped up in the emergency as only he could have. He'd paid and persuaded hundreds of Eskimos to hunt for food to feed the stranded men, and even though he anticipated submitting a bill to the whaling companies for his services, it was an unselfish effort. Those Eskimos would normally have spent all their time hunting to insure their families' survival. To give this food to the men was a sacrifice, but because of this arrangement, a constant flow of seal, walrus, and wild deer came into the station. If not for Brower and the hard work of the Eskimos, the men would already be dead.

Brower and the men had listened to the mate intently. He seemed to be making a genuine effort at reason. "Yes," confirmed Brower, "our Eskimo friends are the only reason we're alive."

"So we take orders from Brower and McIlhenny only," interjected Joiner.

The men yelled in agreement. "Yeah, to hell with the other buggers."

Brower and McIlhenny looked to the officers for some sort of confirmation. They responded with silence. It was unclear to Jim whether the officer speaking had intended for this to be the outcome, or had accidentally laid the argument for the crew to abandon the chain of command. Given the lack of resources for the captain and officers to provide for the men, it seemed logical to turn to the managers of the whaling station.

"All right then," confirmed Brower, "we'll give the orders. But don't expect it to be easy! We'll have a hell of a time of it trying to survive. We'll need hunting parties, work parties, and the like if we're going to make it."

The sailors generally agreed and seemed to rejoice in their small victory. They patted backs as if they'd just repelled an invader. But the ominous fact remained: The season for caribou in this region was almost over, and this food source would soon run out. To compound matters, Brower had sent word to the captains of the *Rosario, Newport, Fearless,* and *Jeanie* to send their extra men to Point Barrow. There would soon be more mouths to feed.

Chapter Seven

Jarvis...   The Cutter Bear

Lieutenant David Jarvis watched as the crew hauled on the *Bear*'s mooring lines and seagulls circled her rigging looking for a meal. There was nothing like coming home from a tour of sea duty. Gratefully Jarvis squinted up at the sun, relaxing as the breeze caressed his face. It felt good to be in Seattle. After yet another season in the Arctic he couldn't wait for some time in a warm climate with green grass, restaurants, and clean sheets.

Lieutenant Jarvis was not unlike the cutter *Bear*. Tall and thin, with full dark hair and a clean-cut mustache, he had the long, sleek body of an athlete, just as *Bear* was built for speed and service. Jarvis was popular among the crew. He was fair, warm most of the time, and firm when he had to be. On each crew member's first day he made sure the man knew his slot on the watch quarter and station billet, including what watch section he was assigned and where he was supposed to be in an emergency. Jarvis's careful attention to new crew members' introduction to the ship continued as he supervised their shipboard duties. The men appreciated his thoroughness and consistency.

The port was buzzing with activity: Fishing boats hauled in their catches, cargo ships busily unloaded, sailors excitedly strode down gangplanks. Jarvis himself was going to see his young wife. Their child was due in a couple of short months, and he was looking forward to being there to assist her and become a first-time father. He couldn't wait.

The *Bear* had just completed a full season of patrolling over 20,000 square miles of Arctic Ocean. Her mission was to rein in whalers on leave, transport teachers and supplies to mission schools, enforce customs laws, and rescue anyone in need. After her most recent tour of duty, she showed signs of fatigue. Her hull was leaking, the sails needed replacing, and the boilers required refitting. In her own way, *Bear* was glad to be home, too.

As he leaned against the gunwale, Jarvis spotted a messenger waiting impatiently for the gangplank to drop. The moment the gangplank thudded into place, the messenger sprinted up to the deck, clutching a cablegram. "Lieutenant, where might I find Captain Tuttle?" asked the young man breathlessly.

"He's on the aft weather deck," said Jarvis, pointing. Assuming that the lad didn't understand sailor's jargon, he gave him a visual directional.

"Thank you, sir," the messenger called over his shoulder as he scurried to the aft deck.

Like the rest of the crew, Jarvis was anxious to go ashore. But anxious or not, the men had to wait for watch assignments and permission to leave the ship. Even though *Bear* was in port and shipboard duties would be light, she still required a crew.

Jarvis watched attentively as the captain took the cablegram and quickly scanned its contents. Even from this distance, Jarvis noticed that the cable seemed too lengthy to be orders to stand down.

Abruptly the captain left the deck, waving for Jarvis. "Would you follow me below?" he asked cryptically.

"Yes, sir," said Jarvis, suddenly engulfed with foreboding. As executive officer, when *Bear* was at sea he was often consulted in a private meeting with the captain. But what could cause the captain to invoke such a meeting now, as they were preparing for shore leave?

Jarvis strode toward the deck hatch.

"What is it, sir?" asked a young boatswain's mate.

"I don't know," said Jarvis, ducking into the hatch to the wardroom.

The wardroom was a small space, like the other rooms on the *Bear*. With walls of dark wood, it had a porthole on each end and a table at the center. Above the table hung a lantern. The officers were accustomed to assembling there for meals and meetings with the captain. Now, the captain peered out the porthole.

"What is it, Captain?"

"Most of the whaling fleet's been stranded near Point Barrow."

Jarvis recoiled. This was devastating news. Jarvis knew Point Barrow well, having been one of three people to oversee construction of the whaling station there. In fact, *Bear* had left Point Barrow just two months earlier after rescuing the captain and remaining crew of the shipwrecked *Navarch*.

"Why didn't they leave when we did? They had to know that the season was drawing to a close."

"I don't know," the captain said grimly.

Both men stood silently for a moment. The implications for the *Bear* were quite clear.

"We have to return," said Jarvis, disappointment clearly sounding in his voice.

"Yes."

"I'll gather the officers," said Jarvis. Tuttle simply nodded.

As each officer entered the wardroom, he remained standing. It was customary to stay on your feet in the presence of the old man until told otherwise. Finally, with all assembled the captain gave the orders to sit.

"Men," said the captain in an ominous tone, "I know you were looking forward to a long leave . . ." Instantly faces fell; the news couldn't be good.

Captain Tuttle normally spoke very plainly and with authority, in a voice loud enough to be heard above a gale. Now he was quieter— almost tender in his manner. "The ice floes," the captain continued, "are unpredictable, and this year has been worse than most."

The men knew what he was referring to. The signs of winter this year had appeared earlier than expected. As *Bear* had proceeded south through the Bering Strait, the crew saw that some ice was already beginning to form. It was unclear whether it was temporary or a sign of an early season. The Arctic was like that—the weather could change at a moment's notice.

"We also know that whaling season can be cut short in the polar basin," continued the captain. "It was just a matter of time before they would get caught in the ice . . ." the captain paused for a moment, ". . . and the worst has come to pass."

The room was hushed. Every man with Arctic experience had a

premonition of what he was about to hear.

"We've gotten word from the steam bark *Alexander* that the rest of the whaling fleet's been trapped north of Point Barrow. *Alexander* was the last of three other ships that barely escaped through the Bering Strait," said Tuttle slowly.

The wardroom instantly broke into gasps of disbelief. The number of ships and men was a surprise. But a ring of terror was the location, Point Barrow, for all practical purposes the top of the world. Point Barrow, more than 1,500 miles north from where navigable waters ceased in winter and all routes north became solid polar ice. Point Barrow, considered virtually unreachable by land at *any* time, let alone in winter.

Captain Tuttle, usually not one to let subordinates have extraneous words, allowed the group to absorb the impact of the crisis.

"Settle down," said Jarvis finally. As executive officer, it was his duty to be the interface between the captain and the crew in matters of discipline. The room again quieted.

"I'm not going to kid you; this will probably be the biggest rescue attempt in history," continued Tuttle. There was now a collective audible gasp from the group.

"Rescue, sir?" said Chief Engineer Spear. "What do you mean, rescue?"

"Yes, rescue," responded Tuttle. "I don't have to remind you all that we're in the Revenue Cutter Service, and consequently the lifesaving business. Mariners don't get into trouble at our convenience. Crisis is created by bad situations, not just bad judgment."

The room fell silent again. This was a hardy group. Once the initial news wore off, they were all business.

"Sir," said the chief engineer, "I assume you intend to take the *Bear*?"

Captain Tuttle simply nodded.

"We'll need to make repairs quickly and provision the ship," continued Spear, mentally calculating what must be done.

"How long will it take?" asked the captain.

Spear turned to the other men. They quickly conferred, each man representing a different function of the ship, from boilers to food. Jarvis, with the most Arctic experience, made most of the estimations. After just a few moments, the group returned their verdict to the captain.

"Sir, we would normally need well over a month, but we can try to cut that in half by pulling round the clock."

Captain Tuttle was justly proud of his men, for he knew they represented the best in the Cutter Service. Since the *Bear* was almost legendary for her exploits in single-handedly patrolling the entire Alaskan Territory, she attracted the best officers and crew. Now, the men's uncomplaining, quick planning to put back out to sea just as their long-awaited visit home was at hand, confirmed the captain's pride.

Tuttle continued. "Our orders are to make as far north as we can by sea, then land a rescue party to travel overland to the whalers. We're to collect reindeer on the way to sustain the men on our arrival."

The room grew silent again. The plan sounded too fantastic to be real. The captain allowed a long, uncomfortable silence to let each man think through the situation. It was easier than just coming out and telling them that he would need volunteers to go overland.

Finally, Jarvis stated the obvious. "You'll need volunteers to go through the Bering Strait. Going through the ice floes will take the most experienced crew the *Bear*'s ever seen, not to mention an overland expedition going through terrain never tried before in the winter."

"I'm afraid that's the only way," said Captain Tuttle flatly, looking directly at his lieutenant. With over eight years in the Arctic as the executive officer of the *Bear*, Jarvis had more polar qualifications than any man alive, besides himself. And because of his approachability, Jarvis had the most contacts among the native Eskimos. Both Jarvis and the captain knew he would be the logical choice to lead the overland expedition. But how could he, with a pregnant wife due in just a couple of short months?

"I volunteer," said Engineer Spear. Almost all the officers speaking in unison quickly followed him.

The captain waved them off. "Thank you, but I want you to think about it overnight. Talk to your families." Again the captain looked at Jarvis. Then the skipper released the men.

Jarvis left the ship and slowly trudged along the wharf on his way home. He knew he was the obvious choice to lead the overland expedition. But he also knew he had a wife and a child on the way. To leave now would mean abandoning them. As Jarvis walked, he no longer felt the jubilation of coming into port. The seagulls now seemed like a raucous nuisance. What would he do?

Chapter Eight

Jarvis...   Bear Returns

Lieutenant Jarvis watched Nunivak Island recede to starboard. The place
reminded him of the desolate Aleutian Islands they'd passed almost two
weeks ago. The Aleutians looked like nothing so much as a thousand-
mile dam separating the two land masses of the American and Asiatic
continents, with breaks every few miles allowing the sea to flow freely in
between. It was almost like the great wall of an ancient civilization fallen
into disrepair—only in this case, natural volcanoes stretched between the
two continents as far as the eye could see. Jarvis had heard that some
scientists theorized they marked the place where the continents had been
joined millions of years in the past. It seemed a fantastic notion, but why
not? This was 1897. They were on the verge of entering the twentieth
century. Jarvis often marveled at the new technology he enjoyed that his
grandparents could never have imagined, including the steam engine and
the telegraph.

The grand size and scale of the islands against the blue and white
backdrop of the sea was matched only by the sense of loneliness and
desolation. Behemoth windswept rocks completely devoid of any trees
inspired a feeling of foreboding. Snow flowed down to the very water's
edge. Streaks of black showed sheer rock cliffs refusing to be covered by
the blanket of white. And the sense of loneliness was magnified by the
darkness that enveloped the Arctic most of the day, even at these latitudes,
1,500 miles south of Barrow.

The original course had called for Nunivak Island to be far to their
south as they traveled north to Cape Prince of Wales. There the plan

was to land the rescue party near a government reindeer herd, which they would drive north a thousand miles to feed the starving whalers. But the same pack ice that stranded the whaling fleet now extended too far south. As *Bear* desperately tried to press north through channels in the ice, those channels quickly turned to slush on its way to freezing. After a week's struggle, *Bear* narrowly averted being trapped herself; she had had to reverse course at St. Lawrence Island in an attempt to reach land farther south. Now Jarvis looked upon Nunivak once again, after passing it almost a week ago.

Jarvis could barely make out a group of walrus in the gloom along the rocky shore. The islands teamed with life: Cod, halibut, salmon, whales, seals, and birds abounded along shores mostly untouched by commercial profiteers—not that none had tried. Several commercial trading companies were paying the few Aleut natives handsomely for furs. They even erected small wooden structures called "barabaras" for the more productive hunters. Unfortunately, these companies also brought destructive forces, including the crudely fashioned alcohol "kvass" and indebtedness to the company store. The strain of both forces pressed many of the hunters and their families onto hard times.

These recollections brought Jarvis back to wry reflections upon his own wife, languishing alone back home while he went to save whalers caught pursuing commercial riches. The thought put a knot in his stomach. His bitter thoughts were interrupted by the sounds of the jib luffing in the wind. As a seagoing officer, he was conditioned to watch the sails. Small repositionings of the ship and trimming of the sails were constantly required to take full advantage of the polar winds.

He turned as the navigator coughed. The ship's navigator was peering through the lens of his sextant at a star. He used this triangular instrument to determine the angle between a celestial body and the horizon. By taking two or more precise angles of celestial bodies and checking their position against navigation tables, he could determine their position. Lack of landmarks at sea made constant attention to navigation critical.

Jarvis had no shipboard duties assigned him on this journey. This was unusual. Instead, he coordinated food preparation and equipment for the overland expedition. While he carried out these daily duties, his mind returned often to his wife. Their meeting in Seattle had begun as an exciting homecoming. But Mrs. Jarvis, who knew her husband well, detected that something was wrong. That night he told her about the trapped whalers. He told her of his intentions to stay home to help with their new child on the way. And as hard as it was, she encouraged him to go, for this was his life's work. As a Revenue Cutter Service officer, all his training had been designed for such an event. And with over eight years' experience on the only cutter patrolling the Arctic, he was unquestioningly the one best choice to lead the expedition.

As the night's discussion went on, they held each other tightly and cried. But he had to go, even though he might never return.

The ship's doctor interrupted Jarvis's ruminations. "Daydreaming?" asked Surgeon Call. Samuel Call wasn't new to Alaska or the *Bear*. His introduction to the region came as a doctor in Unalaska for five years early in his career. That stint of service taught him the region and the medical conditions most commonly encountered in the Arctic. As the only doctor in the Aleutians, he also came in contact with the *Bear* on many occasions. After one of these encounters, he joined the Revenue Cutter Service, where he was posted to the *Bear* as ship's surgeon. With this much Arctic experience, Dr. Sam Call was the obvious choice to go on the overland expedition with Lieutenant Jarvis. His job would be to tend the rescue party along the way and minister to the 300 whalers when they finally arrived at Point Barrow.

"Just thinking," smiled Jarvis. "I try to do that every month or so."

"Well, lucky thing you have a doctor here to stop the brain hemorrhage," chuckled the doctor. Unlike Jarvis, the doctor was a larger man with a slight pudge around the middle. As a doctor on the ship, he wasn't quite as active as the rest of the crew. There was no climbing out on the long yardarms to work the sails or haul mooring lines. Most days consisted of dealing with the routine medical problems of sailors suffering from anything from frostbite to syphilis.

"Really, I was just thinking about my wife," said Jarvis.

The mood of their discussion changed. The doctor knew the anguish Jarvis must be feeling. "Well, I understand," he responded. "I know your wife is due for your first baby soon."

A nod was all that Jarvis could muster.

"Well," said the doctor, now glancing toward the horizon, "I understand it must be difficult. But there are 300 men out there who also have wives and children. Those men need you. And you could be literally the only man that could pull this off."

The two stood in silence again, watching the waves break across *Bear*'s bow. Large pieces of white gleamed in the water. The sea was littered with pack ice as far as the eye could see; the moonlight flickered ghostly shadows among the floating specters.

"I guess you men can't sleep either," said Second Lieutenant Ellsworth Bertholf, approaching from the stern. Bertholf was young, slightly balding but good-looking, confident in his manner. Stockier than Jarvis, he was nevertheless athletic. He'd have to be. As the third and last member of the overland expedition, he would face both physical and mental hardship.

As difficult as the planned expedition was when they began, the unplanned version that unfolded became even worse. *Bear* had spent a mere eighteen days in port, where steamfitters, sailors, and carpenters worked round the clock to get her under way in record time. She had been repaired, provisioned with extra supplies for the whalers, and fitted for an almost year-long stay in the Arctic—it would be that long before spring thaws could free the whaling fleet.

By the time *Bear* sailed, ice prevented her from reaching Cape Nome, so she headed southeast and made for the village of Tanunak, north of Cape Vancouver, in the bottom third of Alaska. Tanunak had a rocky shore, but was the farthest north the rescue team could hope to land. Unfortunately, that would still leave the three men a journey of over 1,500 miles, a daunting undertaking even for an Eskimo in the spring and summer. For three sailors to make such a journey in the Arctic winter, through mountains and barren sub-zero landscapes, was considered foolhardy. Add the driving of a reindeer herd to feed the whalers, and you had an assignment bordering on suicide.

The three men peered out contemplatively over the ice-strewn water. Of the three, Bertholf had perhaps the most to prove. He had initially been a midshipman at the U.S. Naval Academy. Despite extreme intellect, his playfulness had gotten the better of him and he had been discharged, along with several of his classmates, for hazing younger cadets on a summer cruise. Luckily, the Revenue Cutter Service was looking for a handful of cadets and accepted him on the merits of his entrance exam. Since that time he had proven himself a strong mariner. However, his early failure haunted him.

Dr. Call and Lieutenant Jarvis were the elders of the group at thirty-nine and forty-five respectively. Each had longer terms of Arctic service and blemish-free careers. However, they knew that this rescue would put them to the ultimate test.

Chapter Nine

Jarvis . . .   *The Landing*

Jarvis scanned the activity on the beach in front of the village. Tununak, as it was known, was located near Cape Vancouver off Nelson Island. To say it wasn't much to look at was putting it graciously. Lying at the base of a mountain, the village was barely more than a little patch of beach filled with rocks and boulders. Several huts and an oddly out of place log cabin, the last remnant of a former Catholic mission, now served as home to the half-breed Russian trader Alexis Kalenin, his wife, their family, and the native villagers. The villagers occupied the huts scattered along the water; the trader occupied the cabin. Luckily, the beach itself was free from ice that would have made landing the rescue party more difficult.

"Ho there," yelled Jarvis from the *Bear*'s launch to the kayaks approaching from the village. Faster, lighter, the native kayaks bore Alexis and the island's Eskimo men.

"Welcome," chimed a dark-skinned Inuit with a weathered face. His body wasn't really round, though his thick clothing made it appear so.

"Glad to see you," returned Jarvis with a smile and a wave. The Eskimo was pleased by the response. Tununak was not along the normal travel route for miners. As a result, they didn't get many visitors or many chances to trade for badly needed goods. Jarvis was pleased, as well: Tununak's inaccessibility to miners meant that sled dogs might be available for hire, not having already been sold for a high price to gold seekers.

Jarvis went ashore with the villagers and the Russian trader to enjoy a smoke and what hospitality they could provide. He explained about the trapped whalers and the rescue party's plan to travel overland with reindeer to maintain the sailors until spring, when they could break out of the ice. The audience listened in amazement, not at the bravery of the sailors, but at the apparent suicide mission chosen by the rescue crew. It wasn't lost on the villagers that these were *koblonas*—white men—with no Arctic survival experience. Not even an Inuit, let alone a white man from the south, had ever tried a journey of this magnitude, more than 1,500 miles over the Arctic wasteland. However, the Eskimos were accustomed to going to great lengths to help strangers. Their sharing culture was necessary for survival, for the kindness of a stranger was often the only thing between a freezing man and death.

After some discussion, the Eskimos offered to transport sleds and provisions from *Bear* to the beach. Lashing their kayaks together, they managed, with great skill, to bring ashore over 1,300 pounds of material ranging from pork, beans, and hard bread for the men, to dried fish for sled dogs. It was an amazing operation under less than friendly conditions. At final tally, only a small portion of flour had been exposed to seawater, rendering it unfit for the trip.

The villagers were able to collect forty-one dogs to be harnessed to four cargo sleds. Three of the sleds were provided by the villagers and represented the best of Eskimo construction—light, fast, and strong. Boasting an open framework of hickory and oak, rare commodities in the Arctic, all of the sleds' parts were lashed together with strips of sealskin and walrus. These strips of animal flesh provided flexibility for travel in a rough terrain; rigid nails have no such flexibility.

The harnesses of the dogs were no less cleverly constructed. Their basic materials were strips of heavy sennit, canvas, or seal hide. Cut about two inches wide, the strips wrapped around the dog's neck and chest, each part connecting to its neighbor to form a large collar. This harness attached to a small rope that connected to a longer line tied along the length of all dogs and fastened to the sled. For placement of the dogs, it was decided to use a system deployed by men of the lower Yukon in which an odd number of dogs was tied to each sled in pairs, two by two, with the odd-numbered dog placed singly at the head to act as leader. This method was chosen over a more traditional one that strung the dogs in single file.

Realizing that the delta journey would provide neither brush nor trees for cooking fuel, men aboard the *Bear* had kept busy precooking the food carried in the sleds. One benefit of the frozen Arctic was that no one worried about food perishing along the way. Nevertheless, food, along with the other provisions, was packed with the greatest care on each sled, then covered and tightly lashed. The cover and extensive lashing lines had to stand up to considerable abuse along the rough trails. It was not uncommon for even the most seasoned sled driver to capsize frequently over rough terrain obscured by driving snow.

Doctor Call, young Bertholf, and Jarvis spent the first night in a snow house to get accustomed to the lifestyle, even though the *Bear* was just offshore. Jarvis awoke to the cold, dark, winter morning of the Arctic with feet like ice, his muscles stiff from a difficult night's sleep. At their present location it would be almost noon before the sun would appear. He lay in his sleeping bag for a moment, dreading the start of the day in this inhospitable place. He thought back to his beautiful wife and her concerns with his continued posting to the *Bear*.

When people typically think of the Revenue Cutter Service, they imagine warm climates, the Caribbean, and California. The *Bear*, on the other hand, was now at the tip of a world covered by more than 20,000 square miles of ocean with ice floes, rough seas, and snow. Jarvis longed for the warmth of his cramped bunk on the *Bear*. His wife's look of shock when he told her of the mission remained painfully in his mind. A feeling of guilt, especially now, hung in his stomach.

Lying beside the lieutenant, Doctor Call groaned, "*Semper paratus* all to hell." *Semper paratus*, Latin for "always ready," was the motto of the Cutter Service.

"You don't look very *paratus* today," quipped Jarvis.

"I don't feel very *paratus*. In fact, I think somebody surgically inserted a new hip bone during the night and botched the job," said the doctor. "Caribou hip, I think," he said, rubbing his side.

"Caribou," said Jarvis. "That explains the smell in here." It must be noted that several Eskimo families also occupied the small hut, which featured no ventilation that could dissipate heat. Consequently, the

45

remnants of all imaginable body functions still hung in the air.

Suddenly Alexis, the Russian trader, crawled through the hut's small entrance. Alexis had agreed to guide the group through the local terrain he knew so well. After that, they'd have to find another guide. Without a guide, navigation was problematic at best. Maps were totally inadequate, snow obscured what would otherwise have been landmarks, light reflecting off the snow affected the sky day and night, and dead reckoning became impossible in the maze of snow-covered obstacles.

"Well, the koblonas have survived the night," said Alexis, using the Inuit term for the white man. His tone was neither humorous nor serious, but merely an off-handed observation. The lack of emotion in his voice gave Jarvis an eerie feeling, almost a foreboding of trouble to come.

The word "survived" brought Jarvis back to the urgency of the situation. Almost 1,500 miles away, over 300 men were stranded and freezing. Jarvis jumped to his feet and began dressing as he spoke.

"How could I not survive," returned Jarvis, smiling in the doctor's direction. "I have the entire *Bear* medical staff right next to me."

"Ha, ha, who's going to take care of the medical staff?" retorted the doctor. Jarvis glanced at Bertholf.

"Yeah, sure, always go to the junior lieutenant," he laughed. Bertholf, always a prankster, was quick with a joke. "Sure, doc, if you need any medical procedures, just let me know."

The morning's sparring helped allay the men's nervousness. This was their first day venturing into the great unknown. Pulling together the rest of their gear, they made their way out into the still, dark morning. The dogs, prepared, jumped in their strapping, anxious to go despite the cold.

"Mush!" yelled Alexis, and the group took off. Their initial route would take them along the northern shore of Nelson Island opposite the mainland. This route had been chosen to avoid, as long as possible, crossing the mountain range between Tununak and Ukogamute, the next village on the route. Keeping to the shore would buy them time to find the right pass through the mountains. Their objective: to reach Ukogamute before nightfall. Like Tununak, Ukogamute was barely more than a few huts. However, it contained valuable information regarding conditions, routes, and shelter.

And so they began, the dogs immediately struggling in the soft snow. Ideally, dogs wanted hard, packed snow to run on, for packed snow provided a fast surface for the sled runners to glide across with relative ease. But these snow conditions were just the opposite. The dogs sank to their shoulders and had to literally plow their way through the deep snow. In this situation, a strong lead dog is especially important; the lead dog blazes the trail and finds the quickest path. Each dog in turn follows the lead dog, placing its paws in the footprints of the dog before it.

Worse yet for the men, they had to take turns running ahead of the sleds to check for obstacles, and to navigate. This exhausting work required a frequent change of men in the deep snow. To add to the difficulty, the trail also led up a steady incline as the sleds progressed along the narrows coming closer to the mountains.

Jarvis couldn't help but feel dejected and overwhelmed. They had only traveled twenty-five miles, struggling all the way, with months of travel ahead. And yet he was already exhausted. His legs ached; his breathing was labored from his attempts to guide the sled through the rough trail. Like the other drivers, he was forced to spend more time off the sled than on, actually pushing it through the thick snow to assist the struggling dogs.

To make matters worse, the wind and snow increased steadily until the party was engulfed in a full-fledged ice storm. In the thick sheets of falling snow, the lieutenant could only see a few feet ahead of his lead dog.

"Whoa!" yelled the doctor. Jarvis had almost run over the top of the doctor's sled, now stopped immediately in front of him. Luckily, he managed to pull alongside.

"What's happening?" asked Jarvis.

"Alexis has stopped," responded Dr. Call.

"Why, is something wrong?" Jarvis asked, more to himself than to the doctor, whom he knew would have no more information than he.

Ahead they could see Alexis studying out the right direction. Since they were paralleling the mainland, with the thick snow acting as a blinder, there was real danger of their running over a precipice into the icy sea.

"What do you think, Alexis?" asked Jarvis, walking to the guide.

"We've made the summit," Alexis responded.

"I never thought we'd do it," said Jarvis with a smile of relief. "Now that we're done with the incline, we can progress downhill," he said, spirits lifting.

"Ah, but now things are going to get more difficult," responded Alexis.

The lieutenant's smile instantly turned into a look of dismay. "I don't understand," said Jarvis.

Alexis, in his characteristically unemotional way, simply gestured toward the edge of the summit just ahead. Even though the snow made visibility almost impossible, Jarvis could still make out the steep and rocky slope. It looked like the side of a mountain barren of trees.

"That doesn't look good," said Bertholf, now standing beside Jarvis and the doctor. "In fact, that looks downright unfriendly."

"Are we going down there?" asked the doctor plaintively.

"Yes," responded Alexis, "First the dogs, then us."

"That's pretty much been the system all day," responded the doctor with a twinge of sarcasm. He was gritting his teeth partly from exhaustion and partly from anxiety about the overwhelming mission ahead.

"No," said Alexis, "The dogs won't be able to outrun the sleds on that steep slope. They'd be crushed."

"So what do we do?" asked Jarvis.

"The dogs will have to go by themselves; the sleds will go separately," said Alexis in his usual unemotional tone. Looking down the steep slope it was easy to see why the sleds would need no help with the down trip. It was almost a free-fall.

As Jarvis peered apprehensively down the slope he was hit with a feeling of desperation. Rocks and crevices were strewn along its face. Here they were on only the first day, facing exhaustion and a major obstacle.

"Let's get out the chains," said Alexis. "We'll need to wrap them around the sled runners to slow them down in the snow."

With that, each man fell to work attaching the chains in hopes of giving their descent some measure of control—a controlled crash would be better than a crash with no control at all. Chains installed, the four men paired up, two to a sled, for the downhill ride, hoping that the doubled weight would give the sled more drag. They would return for the two sleds thus left behind and repeat the exercise.

"Are you ready?" Jarvis asked Alexis, his partner for the ride, trying to disguise his anxiety.

"Yep," said Alexis, and he began pushing the sled, which instantly began sliding down the hill; Jarvis and Alexis barely jumped on before the sled was speeding downhill. Each grasped the lashing, trying to hold on. The almost half-ton fully loaded sled bounced and skidded downhill, its riders desperately trying to keep it straight by throwing their legs out into the snow as rudders. With each such steering attempt, however, they risked falling off or breaking their legs under the runners. Any injury now would be disastrous. Likewise, any loss of equipment or provisions could doom the expedition—and several hundred men—to death.

Several times the sled almost rolled over as it hurtled downward through the snow, striking rocks in its path. After ten harrowing minutes that seemed an eternity, the sled reached the bottom. Jarvis and the Russian guide just sat on the sled trying to catch their breath. They had made it down the 2,000-foot trip in one piece. Looking back over their steep path, they could see the dogs still running down the hill. Running at full speed and with a head start, the dogs hadn't been able to match the rapid descent of the sled—even with chains on its runners.

"We made it," said Jarvis almost in a whisper. He was still panting from his ordeal.

"Yep," responded Alexis with his usual brevity.

"You OK?"

Alexis moved his arms and legs to check which aches were bruises and which might be broken bones. After a cursory check he simply nodded. Like Jarvis, he was still out of breath and not inclined to waste his lungs on words.

"Here they come!" said Jarvis, pointing up the slope to a barely visible sled. Apparently Bertholf and the doctor had been able to see that Jarvis and Alexis were standing and not lying mangled in a heap after their controlled crash.

As Jarvis anxiously watched, the second sled began its descent with Bertholf and Call aboard.

The sled moved slowly for about five seconds, then suddenly shot down the hill. Jarvis gasped as it hit a rock and launched into the air. Rolling to the right, it hit the snow at an angle semi-perpendicular to the slope, then started skidding partly on its side. Jarvis could see the passenger on the left side dragging his feet in a vain attempt to right the sled. Then he suddenly lifted his legs as the sled struck another rock. Despite the impact, the passengers clung on fiercely as the sled, now upright and miraculously still in one piece, careened on down the hill in a relatively straight course. The last rock had hit the left rear part of the tilted sled, actually driving it straight again.

"That was close!" exclaimed Alexis with an uncharacteristic burst of emotion and relatively good English.

"Yes!" said Jarvis, likewise gazing up the slope at the surreal scene. The little sled bounded down the jagged mountain, with Bertholf and the doctor struggling futilely to avoid hitting more rocks. It seemed luck, or Providence, was the only thing keeping the sled and men from being broken into pieces.

Jarvis and Alexis watched the sled finally come sliding to a stop about a hundred yards in front of them. During the whole spectacle, they had barely noticed that the dogs from their own sled had reached the bottom and were surrounding them, unaware of the drama. Still panting, the dogs gathered by the sled and waited.

The two men walked the short distance, to find Bertholf and the doctor still clutching their sled with heaving lungs. "You all right?" asked Jarvis, extending his arm to Bertholf.

Bertholf paused to catch enough wind to answer. Taking Jarvis's hand to right himself, he choked out, "I guess I'm still alive."

Jarvis laughed, "Alive enough to climb up and do it again?"

Bertholf let out a barely discernible groan.

"I'm sure the mountain will be more forgiving next time," said the doctor as he struggled to his feet with the help of Alexis.

Jarvis just smiled in return. He didn't have to explain the need to climb the hill for the remaining sleds. They all knew they had no choice.

"Well, look at the bright side," offered Bertholf. "All these trees and rocks we tried to avoid on the way down will help make climbing up that much easier." The other three just stared back without comment.

"No, really," exclaimed Bertholf. They all peered up the hill, assessing the next task of ascending the summit. Finally Jarvis broke the silence.

"Ready?" he asked, nodding at the other three. They simply grunted and began trudging through the snow.

For the next two hours the men pulled and crawled their way up the slope, occasionally pausing to look down and see how far they'd come. As mariners, they were accustomed to scaling heights. They routinely had to climb aloft, high into the ship's rigging, while the masts and yardarms creaked and swayed. Their movements were often fast and violent as the ship pitched and rolled, creating a major challenge to hold onto wet timbers with cold hands. But cling they did, for the alternative was a quick death on the deck below.

Finally, the exhausted four reached the top and simply collapsed in the snow next to their remaining two sleds. They remained silent, almost fearing that whoever spoke first would cause the group to rise and start the hellish descent again.

"I'm not sure what was worse, the climb or the descent," said Jarvis, finally breaking the silence.

Almost in perfect unison the three immediately shot back, "The climb!" They all laughed at the joke.

Jarvis rose to check the sleds for the trip down. Peering down the cliff, they readied themselves for the next flight to the bottom. Hopefully, Providence would again insure no broken bones—or lost lives.

Chapter Ten

Jarvis...   *The Split*

Gratefully, Jarvis and the group approached the village of Ukogamote on their way to the government reindeer station. Like Tununak, this village was a small scattering of icehouses, each sheltering one or more families. It had been a difficult two days' travel, what with the horrendous mountain descent and generally bad conditions. Their route had taken them farther inland than expected, for bad ice conditions along the coast had created exposed ground and water, terrain unsuited for snow sleds. They were, however, still traveling in a northerly direction in pursuit of the reindeer herd.

Jarvis paused for a moment, stopping his sled before the village. It was a strange sight. Several hundred feet earlier as they'd approached, in the relative darkness they'd observed the villagers milling about and excitedly watching their progress. Now, just a few moments later, the village was almost deserted. The seven small igloos and one larger meeting house seemed larger without the people present. Even the few village dogs seemed to be looking on in puzzlement, trying to figure out what had happened.

As Jarvis scanned the scene, two Eskimo men came from behind the main hut in an apparent move to greet the travelers. Jarvis mushed toward them, with Alexis and his sled alongside. When he stopped, the two Eskimos gestured them inside the larger central hut. Like many they'd already seen along the way, it was a large hut generally known as a *kazheem*, the center of village life. Most established villages had one for community functions such as dances and council meetings, and for housing travelers and single men of the village. The invitation came not a moment too soon. Jarvis was exhausted.

Jarvis pulled up the animal skin covering the entrance to the kazheem and crawled through the long descending tunnel. He was so exhausted that he was tempted to lie right there and go to sleep.

He emerged four feet below ground level in the large room comprising the hut. Light filtered down from a small opening in the roof, illuminating the compartment and its occupants, the men of the village, who sat naked to the waist, eyeing them warily. Glancing quickly around, Jarvis saw a dirt floor roughly covered with driftwood lashed together, meeting dirt walls equally lined. The walls began four feet below the soil's surface and continued vertically for eight feet, where they ended in a domed roof above ground. Cracks and gaps in the lashed driftwood had been filled with dirt and brush. At the center of the roof a small three-foot hole, covered in seal or walrus intestines sewn together, acted as a skylight to bring in the sun's rays while retaining the heat of the room. Even in the dead of winter, these huts didn't require fires for heat; the warmth generated by the Eskimos' bodies was sufficient to heat the igloo. Sometimes a small oil lamp provided light.

Alexis, following Jarvis into the kazheem, spoke to an older man who seemed to lead the village. They exchanged words in Inupik, glancing occasionally at Jarvis. Finally, Alexis turned to Jarvis.

"He said he send two men to lift sleds and feed dogs," explained Alexis in his normal Russian accent.

"What about acquiring dogs? Does he have any to spare?"

"No. I ask; he said they with hunting party."

Jarvis paused for a moment. The conversation between the two had seemed brief compared to exchanges in other villages they'd visited, and these people seemed somehow wary of the visitors. Jarvis noticed that all the women and children were conspicuously absent, which only added to his strange feeling of foreboding.

"Where are the women and little ones?" he asked.

"You're right," said Alexis. "Seems only the men are here." He then turned to the elder and asked in Inupik, "Why only men, no women, no young ones?"

The old man answered testily.

"He said they were taken to safe place," Alexis translated. Then seeing Jarvis's look of confusion, he continued, "The village has had problems with koblonas taking women."

Jarvis could envision it clearly. Somewhere in the recent past, unscrupulous visitors, probably trappers, had overpowered the small, remote village and taken their women, whom they generally abused. Jarvis could certainly understand the elder's affront at being questioned.

"Tell him that we're here just for the night and then will move on," said Jarvis, facing the old man with the warmest smile he could muster. "And tell him we're with the government."

Alexis translated the thought to the elder, who seemed somewhat more comfortable, but still suspicious of the travelers. He returned something in his native dialect.

"He says that we are the first whites they see in two years. Others were missionaries," conveyed Alexis.

"Well, at least the last ones were good guys," said Jarvis with a slight smile. "Tell him thank you."

With that, Jarvis and Alexis crawled back through the entrance to set up their tent and secure their sleds on top of the village racks, where their supplies would be out of reach of ravenous sled dogs—in their typically half-starved state, sled dogs will eat anything not made of wood or iron.

With the help of two Eskimos, the four travelers took on the arduous task of feeding the dogs their ration of dried fish. This was no easy task, for it required the entire party to have clubs in hand. As the food was brought out, the dogs typically circled and broke into a fight. It took club-wielding men to protect the smaller dogs and insure they got their share. As soon as they were fed, the exhausted dogs immediately settled down, curled up in the snow, and went to sleep.

After pitching their tent, the men settled down for the night and were soon asleep—except for one. Despite his weariness, Jarvis, haunted by the images of the villagers hiding their women and children, tossed restlessly. He seethed at the knowledge that other koblonas had abused these generous people so severely that they had to hide their loved ones. He was even angrier to think that these abusers, being white, were generally considered more civilized and higher in social stature than the Eskimos, who were considered lie-abouts lacking family values.

The thought of these little children huddled away from the scary travelers caused him even greater anguish about his wife. By now, their baby would have been born, and he didn't even know whether it was a boy or a girl. His wife was alone, save for friends and the families of shipmates who would take care of her. The Revenue Cutter Service itself would deliver his wages and provide for their medical care. But his family was still without his protection. Could *they* fall prey to some unscrupulous men like those encountered by the villagers? Or had his wife even survived the baby's birth?

In the pit of his stomach boiled fear and bitterness—not against the Cutter Service for sending him, but with himself for being there. What kind of man would volunteer for a mission while his family needed him? These Eskimo men would never have done it. *What kind of fool am I?* he anguished.

A cold northeast wind violently flapped the tent's fabric walls, increasing Jarvis's bitterness. He wanted to be home, but there could be no turning back. He was deep in the Arctic on a mission that would take him more than fifteen hundred miles into a frozen hell. It was like a bad dream.

"Bertholf, you seem good with the Eskimos," commented the doctor as they gulped down a quick breakfast of crackers and beans in the dark morning.

"How do you mean?"

"You seem to take their customs in stride. I've never seen you comment in a negative way on anything they do—you know, their different traditions. In fact, during discussions on the ship, I remember your defending them a few times."

Bertholf paused for a moment to process the compliment. "My family has always had a stake in defending other races," he said quietly.

"How so?" asked Jarvis.

"My dad was recruited in New York by General Ullman to lead a brigade of Negro troops in the Civil War."

"Really," commented the doctor. This was a major find about Bertholf. Up to this point, all they had known was that Bertholf's father was an accountant.

"Yes, he was a first lieutenant in the 7th Infantry Regiment, Corps d' Afrique. He saw combat at the siege of Port Hudson and survived. Throughout his time in the army, he had to stand up against prejudice toward his men. Because of that, he instilled in all his children the need to appreciate other cultures and do the same."

Dr. Call and Alexis were both silent at this new revelation about the young officer.

"Well, I'm that much gladder to have you along, Bertholf," said Jarvis.

And then they were back at the task of survival and fast travel. Snow conditions were light, making things worse. A small film of ice had formed on top of the lightly packed snow—ice too thin to support the weight of a dog. The teams struggled as their feet kept breaking through the crust to the snow beneath.

For several days, through several villages, the rescue team tried to replace their exhausted dogs, but could find none to trade. At their last stop, beside the evening fire Alexis confirmed the worst.

"The dogs, they are too tired."

"Yes," agreed Jarvis, "it's been hard."

"No, I mean many will have to stay behind. Mainly the young ones."

Jarvis's jaw tightened. Not a week into the expedition, and already they were stalled.

"How many dogs have to stay?" asked Bertholf.

"Maybe two teams," replied Alexis.

"I could stay behind," said Bertholf, turning to face Jarvis.

"What?"

"No, really, I can stay behind and catch up once we get fresh dogs. I'll get directions from a local guide. I'll be all right."

Jarvis appraised the young officer. He was certainly capable; that's why he had been chosen for the mission. If anybody could improvise, he could. This would also be his chance to prove, once and for all, that he was not the same midshipman who had been dismissed from the naval academy.

"Permission granted. But Alexis will stay with you. The doctor and I will go ahead with the local guides."

Bertholf started to protest but Jarvis raised his hand and continued. "I appreciate the gesture, but you go with Alexis. He'll help you barter for the dogs and any other supplies you can get along the way. We'll meet up at St. Michael." St. Michael, a large outpost perhaps a week ahead, contained a large government herd of reindeer they hoped to acquire. Formerly a mission, St. Michael was conveniently located and large enough for both groups to find with relative ease. After some further discussion about the upcoming travel, they fell off to sleep.

Early the next morning, in the darkness Jarvis and the doctor got up to leave for the next village along the route. As on the previous day, the sleds had to be dragged through the delta country's network of streams and small lakes. In the summer when the snow and ice melted, this area would be one vast swamp. Now, with the snow and ice, it was a very bad—but passable—trail.

Zigzagging past small lakes and bad terrain, their route tripled the distance to the next village of Akoolukpugamute, at the edge of the Azoon River.

Upon arrival, Dr. Call and Jarvis found the villagers were very much like those encountered earlier. Sociable and attentive, they helped the travelers unload their tent and store their sleds on fish racks.

That evening, after the dogs were fed, Jarvis and the doctor huddled by the fire, tired, discouraged, lost in thought.

Finally, Jarvis spoke. "It's only five days until Christmas," he said, leaning forward, elbows on knees, chin in hands, gazing into the flames.

"I know," responded the doctor.

"What does your family typically do for the holidays?" Jarvis asked, his chin now perched on steepled fingertips.

The doctor sat motionless, staring into the fire, wondering whether to be depressed or happy recalling Christmases past. After a long, uncomfortable pause, he broke out of his reverie. They both needed a diversion from stress and exhaustion.

"Well, Christmas has always been a big event in my family. Food, presents, the whole traditional scene."

Jarvis nodded. "Mine, too. It's become quite an event since I got married two years ago. My wife loves Christmas and really does it up."

"Yes, Christmas is made for family. Is your wife going to be all right this season?"

"She'll be all right," responded Jarvis. "As the wife of a sailor, she knew that we couldn't be together for a lot of things."

"Does she know much about how this is going to work?"

"I mailed her a letter before I left the ship," Jarvis replied, remembering his struggle to find the right words. How do you write a loved one what may be your last letter before dying and not reveal your anxiety? With an unexpected surge of emotion, Jarvis thought of the precious satchel that lay among their cargo.

Many weeks before, the postmaster in Seattle had entrusted *Bear* with all the mail destined for the Yukon River, reasoning that with this year's early winter, the only chance of delivering mail to the region lay in giving it to the rescue expedition, who on their route along the Yukon River would pass a small trading post of the Alaska Commercial Company. Located on a pocket off the main river, the trader's camp and the village rising up around it were safe from ice traveling downriver. Because this made it a safe anchorage of sorts, the trading post also served as an emergency winter layover spot for river steamers caught in the ice floes too far from their winter quarters. This year, several steamers there lay anchored, stranded until spring. Unlike the whalers almost 1,500 miles north of Tununak and Vancouver Island, the steamers were well provisioned and ready for winter. Their crews, however, were confined to the anchored vessels with nothing to occupy their time but thoughts of home.

Letters to these men would be like nuggets of gold. As a sailor, Jarvis understood the importance of the mail satchel. For a man at sea for months or years at a time, letters were the only connection to family and friends. Letters were read and reread for months. Shipmates with no letters borrowed those of their buddies.

When Jarvis was asked to consider carrying the seventy-pound satchel, he knew it added significantly to the sled's weight. He knew it took critical space that could have been used for food and gear. But he also knew from experience how important those letters would be to men isolated in the Yukon.

"You know that mail satchel?" said the doctor. The mention of a letter had triggered for him the same recollections.

"Yes," replied Lieutenant Jarvis. "I've been packing it like fine china every day, making sure it stays dry."

"Well, if you think about it, we're within reach of the Alaska Trading Company. A little extra effort *could* put us there by Christmas," said the doctor, lacing his fingers and gazing significantly at Jarvis.

"I was just thinking the same thing," said Jarvis, meeting and holding the doctor's steady gaze.

"If we were to travel relentlessly for the next four days, stopping only at night, we might be able to reach the men with letters in time for Christmas. These notes from home would probably be the only Christmas present the men would receive—and the only one they'd need."

"Do you want to try?" asked Jarvis. Although he was in charge, Jarvis knew that the rush to make it by Christmas would mean a sacrifice for both men in their already exhausted state. Nor was it part of their official mission.

"That's what Christmas is all about, isn't it?" replied the doctor. "A sacrifice for humanity."

With that, they both fell silent, their eyes turned to the night sky. In the Arctic, with no city lights to interfere, the sky somehow always seemed larger than anywhere else in the world. To the observer that infinite blackness studded with an infinitude of twinkling lights swallowed up the world and everything in it.

Jarvis adjusted his blanket over his shoulders and broke the silence with a grunt. "I just wish I didn't have to spend Christmas curled up next to a guy who won't see the inside of a bathtub for six months." With that they both burst into laughter. Their mirth echoed off the snowy landscape for miles.

The next morning, Jarvis emerged from his tent to gaze at the dark forms of the mountains extending from east to west along their route to the government reindeer station.

He immediately winced as a cold north wind bit at his sore muscles. Their trip thermometer read -4 degrees. The wind chill reduced that by 20 degrees. Twenty-four below zero was too cold for any koblonas to be outside.

They'd intended to cross these mountains, but the villagers warned against the effort as folly: deep snow in the mountain passes would make travel slow and dangerous. Instead, the locals recommended that the party travel around the mountain range where it terminated in the west. This would make their task to deliver the mail by Christmas more difficult, but not impossible.

So Jarvis and Dr. Call set out for the end of the mountain range, following the winding streams known as the *agoocharuk*, as directed by the villagers. At the streams' end they struck out cross-country to Lake Agoo, whose frozen surface, like the congealed streams they had just traversed, would give the dogs and sleds an easy glide.

After crossing the five-mile width of the lake, the group arrived at the village of Chukouokulieugamute. Jarvis and the doctor were exhausted. Traveling against the biting wind had tapped their strength beyond expectations. They knew that their Christmas pact was a long shot at best.

More serious, however, was their lack of warm clothing. The woolens they wore had served them well in more temperate climes. But now, faced with temperatures dropping to -15 degrees with a much colder wind-chill, they had to secure warmer clothing or risk freezing to death. With darkness claiming most of the day, the cold seemed even more insidious. Shivering, they built a small fire and huddled next to it.

"The weather is turning worse," said the doctor.

"I know," said Jarvis. "My feet and hands are freezing. I can hardly grasp the sled or feel if my boots are on the tracks."

"Let me look at your feet," ordered the doctor.

Reluctantly, Jarvis pulled off his boots. Anxiously, he watched the doctor search his feet for a darkening at their edges, a telltale sign of frostbite.

"You're at the limit," said the doctor. "If you don't get better clothing or if the weather doesn't break, we can't continue. Frostbitten limbs must be amputated."

"Well, we're only days from the trading post. I guess now we have an added motivation to get there as soon as possible," replied Jarvis.

"That may not be soon enough," the doctor said ominously.

Jarvis sat in silence for a long moment. He had known that at each point of the journey, he would be faced with weighing the needs of his men against the needs of the whalers they were attempting to reach. Now he grimly contemplated their position. The Eskimos thought it almost impossible to reach the stranded ships, especially in the dead of winter. Already, just a short way into the journey the rescue party had been forced to split up. They found their clothing inadequate and were on the verge of severe frostbite. The men were at their limit; so were the dogs. Dr. Call and Jarvis desperately needed a break in the weather, new dogs, and warmer clothes—as soon as possible. If they didn't get them soon, this would turn into a suicide mission.

They emerged from their tent in the dark morning to greet Sojeena, a guide from the village, who had agreed to join their party. For the next three days, with Sojeena's help they wove through uncharted terrain before finally reaching the headwaters of the Kashukak River. Kashukak meant they were getting close to the wintering steamers and the target of their Christmas delivery.

After one more layover, the trio arose on the ever-dark morning of Christmas Eve. For them, today would bring no well-wishers, no carolers, no Christmas revelry. There would only be the frigid Arctic cold. But perhaps there would be one gift after all, for the group now found themselves at the timberline, only seven miles from the start of the Yukon. Here they would find the reindeer herd. There would be trees for shelter. Best of all, from here they had a fighting chance of delivering their satchel by Christmas.

They traveled rapidly along the Kashukak and then the Kwikpuk, or big river, more commonly known as the Yukon to the white man. The going was relatively easy as they worked their way through snowdrifts for twenty miles.

Finally, as twilight approached, the triumphant little group pulled into the village near which the wintering steamers lay anchored. Spotting the new arrivals, two sailors strolled toward the group, seeing nothing unusual in their visitors, since Eskimo traveled up and down the river to trade and hunt.

Jarvis pulled back his hood, startling the first sailor: a white man this far north on a dog sled was unusual.

"I'm Jarvis of the Revenue Cutter Service," he said, removing his large mitten and extending his hand.

The first man was still taken aback. Finally he spluttered, "I'm Smitty, and this here's Jones. We're off of that steamer over there."

"What brings you way up here?" asked Smitty.

Jarvis glanced at Call, as if asking permission to reveal the news. At a hearty nod from the doctor, he said, "We've brought your mail."

"Mail!" said Jones. "Oh, my God!" With that he turned and yelled at the top of his lungs, "Mail!" Instantly men appeared from everywhere. Within just thirty seconds, sailors had surrounded Jarvis. They didn't ask how or why Jarvis had gotten there; they just looked on as excited as children by a Christmas tree.

Jarvis removed the satchel carefully packed in the sled and began reading off names. With each name, a man yelled and stepped forward. Some cried; others just quietly took their letters inside. Some opened their correspondence and ravenously scanned the text for news. Nobody threw away even an envelope. Each letter received was treated like a delicate object of beauty. Most tried to utter a thank you when handed their letter, but many were too choked with emotion to get out the words.

It was truly a Christmas miracle.

Having delivered the letters, Jarvis and Call finally obtained some wood for a fire and warmed some tea and beans. They sat, well pleased with the day.

"We did it," said the doctor. "Did you see the look on their faces?

62

Medical school was right; everyone has a mother, after all."

"Yeah, it's something to see some of the bigger, burly guys break down when they get a letter," responded Jarvis. A long pause ensued as they both reflected on the joyous day's events.

"I needed that," said Jarvis finally. "No matter what happens on the expedition, at least I have the memory of this. Nobody can take that away." Jarvis's face showed the weight of his awesome responsibility. He was in charge of a barely equipped rescue party tasked with an impossible assignment. None, including himself, had the experience to navigate over 1,500 miles through the desolate Arctic—probably no one with those qualifications existed. If the mission failed, 300 men would die a slow, miserable death. Such a leadership assignment surely would be more than most men could bear.

The doctor looked at his friend compassionately. As a physician, he was accustomed to being responsible for the lives of many people. Today, however, he only had to worry about his own survival. In keeping with the Christmas theme he said, "Don't worry. God doesn't choose the qualified; God qualifies the chosen."

Jarvis wrinkled his brow while he tried to process that statement.

"You know," continued the doctor, "like Joseph and Mary." He paused again. "And the manger."

Again Jarvis looked perplexed, too tired for so deep a statement. "I'll think on that tomorrow," he said, rising to go to his sleeping bag. He took three steps and stopped with a thought, paused, and turned to face the doctor. "I certainly get the manger part," he said with a mischievous grin, glancing at one of the many dogs sharing their camp. With that they both laughed.

It would be a good Christmas night's sleep.

Chapter Eleven

Jarvis...   *No Deer*

It had been a week since they delivered the mail to the steamers. Since that time they had traveled along the northern bank of the Yukon River en route to the government reindeer herd at St. Michael. Two guides, acquired following the visit to the trading post a few days before, came down with pneumonia. Fearing that the guides could die, Jarvis and Call rushed them to the next trading post, where they found another wintering steamer with a purser who agreed to take on the guides' care. Jarvis and the doctor said goodbye to their new friends on the steamer and continued on their way.

The next day they pushed to Aproon at the mouth of the Yukon River, a short distance from the seacoast. The sun appeared after noon now and remained for almost five hours before it disappeared again. The men at Point Barrow, to the north, had more darkness to contend with.

Coming to the abandoned village of Kotlik, they started down the last part of the Yukon River. Then, having traversed the length of the Yukon, they traveled along the seacoast and struck off across the ice to Cape Romanoff. This was tricky business, for they could see open water and had to travel carefully through ice crushes—walls of ice formed by the ice pushing upon itself.

After almost a month of grueling travel, Jarvis and Call were exhausted. It was twilight as they finally arrived at St. Michael where they were to pick up deer from the government herd for the long haul to Point Barrow.

As they approached the government station with its three or four small buildings, each the size of a large cabin, it seemed like New York City compared to the small huts—mostly buried underground—they'd become accustomed to seeing. They half expected a trolley to pick them up.

"Dr. Livingston, I presume," said a tall, handsome man in a green uniform, obviously referring to the fact that everyone up and down the Yukon knew of the curious rescue party. News traveled fast, even in these parts.

"No, just a sailor who's lost his way," responded Lieutenant Jarvis, removing his mittens. Unlike Jarvis, who was bundled head to toe in thick skins, the green-uniformed man had just come from a warm cabin with a fire. Since the weather was unseasonably warm, just below freezing, he hadn't bothered to put on a coat, appearing only in the long-sleeved shirt and wool pants of his army uniform.

"Well, we're glad to see you anyway. I'm George Randall." He was actually Lieutenant Colonel George Randall, Commanding Officer of the U.S. Government Military Station at St. Michael. Typically he would have introduced himself as such, in accordance with military custom and courtesy. However, this was the Alaskan territory. Things were a bit more informal than in the U.S. Here he addressed Jarvis, a junior officer, on a first-name basis to signal that he was dispensing with the usual military formality.

"I'm David Jarvis," responded the lieutenant, reaching out to shake the colonel's hand. Under normal circumstances Jarvis would have saluted and waited for the colonel to return same. However, he gladly followed the colonel's lead and simply smiled while he warmly shook his hand.

Now a small crowd composed of three government workers and almost twenty villagers converged on Jarvis. He had kept from the satchel letters destined for the government station; now he handed them out to the eager recipients. After the excitement, Jarvis and Call turned to their normal routine of securing dogs and sleds.

"Your dogs look pretty rough," said the colonel, bending down to examine one of the young dogs sprawled in the snow. After twenty-one days with no rest, this would be their last stop.

"I know," said Jarvis, embarrassed at the necessary harsh treatment of the dogs. "If I could have found other dogs to give them relief, I would have."

"I know," consoled the colonel, sensing Jarvis' unease. "The dogs' lives or the whalers': you had to make a choice. Maybe I can help. I'll rustle up some dogs and keep these. They'll have to rest for a week before they can be used again. But it's the least I can do."

Jarvis just looked at the colonel. His final comment felt ominous. Something was wrong.

"Well, giving us the reindeer is more than enough."

The colonel cleared his throat, manifestly uncomfortable.

"Let's go inside for some tea and warm food. You must be exhausted," said the colonel, stalling. Jarvis nodded his agreement and went inside, followed by the doctor. After ravenously eating, they went back to the subject of deer.

"Well, about the deer. You know that the Inuit need food here," said the colonel. This was going badly. Jarvis could feel anger beginning to swell in his chest. It was obvious that the colonel was leading to something not in their favor.

"Yes, and the Inuit have been surviving for a long time before the government deer herd was established. The whalers have no such survival skills," said Jarvis, almost sarcastically.

The colonel bristled at Jarvis's tone. "Well, lieutenant," he snapped, all pretense of non-military informality now gone, "there's also some miners here, and they need deer." The colonel had obviously decided to exercise the privileges of his rank.

Jarvis clenched his fists. He hadn't traveled almost 400 miles by dog sled to come up empty-handed.

"My orders . . . *our* orders from Washington clearly state that I'm to get these deer and drive them to Point Barrow," he persisted.

The colonel, now red with anger, scowled. "I'm in charge of the deer, and my orders are to use them here."

"Here?! There's nobody starving here!" said Jarvis, now in a rage.

"There will be if you take the deer! My orders are to support the miners and Inuit of the upper Yukon. These orders supercede all other requests. I'll not choose who lives and who starves!" said the colonel, making no effort to lower his voice.

They were now clearly at a standoff, with the colonel holding all the cards. Jarvis realized his predicament. A letter from a Washington bureaucrat didn't go far in the Arctic.

"Well, sir," said Jarvis, now conciliatory, "as a colonel in charge of the welfare of this region, I ask you: how can we both fulfill our orders?"

The colonel took a breath. He now had to respond to a reasonable question that didn't challenge his authority but, rather, recognized his position and experience.

"You're probably aware that there are more government deer. The rest are under the control of Superintendent Kettleson at Unalakik. He may have some available. He also works with some missionary teachers who manage herds in nearby villages. Tom Lopp, one of these missionaries, has a large herd."

Jarvis made no attempt to hide his disappointment. It was clear that he couldn't get the main government herd. He'd have to turn to Kettleson and the Christians.

"Yes, I'm aware of the other herds and Tom Lopp specifically. He's well known for his work in the region and his herding skills. But what if they say no?" Jarvis had given up trying to get the government herd; he now needed help in securing the other deer still hundreds of miles away.

The colonel was now himself deep in thought. Finally he said, "I'll write a letter for you to take to Dr. Kettleson. It will explain the situation and request, based on my personal authority, that he give you the deer. I'll also guarantee that he'll be repaid for the deer."

Jarvis looked intently at the colonel. Such a letter could have even less influence on the missionaries than the orders from Washington were supposed to have had on the colonel.

The colonel, seeing doubt on Jarvis's face, continued. "Lieutenant, this Kettleson and the missionaries got their training here at the station. I know them. They'll listen."

It looked as if the letter was all Jarvis was going to get. "OK, but if they refuse, I'll be back," said Jarvis with a firm stare. He was not about to let anybody, including a higher-ranking officer, stand in the way of completing his mission.

"Fair enough," said the colonel. He, too, knew whom he was dealing with.

Chapter Twelve

Jim . . .   Navarch

It was now January 10th, just two weeks after Christmas—not that it mattered: there had been no Christmas celebration to remember. The holiday was drenched in darkness day and night, with nothing to mark the passage of time. Jim crouched in the Old Kelley House, shivering uncontrollably. His companions were covered in soot. Weak, demoralized, they felt abandoned. Many were sick from the filth and lack of proper food. More and more conflict arose as they fought for their rights.

More importantly, they were freezing. The destroyed ships had long ago been stripped of wood to build fires; a number of the men had then taken to robbing Eskimo graves for timber. In some cases, they even took the clothes off the bodies.

At least *they* had graves to rob. The men on the outlying icebound ships, like *Rosario* to the west and *Wanderer* to the east, had nothing but the ship's dwindling stores to draw upon.

Brower had been called upon to mediate more than one dispute between the villagers and the men, who were merely trying to keep from freezing. The fact was, there was no wood and the alternative, seal oil, was running out.

As Jim sat in the cold, dark recesses of his berth, he heard a commotion outside. With all the ongoing conflicts, this was not an unusual situation. But these sounds were different: they actually sounded positive. He crawled out to the frigid Arctic air, whereupon he could barely make out twenty or so men taking turns looking through a spyglass toward a channel of open water.

"Is it the *Navarch*?" one asked hopefully, unable to see much in the darkness.

"No. It can't be. *Navarch* was crushed. Anyway, she's too far away and completely frozen in."

Brower strode up to the group. Since he was one of only two men the crew now recognized for authority, they handed him the glass.

"Well, I'll be damned; it's the *Navarch*." Having left the *Navarch* just three months earlier—and barely having survived the trip—Brower knew her markings well, even if only in silhouette.

"How can that be?" asked Tom Gordon, his assistant.

"It can't. It's impossible."

They both paused for a moment. A channel must have opened right where the ship had been abandoned. Apparently she had floated through miles of killer ice floes and managed to come directly to Point Barrow.

"This can't be happening!" cried one of the men.

"It's Providence," declared another.

Brower continued to stare in disbelief. He was a non-believer, at least in the traditional Christian sense.

"Well, I can't explain it, but our heating problem is solved."

At that, Jim realized the importance of the *Navarch*'s arrival. The *Navarch* was a steamer; a steamer carried tons and tons of coal in its hold. It *must* be Divine Providence. How else could a ship full of coal, left for dead, suddenly float to their ice-locked location where no channel existed? More amazingly yet, how could she have come to this exact spot without the aid of a crew or navigator?

The men whooped and hollered with excitement. All that now stood between them and the warmth of a coal fire were six miles of ice crushes.

Quickly, crewmen and Eskimos were organized into work parties. For days and days, they chipped and hacked a makeshift road to the *Navarch*. Upon reaching the vessel, they found her in pristine condition. More importantly, in her hold were eighty tons of coal. This would be enough to keep them from freezing until spring.

Because of unpredictable weather, unloading *Navarch's* lifesaving cargo took more than three weeks. Exhausted, many of the men started bitterly complaining.

"We got enough coal," growled one of the men.

"No. Mr. McIlhenny's calculated that we need at least one more day's haul to make it," responded Jim.

"Just you shut up."

Jim knew when to leave it alone; he went back to the Old Kelley House, looking forward to some sleep.

He was awakened by another commotion. This time it didn't sound good. Alarmed, most of the building's occupants rushed outside, only to be greeted by the sight of flames rising on the black horizon. The *Navarch* was on fire.

"What happened?" cried Jim.

"I don't know, but I think I can guess," replied a crewman, pointing to two men walking up the six-mile, makeshift road from the burning ship to the station. Jim, peering at the outline of the men, recognized two foremast hands from the *Orca*, like himself. But these two were generally troublemakers.

The angry group descended on the men. Brower, who had become the peacekeeper for most conflicts, separated the mob from the suspects. Then he turned to the two.

"Tell me, what did you do?"

They hesitated.

"I mean it," continued Brower. "Tell me . . . or would you prefer to be questioned by your crewmates?"

They exchanged hesitant glances. Finally one decided to speak. "We accidentally started the fire," he blurted.

At this, the restless crowd started to get ugly. Brower turned to them and demanded quiet.

"What do you mean, 'accidentally'? You weren't even supposed to be on the ship."

"I don't know. It just started in the blubber room and spread to the coal bunkers. We barely got off."

Brower was irritated. "It just started for no reason?"

After a few seconds' hesitation, the second crewman responded. "We was trying to get rope to make pads for our boots. We gathered straw from the foremast bunks and made a fire in the blubber room. It just spread."

The crowd was livid, enraged, disbelieving such an obvious fabrication. Brower spirited off the culprits, ordering the rest of the crews back to the Old Kelley House. Leaving the two with their crewmates might have resulted in their deaths.

The next day, the men wanted answers but Brower had none to give. The two miscreants were unwilling to give any additional information. But it was obvious; they were tired of moving coal and decided they had enough. To keep from working any more, they destroyed the ship.

The irony of the situation was remarkable. The memory of frigid conditions just a few short weeks ago hadn't affected the actions of the present. What had so recently seemed like divine intervention had now been lost to the exhaustion and frustration of the moment.

Speculation as to what should be the guilty ones' fate ran rampant. Opinions among the crew ranged from hanging to flogging. But in the end, Brower left them alone. He told the group, "If you get cold in a couple of months, take out your frustration on these fellows then."

For their sakes, Jim thought, *the coal had better last until spring.*

Chapter Thirteen

Jarvis...   *Tilton*

The next morning David Jarvis and Dr. Call again set forth on their journey. This time they were more adequately outfitted. As a consolation for being denied the government deer herd, the colonel had found them warmer clothing better suited for the Arctic winter. Their existing clothing constructed of wool and dog skin proved to be heavy, cumbersome, and not particularly warm. Likewise, the goatskin sleeping bags taken from the ship, with their canvas and rubber covers, were both too heavy to haul and too cold to sleep in. Now the group enjoyed clothing—including boots, socks, and sleeping bags—made of reindeer skins with the fur still on. Even in the Yukon, clothing of this material was at a premium, especially given the influx of gold miners. Such garments, treasured by Inuits and old Arctic hands, cost a king's ransom, if you were lucky enough to find them.

Another problem facing the intrepid travelers was an adequate, portable food supply. They had to move quickly, yet carry enough food to insure the mission's—and their own—survival. To that end, and considering the length of the journey, they loaded each sled with provisions to the sled's full capacity of 300 pounds. These supplies not only had to sustain the travelers until summer, up to six months away, but also had to provide for the whalers at journey's end.

To lessen the strain on Jarvis's and Call's dogs, the colonel sent food ahead by dogsled across the divide from the head of Norton Bay to Kotzebue Sound. This extra food would be needed to replace what Jarvis and Call would eat on the way.

In a month, they expected to meet up with Lieutenant Bertholf, who'd been sent by another route farther inland. Thus the group set out from St. Michael to obtain deer by going inland, across the tundra to Cape Prince of Wales, a long and precarious trip. Meeting Bertholf on time would be a long shot.

The easterly winds had warmed the shores of the sound and forced Jarvis and Call to the rougher inland terrain earlier than planned. Ironically, now that the group had obtained warm clothing, the weather turned uncomfortably warm.

"Well, I'm sure glad we got the reindeer skins," said the doctor mockingly as he wiped the sweat from his head.

"Yeah," replied Jarvis, "I think the deer sold them to get cool." He chuckled at his own joke.

In addition to making them uncomfortable, the warmer weather also made the rougher trail even more difficult. Wind and sun had cleared off the snow, forcing the men and dogs to slowly grind and pull the sleds through the dirt and rocks. Grassy mounds and boulders compelled them to haul sleds slowly up and around gullies and cliffs. It took all day to travel eighteen miles to Kikikaruk. The next day wasn't any better.

On the third day, the group found better conditions with small bays covered with snow and ice. They also had an astonishing encounter. In the Arctic, small dark objects stand out against a white landscape. Visible for miles, they can appear larger than they are. Thus they saw her from far away, the Eskimo woman in snowshoes crossing a bay to the south. And they saw that she saw *them* approaching her on dogsleds.

Now, in this area, a lone woman could be in a very dangerous position. Alone, on snowshoes in the middle of a bay, she had no escape. She froze as the dogs approached her at a run.

White trappers had been known to kidnap and abuse native women; consequently, Eskimos were very leery of white travelers. Knowing this, Jarvis and Call held their sleds off at a distance so as not to heighten the woman's obvious fear. Then slowly, carefully, Lieutenant Jarvis walked toward her, smiling warmly. He held his hands out from his side, palms forward to show that he wasn't armed.

"Don't be afraid," he said gently. "I'm Lieutenant Jarvis of the United

States government. I'm here to rescue some whalers north of Point Barrow."

Her look of fear was instantly replaced with wide-eyed amazement. "Koblonas going to save *Jeanie*?" she asked incredulously.

It was Lieutenant Jarvis's turn to look stunned. How could an Eskimo woman over 1,000 miles from the stranded men know the name of one of the trapped ships?

"How do you . . . where . . . who . . . ?" stammered Jarvis.

"Koblonas," she repeated.

"What koblonas?" asked Jarvis.

"Tilton," the woman said haltingly. Being Inuit, it was lucky she spoke any English at all.

"Tilton?" echoed Jarvis.

"Yes, Tilton. From ship, *Jeanie*." Instantly it became clear. One of the whalers had managed, alone, to travel over 1,000 miles. He had either been sent to get help or had abandoned his post in an effort to survive.

"Where's Tilton?" Jarvis questioned eagerly.

She silently pointed ahead over a route that must have taken Tilton under the bluff they had just crossed. Apparently they had been within a couple hundred yards but had not seen each other because of the difference in elevations.

Creating a small berth for the woman atop one of the sleds, the group set off to find Tilton. As they skimmed along, she mentioned that Tilton was traveling with her husband. Why she was on the bay alone, they couldn't determine.

Before long they encountered Tilton and the Inuit lying asleep on a dogsled, exhausted from their travels. The dogs were strewn about in the snow, still in their harnesses. They were entirely played out.

"Tilton," said Jarvis, shaking the man vigorously. Covered in wool clothing and dog skins, he couldn't have been warm; he was surely uncomfortable.

"What, what?" responded Tilton in a daze. "What's going on?"

"Are you Tilton?" asked Jarvis, shaking the man again.

"Yes," responded Tilton groggily as he sat up. "Who are you?"

"I'm Lieutenant Jarvis of the Revenue Cutter Service. I'm going to Point Barrow to save your shipmates."

"You know about us?" asked Tilton, eyes now wide. "Thank God. Thank God," he said as he collapsed back onto the dogsled. "I've been traveling like a madman to get the word out!"

"I had all but given up on getting news to the government," said Tilton, cupping his hands around a hot mug of tea while the doctor closely examined his extremities in a makeshift medical examination.

"I can't believe you made it, Tilton," said the doctor.

"How's he faring, Doc?" asked Jarvis.

"He has some frostbite on his extremities," said the doctor. Jarvis could see the blackness on Tilton's nose, parts of his cheeks, and toes. When skin or limbs become totally frozen, they die, slowly turning black. Typically, limbs have to be amputated, skin must be excised. "He's also suffering from total exhaustion."

"His dogs are in pretty much the same shape," said Jarvis.

"The dogs won't go no more, poor fellows," said Tilton. "They's been all that saved me, besides these Eskimos," he said, gesturing at the Eskimo couple.

"Tilton, we'll take you and your friends to Unalakik to get healthy," said Jarvis. It was not his responsibility to care for the three; however, he found it necessary somehow to reward their stamina and charity in helping each other.

"God bless you," said Tilton.

Jarvis got the impression that he was grateful not so much for the aid of his little party, but for Jarvis's taking on the responsibility of helping his shipmates.

"What else can you tell us about your mates?" asked the doctor.

"Yes, and their supplies?" added Jarvis.

It was obvious that Tilton was almost ready to drop.

"Look at the letters," he said, wearily gesturing toward the sled.

"What letters?" asked Jarvis.

"In the bag there. The letters from the Old Men and me mates," responded Tilton.

Jarvis and the doctor instantly went to the letter bag. From its contents they learned that the *Orca, Jesse Freeman,* and *Belvedere* had gotten the farthest south before being stuck in the ice near the Sea Horse Islands. The ice crushed the *Orca* and *Freeman; Freeman's* food was lost. Both crews escaped to the *Belvedere,* but ultimately moved to land at Point Barrow. The *Belvedere* was spared by a safer anchorage behind Point Franklin. The *Rosario, Newport, Fearless,* and *Jeanie* were likewise caught in the ice but remained safe to this point. The fate of the *Wanderer* was unknown; she had last been seen west of Herschel Island in early September. The *Mary D. Hume* was temporarily safe near Herschel Island. The wreckage of the last ship, the *Navarch,* was trapped in the ice. It was conjectured that her crew had escaped to safety, but their whereabouts were unknown. In short, as of three months ago, most of the men were still alive and had some food.

The news that three ships and all their provisions were lost was a blow. Jarvis and Call now knew that the stranded whalers' food supplies would never make it to spring—or even the next couple of months. The race was on to reach the men as soon as possible.

Chapter Fourteen

Jarvis...   *The Herd*

Jarvis and the doctor continued along the east coast of Norton Sound with the help of local Eskimo guides. In case Lieutenant Bertholf should come this way, they left a letter instructing him to proceed across the portage to Cape Blossom and wait for the main rescue party to arrive once they had obtained reindeer from Cape Prince of Wales. Hopefully, the deer would not be withheld as they had been at St. Michael.

There was still no snow or ice along the shores, so they moved farther inland, pushing over the hills and mountains of the back coast, traveling a route that had been established by an unsuccessful telegraph expedition in 1865. The going was rough until they arrived at Norton Bay. There they hoped that recent cold north winds had firmed the ice sufficiently to support the heavy sleds and dogs. Running over smooth ice would make an easier stretch of journey. Determining that the bay was indeed firm, they ran the dogs across to the north shore. Unfortunately, heavy wind had driven waves over areas previously frozen, creating jagged piles of ice covered by deep snowdrifts near the sides of the bay. It was a major struggle getting the sleds through the deep snow and over the ice cliffs—they had to relieve Tilton's dogs of their loads for this rugged stretch.

On the morning of January 8th, the men arose to a blizzard. They were compelled to switch to snowshoes to keep from wading through snow up to their waists. But the sled runners sank in the deep powder, burying the main body of the sled and its cargo. The dogs had to jump, plow, and struggle with each tug of their harnesses to pull the dead weight. Visibility was almost zero. Finally, the four men tramped down snow with their snowshoes to clear the trail so the dogs could drag the sleds along. The group literally inched along in the storm. The next day was no better.

This was the nature of travel for the next several days, deeply disheartening the rescue party. At this rate, they wouldn't make it to the stranded whalers anytime in the nineteenth century.

By January 10th, almost a month into the overland expedition, Jarvis and his group were completely played out. Exhausted and discouraged, with a thousand miles to go, they now saw their mission as almost impossible. Given the deep snow and cold, not only was the rescue now seriously in doubt, but questions about their own survival lurked. They were days or weeks from the reindeer herd at Cape Prince of Wales—which lay only a third of the way to Point Barrow—and had no guarantees that they could even get the deer. They needed a miracle now.

Jarvis and the group paused at twilight to rest a moment. They'd have to make camp soon. But for now the gently falling snow brought a moment of serenity. Jarvis sat savoring the scene.

Suddenly, in the distance, through the large, soft snowflakes he made out a solitary deer . . . then another. *How strange*, he thought. *They didn't run. How can they be way out here? Could they have run away from the government herd? Or a private family? It can't be the government herd. They're still weeks away.*

"What's this?" whispered the doctor, sliding next to Jarvis. "Wild deer?"

"No, domestic," returned Jarvis in a hushed tone. "I just don't know what they're doing here."

"I see two," whispered the doctor, straining his neck higher. "Do you think there's more?"

"I don't know," returned Jarvis, "I just hope nothing's happened to the Kettleson's herd."

Each man stood with a knot in his stomach. They were exhausted from literally plowing a path through deep snow with their snowshoes. If they came up empty-handed now with no deer to bring to the starving whalers, it would be the end of their mission. If something happened to scatter Kettleson's deer across the Yukon, it would be devastating.

"Could wolves have driven them away?" asked the doctor.

"The herd is protected," said Jarvis. "Anyway, the Kettleson's outpost is still weeks away. I can't imagine anything that could scatter them this far."

Suddenly, they heard reindeer bells. Creeping forward, they saw more deer and a fire, around which huddled a handful of men. These deer were definitely domestic.

Jarvis and Call stopped to secure their dogs, that had scented the deer. Sled dogs are natural hunters; they would kill game, given a chance. The closest deer, startled, sprang away from the sleds. Some of the dogs barked, alerting the men standing by the fire. They were obviously deer herders, intent on protecting their investment.

"Oh, no," Jarvis groaned.

Guns in hand, the men quickly approached. Jarvis moved to the front of the sled train, expecting trouble. If he got the rifle out of his gear, it would provoke shooting. So instead, he approached the men with hands wide, just as he had approached the woman days earlier. As the herders drew closer, the knot in his stomach tightened.

At a short distance he yelled, "Ho there."

No response.

"Ho there!" yelled Jarvis, louder this time. The men continued approaching at a determined pace.

Jarvis braced himself for the inevitable. But the moment the herders drew close enough to make out that at least two of these travelers were white men, their leader called out. "Are you Lieutenant Jarvis?" The words echoed across the snow.

Jarvis's jaw dropped. How could anybody know his name in the middle of the Arctic? This wasn't exactly Main Street in his hometown. "Yes, I'm Jarvis," he finally responded.

"I'm Kettleson, caretaker of the government herd at Port Clarence."

"What?" said Jarvis, "I don't understand." His eyes were wide. None of it made sense. How could this be? It had been less than two weeks since, empty-handed, he had left the government herd at St. Michael and traveled almost two hundred miles.

80

"We heard from an Eskimo who'd traveled from the government station that you were coming. We knew you'd be here next and thought we'd save you a trip," said Kettleson, smiling. "Would have made it sooner if it weren't for the blasted snow."

Jarvis stood dumbfounded. In his wildest dreams he couldn't have imagined such a break. "I can't believe it. You must have started as soon as you heard," he gulped, now almost in tears. That Kettleson and the herders had driven the deer to meet the rescue party had cut almost two weeks from their time.

"Almost," said a herder named Mikkel. He had a slight Russian accent and must have been brought over from Siberia to train the Americans in deer herding. "We begin January. We drive deer nonstop."

"Call it a late Christmas present," said Kettleson with a grin.

"Well, thank God," said the doctor, who had now joined Jarvis. It was truly a miracle. Just when they were in despair, the deer arrived. All this time, another group—Bertholf's—was enduring the same struggles to secure the deer they needed so badly.

Now that the shock was wearing off, Jarvis asked, "How many deer do you have?"

"Over a hundred in all," replied Kettleson.

That wouldn't be enough to last the whalers until spring, but it was a start. Jarvis instantly felt a great weight lift from his shoulders. He still had a long way to go and needed a great many more deer, but it was a milestone, nonetheless. And there *were* more sources to try, including the herd of the two missionaries and some small stations that Bertholf had been dispatched to get. At least he now actually had something to show for his efforts, instead of a few letters delivered to stranded river steamers encountered on his way.

His euphoria would be short-lived.

After setting up camp and resting for the night, Jarvis and the men prepared to move out again. But first, the dogs had to be taken several miles away, out of sight and smell of the deer herd. If they were to form into packs and hunt the deer, it would scatter the frightened herd across the Yukon. Dogs and deer don't mix, so the dogs were sent back to St.

Michael and Unalalkik with two Eskimo volunteers. From now on, deer would pull the sleds.

As they were about to start inland, Mikkel addressed Jarvis. "This will be an interesting experience for you," he said.

"Interesting how?" asked Jarvis.

"Deer aren't as smart as dogs," interjected Kettleson. "Once the lead sled starts, they all start running. If you're not securely on your sled, you'll be left on the trail. Deer also run until they're tired, then they slow down. They don't have the strength and endurance of a dog. They also don't have a dog's judgment or sense of direction.

"And don't forget to mind your clothes and skin. Since it's a faster ride, you'll have wind whipping through your clothes. Men have gotten frostbite before they knew it."

Jarvis tried to take it all in. "Thanks for the training," he said with a smile. "On this whole overland mission, this has been the first time I've actually gotten advance notice, instead of learning the hard way." And it was true. The sailors generally learned as they went, typically after something went wrong.

With that, Kettleson returned to his sled. Unlike the others, his, the lead sled, was drawn by two deer whose job it was to break a trail and maintain a good pace. This arduous task required the strength of two deer instead of one. Behind Mikkel's lead sled came two "poulkas"—boat-shaped freight sleds. Each deer pulling a trailing sled was secured to its front by a tight-fitting collar made of two pieces of wood with a short trace reaching back to a breast piece and continuing the length of the deer's body. Where this trace continued between the deer's legs to the sled, fur was wrapped to prevent chafing. A line secured along the left side of the deer from the halter to the sled served as a guide. Normally left slack, this line was only used to stop the deer, and then only when absolutely necessary. For much to the exasperation of the driver, when the line was pulled, the deer ran in a circle several times before stopping. Once the deer train began, it rarely stopped.

By agreement, Mikkel and Kettleson would accompany the party as far as Port Clarence, where they had business to attend to, but one of his parties had volunteered to continue part way to Point Barrow. Kettleson was in charge of his group; Mikkel ran the herd and herders.

Mikkel started the lead sled with a jump. Forewarned, Jarvis and the doctor had secured themselves to their sleds by wrapping the reins around the sled and their hands. True to Mikkel's warning, the deer leading the sled train jumped, instantly breaking into a gallop. Jarvis and the doctor clung fiercely to their sleds. If they slipped and fell, they'd be dragged through the snow with no hope of climbing back on board. Since all the sleds were linked as a train, each deer tied to the sled in front of it, there would be no chance of stopping an individual sled.

Luck delivered them a clean, smooth trail up Golovin Sound to the mountains of Stony Cape. At Stony Cape they encountered a steep climb and dangerous descents to the village of Seookuk at the base of the mountain. The deer herd had to be kept out of scenting range of this and all villages that maintained sled dogs. From here on there would be almost no trees anywhere on the horizon. It was a cold, desolate landscape with a biting north wind—no place for a sailor.

The sleds, Jarvis in the rear, continued along the shore of Norton Sound until they encountered crushed ice too large and boulder-like to pass. They were then forced to travel higher ground, along hills that lined the coast. This was difficult terrain, for the deer had to haul the heavy sleds up an incline, then outrun the burdens as they skidded down the hill behind them.

The weather worsened, the wind now increasing to a full-blown gale. Jarvis and his men winced with pain as gusts of Arctic ice-laden wind stung their faces. The next village lay some thirty-five miles away; it was obvious they might not make it before nightfall.

In the darkness and blowing snow, Jarvis couldn't see much past his sled, in the rear of the train. Suddenly a pile of snow-covered driftwood loomed. Before he could react, his deer had become tangled in its crossed timbers. Panicked, the deer struggled, running back and forth to free its hooves. Jarvis pulled on the guideline, in a vain attempt to restrain the deer and calm it down, but the deer became even more panicked. Finally, the deer lurched forward and ran the sled headlong into a large stump rising out of the snow. With the sled held tightly against the stump, the deer continued to plunge ahead with all its strength until suddenly the harness snapped, which now left Jarvis holding the guideline directly tied to the running deer. Jarvis, flying forward, instantly saw his two only choices: hold onto the harness and be pulled headfirst into the stump, or let go and lose the deer. Either decision spelled disaster. The former meant instant injury and probably broken bones, while the latter meant freezing to death alone in the darkness. Since Jarvis was now trailing the team, they wouldn't realize he was gone for several hours. It might take them until the next day to find him. By that time, in the frigid Arctic, with no food, shelter, or heat, he could be dead.

Jarvis let go of the guideline.

Lying in shock, Jarvis watched the deer as it disappeared in the falling snow. His deer was gone. The cargo train was gone, and the rest of the herd was being driven ahead of that. He sat in the darkness pondering his fate.

"Help!" he yelled, hoping the group was still close enough to hear him. He knew he called in vain. His voice had been lost in the wind-blown snow.

Near panic, he jumped to his feet and staggered forward a few steps into the darkness. Then he settled down to a walk, yelling as he went. Finally he stopped altogether. He had to think fast. Should he continue and try to stop the group, or wait here for them to find him? Better yet, should he go in the direction of the deer, to find it and bring it back? Adrenaline flowing, it took him just a few brief seconds to analyze his limited options. Realizing the folly of trying to look for man or deer in the blizzard, Jarvis decided to remain and try to survive the night.

Before the train began several days earlier, Jarvis had instructed each man to carry his sleeping bag and clothing in his own sled. Now, split from the group, he was the beneficiary of his own foresight. With the snow and wind hammering him relentlessly, he trudged back to the cargo. It was lying on its side against the stump. He struggled to right the several-hundred-pound sled. Righting it at last, he placed it broadside to the wind to create a windbreak. Then he unlashed the tarp covering the gear on one side.

With the tarp wildly flapping in the wind, Jarvis managed to extract his sleeping bag in the biting cold. Numb fingers made the task more difficult. Finally after unfurling his bag next to the sled, he popped inside and curled up. The sled was low to the ground and provided little protection from the wind, but he held the tarp over his head to stay as warm as possible. Hopefully, he would survive the night.

With feeling slowly leaving his hands and feet, the gravity of his situation was becoming painfully evident. He strained to hear any sound in the howling wind. He didn't dare look up over the sled to see any movement in the darkness, lest he freeze even faster. Minutes hung like hours as he contemplated his fate—lost, alone, in the Arctic.

Finally he heard a sound, faint but unmistakable. "Hello!" came the distant shout.

Jarvis instantly jumped to his feet and shouted, "Here! Here!"

Peering straight into the stinging gale, he could barely make out the outline of men groping slowly in his direction. They were literally inching along with arms outstretched, as a person feels his way through a darkened house.

"There he is!" yelled one of the men.

Jarvis stood waving his arms in the blizzard until the men reached him.

"My God, am I glad to see you!" he said.

"I never thought we'd find you," came the reply from Mikkel.

"How'd you know I was gone?" yelled Jarvis above the howling wind.

"Your deer," responded one of the Eskimos. "He trotting behind sleds. We thought you attached. We not see in blizzard."

"The deer must have found his way back to the group after he broke away from the sled," responded Jarvis. The wind was now battering the men so painfully that they huddled together only inches from each other's face. Even at this proximity they had to shout to be heard.

"Thank God we decided to halt and talk to you about stopping for the night," said Mikkel. "We walked back and discovered the deer with no sled."

"How did you find me here?" yelled Jarvis. Their route throughout the day had taken the train zigzagging through obstacles in white-out conditions. Two men standing six feet apart could easily miss each other in the blinding snow. The probability that the group could have found Jarvis in this vast landscape was almost zero.

"The sled tracks," yelled Mikkel. "Somehow they still showed in the snow." It was truly uncanny. Hurricane-force winds and heavy falling snow should have instantly obliterated the tracks. But they didn't. Providence once again had staved off certain disaster.

The reunited men then turned their attention to surviving the night. On their way back to find Jarvis the group had passed an old, abandoned hut. It wasn't much, but it might be usable as a temporary shelter against the blizzard.

Chapter Fifteen

Jim . . .   *The Seal Hunt*

Jim looked on as the Inupiat Eskimo guides prepared to go seal hunting. He marveled at their harpoon. It was like nothing he'd ever seen before. Its blade had a hole at the base to receive the foreshaft, which was held in place with thongs. A throwing board was attached to the shaft by two pegs and two bone feathers that stood at the shaft's base and served as counterweights. In all, it looked like a spear with a piece of wood attached to fling the harpoon forward.

The stranded whalers would starve if they had to rely on the rotten meat contained at Point Barrow. Gathering meat was crucial for their survival as they waited for spring. Since the whalers themselves were unaccustomed to hunting and fishing in the Arctic, they had to turn to the Eskimo villagers.

It had been difficult enough for the villagers to maintain food for themselves and their families until spring. Their sense of humanity urged them to help the koblonas. Therefore, some of the men were selected to form joint hunting parties and share the kill.

The Eskimos were a point of great curiosity to Jim. On the whaling ship, the foremast hands had generally referred to them as a dirty, lazy people, not up to civilization's standards. But that opinion didn't seem to fit this group of Inuit. They had given to the stranded men of their meager possessions, an act of charity above and beyond any found in traditional society. He surmised that it was in part due to their strong sense of community. They seemed to care for those beyond their own family and even share communal possessions. Jim thought that the white men could

87

learn much from the Eskimos. In fact, they must if they were to have any hope of survival.

They started out on two dogsleds over the ice. The Eskimos seemed to guide the teams as easily as a rider guides a horse. Jim was amazed at the apparent strength of the sleds, for they were a light apparatus kept together only by lashed animal skins. The dog harnesses were likewise made of strips of heavy tacking and connected to a larger line tied along the length of all the dogs to the sled. As a seaman, Jim could appreciate the handiwork of knots and line that held man, dog, wood, and cargo together.

The Eskimos progressed in a line for over an hour, looking intently at the landscape—for what, Jim wasn't quite sure. Finally, the Eskimo in the lead stopped abruptly. Jim peered ahead but could see only ice and snow.

"What is it?" Jim asked the guide.

The guide raised his hand wordlessly, commanding silence.

The lead hunter then gestured for the others to advance. Silently the hunters crept forward, then crouched in the snow and peered intently at a small hole in the ice—a seal's breathing hole.

As he hunkered beside the hunters, Jim could feel the chill permeate his bones. He ached from the cold. His feet and hands were numb, just as they'd been when he first left the *Orca*. He thought of the dramatic contrast between the hunt on a whale ship and the Inuit's seal hunt. Here he sat in perfect silence; in the whale hunt, everything had been noise and movement.

His heart began to quicken as he recalled his first kill. He had been on deck when the lookout called, "There she blows!" Immediately the crew jumped into frenzied action. Deck hands determined the exact position of the whales; the helmsman turned the ship windward of their prey. The hands scrambled aboard the whaleboats hung on davits at the side of the ship. The boat steerer readied the craft for lowering while the rest of the crew clambered inside. When they'd barely gotten into their positions, the captain yelled "Away boats." With a jolt, the boats were lowered into the water. If the wind was up, a sail powered the boat, lest the sounds of oars frighten their prey. Without a sail, each man put his oar into the water and began to pull hard against the waves that were tossing the boat from side to side, and all the while the boat steerer yelled, "Pull! Pull, you buggers!"

Backs straining, arms pumping, they pulled at the oars with all their might. As they approached their prey, their hearts raced from the excitement of fear laced with killer instinct. Fear came from the knowledge that many a crewman had been lost when whales dove beneath the boat and rammed it. Such stoving typically overturned the boat and drowned the men—those who were not bitten in half by the whale. On the other hand, the whale could turn flukes and dive, never to be seen again.

Jim recalled how they had pulled and pulled on the oars. It seemed to take forever. But soon, even though their backs were turned to the bow, they could hear the loud breathing of those tremendous beasts and their tails hitting the water as they slowly swam ahead. As the boats drew closer and the whales' noise became louder, each man came to grips with the immediacy of his fate. Would he be maimed? Would he be killed? Or would he win the ultimate contest against his powerful prey?

Reaching their deadly quarry, the mate ordered the boat's steerer to stand. He rose and positioned the boat to deliver the harpoon. With the boat maneuvered into exactly the correct position, the mate yelled, "Stern all!" At that command, each man instantly stopped rowing and lifted his oar out of the water, lest the giant flukes and tail strike it. Anxiously they bobbed in the water as the line was checked and wrapped around the loggerhead. Then the mate aimed his darting gun and pulled the trigger, shooting a bomb lance into the whale.

"Hold onto him!" yelled the mate to the bowman, who held the line attached to a lance being pulled under by the struggling whale. The whale seemed to slow to a halt. Jim thought their prey was dead when it suddenly convulsed and threw itself above the water with an earsplitting crash, but the whale turned and rushed at their boat. Just as Jim was expecting to ride a stoved boat to his death, the whale stopped dead from its wound.

Jim could still see that charging whale's eye. He shuddered at the memory.

Suddenly a small wisp of water spewed from the seal hole. The Inupiat Eskimo immediately flung his harpoon at the unseen seal beneath.

Jim thought he must have missed, but the convulsions of the seal beneath the ice signaled otherwise. The skilled hunter had killed his prey.

Jim was amazed that the Eskimo could have kept his concentration at hair-trigger alert for that long. In the same split second that the seal appeared, he had accurately thrust his spear into the water with deadly accuracy.

With some effort the hunters dragged the limp seal out of the hole, onto the ice, and to the sled. Once back at the village, they quickly dressed the seal and prepared it for the villagers and the stranded whalers. The Eskimos took every part of the seal and wasted nothing. Its skin became clothes, blubber provided lamp oil, intestines turned into snow-house windows, and its body was consumed as food. But even an animal of this size couldn't feed such a big group of men for long. When all the food was divided, each person received only a very small morsel from the catch. It was obvious that even hunting and fishing in the Arctic wouldn't save them until spring.

Jim lay in his berth that night, miserable from the damp, the cold, and the foul air. He could barely stand the filth and the smell. If it had been a warm environment it would still be barely tolerable. Freezing, it was unbearable.

As he lay shivering, Jim reflected on the day's hunt. He liked the feeling of power from being in the party that had triumphed over the seal. That gave him a small ray of hope: If they devoted more men to the hunt, maybe they could make it part way until spring. One seal wasn't much, but at least it showed they could supplement the often-rotten meat they were forced to live on.

Chapter Sixteen

After the blizzard had sidelined them in an abandoned shack for several days, Jarvis and Mikkel decided they couldn't wait any longer. Harnessing the reindeer, they set out and crept along through the storm at a slow pace, Jarvis following virtually next to Mikkel so as not to lose the lead sled. He couldn't see the sled behind him, but assumed it was close.

The wind increased. Now the men couldn't stay upright no matter how much they anchored their feet. Only their hold on the sleds kept them from being blown away.

Finally, after a grueling day still mostly filled with darkness, Mikkel drew into the village of Opiktillik. Jarvis was amazed. They could only see two feet past their faces. How had the man navigated? Grasping his sled and fighting his way to Mikkel's, he grabbed the Russian.

"I can't believe it," said Jarvis in amazement. "How did you do it?"

"The deer led the way," yelled Mikkel.

"No, seriously," retorted Jarvis.

"I *am* serious," yelled Mikkel. "I couldn't see where we were going. The deer kept moving forward so I hoped and prayed that they remembered the route from having been here before, and they did."

Once again Jarvis was stunned. They were lost in the blizzard, and the deer led the way. Up until now, Jarvis had been frustrated with the stupidity and erratic behavior of the deer. He'd longed for a dogsled once again. But today the deer's hidden abilities took him totally by surprise. Once again the rescue party had received a miraculous break.

In the howling wind, Mikkel and Jarvis crawled through the long tunnel-like opening of the main hut of the village. Inside, the villagers seemed stunned at their arrival. In a blizzard like this, two men casually entered their hut as if out for a Sunday stroll. How could they have traveled in this blizzard and survived, let alone found the village?

After exchanging pleasantries and removing their outer garments, Jarvis and Mikkel squatted beside the villagers, enjoying the warmth and comfort while outside the blizzard raged. They would wait here for the rest of their party; it made no sense to stand outside, for who could see anything in this blowing snow?

Even with the presence of unexpected visitors, the Eskimos went about their chores of mending clothes and preparing food. It was as if they were accustomed to strangers dropping in to find refuge in bad weather.

Minutes passed, then an hour. Jarvis and Mikkel knew there was trouble. The rest of the sled train obviously wasn't right behind them. In fact, they weren't anywhere close.

"What do we do?" asked Jarvis.

"There's nothing we *can* do," responded Mikkel with a look of great anxiety.

"You found me yesterday when I was lost," said Jarvis.

"That was different," responded Mikkel. Jarvis didn't need an explanation and Mikkel knew it. Yesterday the blizzard hadn't been what it was today. In addition, they had been along the coast, which provided a natural delimiting boundary for their search. Today they had no such luck.

"How about the natives, can they help?" asked Jarvis. Again he already knew the answer; Mikkel simply shook his head.

One of the villagers listened with great concern. "We'll go out for them in a while," he said, gesturing toward the blizzard raging outside. Everyone knew that it was foolhardy to attempt finding the rescuers now.

Jarvis became more agitated with each passing moment. He couldn't sit idly by and wait, yet he had no other choice.

Suddenly the flap at the head of the tunnel opened and a head emerged. It was one of the herders. He was followed by another herder, then Kettleson and the doctor.

"How did you find us?" Jarvis asked the doctor in amazement.

"It wasn't easy," responded Dr. Call. "If it weren't for our young friend here," he said, nodding at one of the herders, "we wouldn't have made it."

Jarvis and Mikkel looked admiringly at the young man as he removed his hood and deerskin coat. He quickly sat down with some embarrassment and smiled back at the pair.

"So," Jarvis asked the young herder, "what did you do?"

"We lost the trail in the blizzard. The wind blew away the tracks and we couldn't see beyond our faces." He paused to remove his outer deerskin pants.

"Yes, yes," interjected Mikkel. "Then what?"

"We couldn't see the trail, so I felt it," the herder responded.

"What do you mean, you felt it?" asked Jarvis.

"I felt it, on my hands and knees."

"You mean to tell me you crawled all the way here, feeling your way?" asked Jarvis. "That was at least a mile, maybe a lot more."

"He sure did," confirmed Kettleson. "Damnedest thing I ever saw. He saved our lives." Jarvis sat back in gratitude and pride—pride that he had been given men such as this to step up and do the impossible, and gratitude that they had all received such help.

Despite five more bodies to accommodate, the villagers shared their space with good grace. And with equally good grace, Jarvis shared food from the rescuers' supplies with the Eskimos. Before long the adventurers fell asleep, exhausted.

The blizzard pounded through the night and into the morning. Jarvis and the team were forced to bide their time in the igloo as prisoners of the storm. Though this provided a much needed rest, for Jarvis it was torture. Already torn about the need to rescue the whalers, as he watched the Eskimo women tend to their families he was flooded with concern for the wife and new baby he had left behind. He wondered now if she was exhausted from caring for the infant. Was she crying? It was almost more than he could bear. At one point he pulled on all his outer clothing and stood outside in the blizzard—anything for a distraction. He tried to remind himself that she had urged him to go, and that he was the only man in the Cutter Service with the skills and experience to save the whalers. It was small consolation. He was sick to his stomach.

By the third day of waiting in the hut, Jarvis was frantic. They had to get on their way, but the blizzard continued with the same severity. What if it lasted for several more days, or even weeks? How many lives would be lost by their sitting there waiting out a storm? After some discussion the group reluctantly gathered their belongings and hit the trail.

With the wind at a brutal 15 degrees below zero, they had to take the extra precaution of wrapping their faces so only a little of their eyes showed to the outside. Progress was cruelly slow as they pushed into the wind. The deer leading the sleds continually attempted to turn away from the gale and walk out to sea.

Jarvis began to think that he had made a grave error. If they didn't reach the next village by nightfall, they'd have to find a protected lee, a natural mountain windbreak. Unfortunately, visibility was zero.

Mikkel stopped his sled to determine the direction to the village. Obviously dead reckoning was impossible in the storm. Jarvis stumbled erratically the few short steps over to Mikkel, attempting to stay upright in the pounding wind. Standing beside the Russian herder, holding his coat lest he fall down, Jarvis said nothing, sensing the tension and frustration of the guide.

"We'll be lucky to get out of this one," yelled Mikkel above the wind. The gravity of the statement instantly registered with Jarvis. Mikkel was a tough man, not given to exaggeration. If *he* said they would be lucky to make it, that meant there was a significant chance for death or serious injury.

"That bad?" Jarvis yelled above the storm.

"I've never gone out in a blizzard this bad, and never will again," Mikkel affirmed.

With that, Jarvis simply squeezed the man's arm and continued back to his sled. There was nothing he could do to help Mikkel, who alone had the skill to bring them to the village.

The group continued inching their way along the trail as the afternoon wore on. Every so often, the sun appeared as a fuzzy red glow through the blinding snow above, reminding Jarvis of better days. It was obvious they wouldn't make the village of Kebethluk before nightfall, as they'd hoped. With the temperature holding steady at minus 15 degrees, they had to find some protection to make it through the night. They pressed on—tired, cold, and frightened.

Suddenly the wind seemed to subside. Jarvis opened his hood a crack to make sure. Either the wind force was weakening or they had accidentally found a protecting ridge. They continued forward. To one side they could barely make out the ridge acting as their savior from the biting cold gale. It was the lee of Cape Nome. Again Jarvis walked to Mikkel—it was easier this time—and waited to be recognized and addressed.

"It's better," said Mikkel, still having to raise his voice above a hard wind.

"Is it better from the lee or is the storm subsiding?" asked Jarvis.

"Both, I think," responded Mikkel.

"Will the lee cover us all the way to the village?" asked Jarvis.

"It should," said Mikkel, pulling slowly on his hood. This type of detail could only be obtained from a guide, not a map.

Jarvis wasn't one to continue a conversation when they had to move. He went back to his sled and they pressed forward. Jarvis almost held his breath waiting for the wind to pound them again.

Finally, as the late afternoon sun set, they arrived at Kebethluk on the west side of Cape Nome. It was a large village with comfortable log buildings. Compared to what they'd seen before, it was almost like pulling into Chicago on a train. For a moment Jarvis stood gazing in awe at the log buildings. Then he turned, to see Mikkel greet the villagers and explain their situation, pointing frequently at Jarvis and the rest.

The villagers quickly ushered them into a log building and gathered food, informing the group that they had passed the bulk of the storm. Moving forward would now be easier under the protection of the mountain ridge. As they sat again, Jarvis felt sleep engulf his tired body. There would be no more time to anguish over his family tonight.

The men were in good spirits when they arose in the dark morning. They had made it through the storm to the other side; the days ahead would be easier. Following their usual routine, they went outside and packed the sleds, retrieving the food from the high racks that overnight had kept it out of reach of ravenous Eskimo dogs.

They were now just over a quarter of the way to the whalers, their destination the deer herd near Cape Rodney and Port Clarence. As they had arrived the previous night, they had left most of the deer they were driving about a mile away from the village. Exhausted, seeing no dogs, they had allowed their tired sled deer to remain in camp. It was a terrible mistake.

Walking toward the sled deer, Jarvis spun around as the first three canine attackers came. "Dogs!" he yelled. The first sled deer kicked valiantly at its attacker. Then the pack attacked in force as Jarvis looked on in horror.

As the blizzard had subsided, the village dogs must have picked up the deer scent. Now they snapped their fangs into the legs of the valuable sled deer. The deer reared up, jumping and kicking at their attackers. Jarvis, the doctor, and all the men quickly leaped into the melee, desperately swinging driftwood clubs, knowing, even as the dogs snarled and bit at the men, that it would be a disaster if the dogs killed or maimed one of the irreplaceable trained sled deer.

The men of the deer train and village joined the fray. Dogs and men battled it out as fangs ripped at the arms and legs of the deer's defenders. Jarvis screamed. A dog had his arm clenched in its jaw, shaking its head in an attempt to break the bone. Jarvis pounded the dog's head and neck. Finally the dog let go, deciding no food was worth a deadly beating. Other dogs similarly fell away two or three at a time, and the rest of the pack, seeing that they were badly outnumbered, retreated. Panting, the men stood in a circle around the deer.

"Any deer injured?" asked Jarvis. A quick examination revealed no injuries.

"We've got to move," said Mikkel.

"Yes, let's get out of here before they come back," Jarvis added.

As badly as the men wanted to recover and tend their wounds, there was no time to waste, for if they remained, the dogs would be back for another attack. Hurriedly they wrapped their wounds as they secured the last items of gear and moved out to collect the main herd about a mile away. As they raced toward the bulk of their small herd, they prayed the dogs hadn't scented them and gotten there first.

They arrived to find the deer calmly grazing on moss, unharmed by any predators. Jarvis pulled next to Mikkel. "They look all right," he said with relief.

"Yes, but we've got to get them moving right away."

So they quickly gathered the herd and continued on the trail, constantly checking behind and to each side, scanning for dogs—in a pack, dogs were cunning and could ambush the group. But they found no sign of the canines.

In the excitement and tension, they didn't realize that the temperature was dropping. It was now minus 30 degrees, creating a deadly danger of a different kind. Jarvis painfully felt the change and realized they needed to reach the next village as soon as possible.

The next village wasn't just another group of icehouses along the way. It was the prize. Not only did it contain Jarvis's personal friend Charlie Artisarlook, but it also contained the private deer herd Charlie maintained. Jarvis was hoping to augment the small herd he was driving by acquiring from Charlie enough additional deer to feed the whalers until spring.

Before the trip began, the rescuers had known of four possible sources of reindeer. The main government herd was at St. Michael, where they had been refused. The second, smaller government herd had already been delivered by Kettleson—these were the deer they were driving. Only two other sources existed. These herds were privately owned by missionaries who used them to feed the Eskimos and help them build a local economy. One missionary herd was held by Tom Lopp. The other belonged to Charlie, whose Eskimo name was Artisarlook. Charlie and Jarvis had become friends during Jarvis's eight years on the *Bear*, when Charlie and Mary lived near the coast.

Yet important as was the next village—and Charlie's deer herd—and as keenly as they felt the chill coming on, the travelers saw that night was falling rapidly. For all their eagerness, they realized they wouldn't be able to make their goal this evening, so they stopped for the night and put up their tents.

Now, sleeping in a tent in open terrain at those temperatures is especially dangerous. If one's extremities get too cold during the night, frostbite will set in. David Jarvis discovered this the hard way. During the night, Jarvis accidentally allowed his foot to freeze by lying in a cramped position that denied the limb circulation. Awakening in the night, he noticed that his foot felt like a block of ice. Realizing the danger, he started to kick and pound his foot against the ground to restore feeling. This went on for over an hour. By morning, he'd regained very little feeling but had to begin again on the trail, nevertheless. If he didn't get his foot warm soon, he could lose that limb.

Chapter Seventeen

Jarvis . . .   Charlie Artisarlook

About noon the next day the group reached Charlie Artisarlook's house in the village. Charlie, a rare man, had a rare occupation: he was a missionary and a deer herder. With his wife, he relied on these animals to survive. It was an arrangement like that of a farmer relying on his livestock. Making the herd more critical still, Charlie and his wife had gathered a group of Eskimo families who tended the herd. For their efforts, these families received furs for clothing, a share of the income from fur sales, and actual animals to sustain themselves and their children.

Jarvis, limping badly, was anxious to warm his foot. But aside from his basic need for warmth, Jarvis had more dread than joy at the thought of a reunion with his old friend. Anguish set in as they neared the house, for Jarvis had to ask Charlie for his herd, the herd upon which all those souls depended. In return, Charlie would receive only a promise that at some future date, the U.S. government would replace the deer. It would require a great leap of faith for Charlie, his wife, and their Eskimo families to surrender their livestock, risking their lives and livelihood on the word of a young lieutenant. And the lieutenant wasn't comfortable basing this promise on the often-unreliable bureaucratic machine in Washington. Promises wouldn't keep these people from freezing to death in the Arctic winter.

Jarvis approached the house of his friend with a lump in his throat. He'd rather face dangers in the Arctic than ask his friends for such a sacrifice.

"Hello, Mary," said Jarvis to the woman who appeared as he

approached. Despite years in the Arctic, Mary was an attractive woman. Her hair was long and dark, matching her complexion. The sight of her heightened Jarvis's longing for his own wife.

"David, is that you?" Mary responded. Jarvis did a double-take. It had been a long time since he had heard his first name.

"Yes, it's me, David," he replied with a broad smile and outstretched arms. They embraced for a moment. The rest of the men tended the sleds and the herd while Jarvis walked with Mary into the one room used both for cooking and sleeping—as with most lodging in Alaska, one room could contain everything they needed and was easier to heat.

"How have you been, David?" asked Mary, bringing her friend a warming cup of coffee and gesturing toward a chair by the fire.

"I'm well," said Jarvis, stretching his feet toward the coals. His chilled foot still had not regained its feeling, despite the day's exertion. He was grateful for the fire's healing warmth.

"I wish Charlie could have seen you walk up to the cabin. He'd have been surprised," said Mary with a smile.

"I wish I could have seen his face," said Jarvis, feeling a sudden shot of fear upon hearing Charlie referred to in the past tense. "But where is Charlie?"

"Oh, Charlie's fine," said Mary, reading Jarvis's worried look. "He'll be back soon. He went sealing."

Jarvis breathed a sigh of relief. "I'm glad to hear Charlie's well. I've always had a great deal of affection for both of you."

As the two continued to exchange pleasantries, Jarvis gradually regained the feeling in his foot. He reached down and rubbed it gratefully.

Mary listened intently as Jarvis explained their travels to date and the plight of the whalers. Though he carefully avoided the reason for his visit, Mary knew what he would ask. She waited patiently, realizing that he would save the request until both she and her husband were together. These types of decisions required both people and a long, heartfelt discussion.

Then into the cabin strode a large man dressed in deerskin, with a bright smile and the round features of an Inuit. "Well, David Jarvis, I can't believe it," said Charlie heartily.

"Hello, Charlie," said Jarvis, rising to grasp the outstretched hand of his friend.

"It's been a long time," replied Charlie. "Don't tell me you've given up the Cutter Service to become a deer herder," he said. A laugh came from deep within his stomach.

"Well, I could do worse things," said Jarvis, showing respect for his friend and his occupation. Caring statements like that had endeared Jarvis to Charlie.

They sat down once again and talked over old times. Then Jarvis explained his mission and the need for deer to save the men almost a thousand miles north in the ice. Charlie and Mary listened intently, quietly glancing at each other. There was a long silence when Jarvis finished and the impact of what he was asking set in.

Finishing the conversation, Jarvis said, "Of course, we'll arrange for food through a trader at Golovin Bay and supplies from Port Clarence. That way Mary won't be lacking for food until the deer are replaced. That's assuming, of course, that Charlie can go with us to help drive the deer." Charlie had extensive experience as a deer herder, and now that Mikkel and Kettleson would be leaving shortly, Charlie was badly needed to drive the herd.

"Well, we have to discuss this, David," said Charlie, looking at his wife. The look on his face was like that of a man having to decide between a firing squad and the gallows.

"Of course," said Jarvis. "I have to go outside and check on my men and setup for the night." He rose to leave.

"Please stay in here with us—bring along as many men as you like," offered Mary.

"Thank you, Mary, your hospitality is overwhelming," said Jarvis with a smile. Charlie patted him on the shoulder as he strode out the door. Most men would have instantly balked at the kind of request that had just been made, but Charlie, being Charlie, was sensitive to Jarvis's situation.

As Jarvis approached his sled, he regretted what he'd asked of his friend. It had taken many years of hard work and faithful service to the people around them for Charlie and Mary to accumulate their deer.

Without the herd, they were poor.

"How'd it go?" asked the doctor sympathetically. He and the others had tended to chores while Jarvis went inside. They knew it would be a difficult request and let Jarvis approach his friends alone.

"About as I expected," said Jarvis with downcast eyes. "I half wished they'd thrown me out."

"You did what you had to do," said the doctor, bracing his hand on Jarvis's shoulder. "When will we know?"

"Soon, I think," said Jarvis. "They're talking it over now." By this time Mikkel and Kettleson had walked up and caught the tail end of the conversation. Knowing what Jarvis had had to ask, they were concerned.

"We've been invited to stay in the cabin," said Jarvis. Then he added, "But let's wait a while to leave them their privacy." The others voiced their agreement and continued with their chores.

After finishing their preparations, Jarvis and three of the men approached Charlie's cabin. The others in their group were taken into the surrounding houses of the Eskimo villagers, where, as always, they received selfless hospitality. The hosts collected and mended the travelers' clothing to keep out the freezing wind. Though their possessions were meager, the Eskimos shared what they had without reservation. It was almost as if the less they had, the more they gave.

Mary and Charlie were there to meet Jarvis. "Come in, come in," said Charlie. "We have hot food and coffee waiting."

"Oh my, that sounds good," said Mikkel.

"Thanks so much for having us in your home," said the doctor.

As they ate near the small fire in the center of the room, the conversation was light and pleasant. They talked about how the region had changed with the arrival of the miners and this year's early winter.

"Well," said Charlie finally, taking Mary's hand. This was his signal that they were ready to discuss their decision. Jarvis had partly hoped that this moment would never come. "As you know, Mary and I have spent many years accumulating the deer."

"And the Eskimos you've seen in the village rely on the deer as we do," added Mary, looking in turn at Charlie and Jarvis.

"Yes," affirmed Charlie, "the villagers are like our family. Their welfare is much more important to us than that of the deer herd." With this he paused to take a deep breath. It was obvious that the decision caused both of them deep anguish.

"But we can't sentence the trapped whalers to death," said Mary, continuing Charlie's line of thought. These two had obviously been together so long that they worked as partners in everything. "Therefore, we'll give you our deer and my husband to guide them," said Mary. With that, she directed a forced, affirming smile at Charlie.

Charlie, obviously shaken by the thought of leaving his wife while he traveled almost a thousand miles into the unknown, found himself without words. Tears welled up while he reached for the hands of his wife and looked into her eyes, ignoring the fact that others were watching. This was the first time that they'd be leaving each other for an extended period. They had no idea when they'd see each other again, if ever.

Mary was going to say something to Charlie but stopped herself. Instead, she simply held his hands and returned his look of adoration. Jarvis and the men sat silently as Charlie and Mary took a few moments to gaze lovingly at each other.

Finally, Charlie broke the silence. "Lieutenant Jarvis," he said intently, using his friend's formal title rather than his first name, "I'm relying on your word and authority to take care of my wife while I'm gone. You'll arrange for food for her and the villagers, and replace the herd. They rely on that herd for their livelihood."

Before Jarvis could speak, Mary interrupted. "And you'll take care of my husband," she said. As the officer in charge, Jarvis would be making decisions that could mean the difference between Mary's enjoying a future life with her husband or becoming a widow.

"Yes, Mary," said Jarvis earnestly. "I will treat Charlie's life as my own." Looking back at Charlie, he said, with fire in his voice, "As God is my witness, I'll not rest until your wife and the villagers are well provisioned and your sacrifice is replaced." And it was true; in the days to come, Jarvis would let nothing stand in the way of his taking care of these people.

"And by the way," Charlie said, "while you were setting up camp, we pulled together the villagers one by one. They're unified in their support of this decision. It wasn't ours alone." The tears pooling in Charlie's eyes showed the pride he had in his people.

"They're great people," affirmed the doctor. "We wouldn't have made it this far without them. In every village, we've been met with open arms and selfless giving; our clothes have been mended and meals have been prepared for us. The sacrifices of the Inuit have sustained us, and I know they will continue to do so in our travels to come."

Charlie's face just glowed.

The conversation continued into the night before they finally succumbed to sleep. Jarvis awoke in the still-dark morning and made preparations to begin again. It had been decided that he would continue on his way to acquire more deer from Kettleson, and Mikkel would accompany Jarvis as far as Port Clarence. The doctor would remain behind to help gather and prepare the two deer herds. Charlie would go with Jarvis, who needed the most experienced man to guide him for the remainder of the trip and provide needed expertise in the deer they'd acquire.

This time there were dogs enough for sled teams. Jarvis was happy at the thought of giving up his skittish deer for a speedier dog team, at least for a while. "I see you're not letting grass grow under your feet," said the doctor to Jarvis, playfully sweeping his head from side to side, as if looking for grass.

"Well, it'd have to grow under three feet of snow, anyway," grinned Jarvis as he tightened the last straps around his sled's cargo.

"It's hard to believe we've made it this far," said the doctor, looking back in the direction from which they'd come.

"I know," said Jarvis with a smile. Then patting the doctor on the shoulder, he added, "Let's just keep thinking about what we've accomplished getting here instead of how far we have to go. It works better that way."

"Good advice from a good man," retorted the doctor.

At this point, Kettleson and Mikkel approached and chided the pair, "Well, if you two would prefer to be alone too, we can go find someplace to wait." They were referring to Charlie and Mary, who were still wrapped in a warm embrace saying goodbye.

"Well then, come on, boys," said Jarvis. "It's time we earned our pay."

After two days of hard travel, the group arrived at the government station at Port Clarence along their route to Cape Prince of Wales. They were now five weeks into the overland expedition.

Like the community that had risen around Charlie and Mary in their missionary duties, the government station at Port Clarence had grown into a small community of its own, oriented around its resident reverend, T. L. Brevig and his wife. As missionaries, they not only taught the local children how to read and write, but also provided a service to the Eskimos and the government by manning a station and its supplies. At Port Clarence, Jarvis gathered supplies that would help his group proceed to Cape Prince of Wales and beyond on the Arctic side of the Bering Strait.

Once again a blizzard overtook the group. This time they were forced to stay with the Brevigs, who took the time to repair their clothing and acquire extra supplies for them.

Two days later, on the morning of the 23rd, Jarvis decided he couldn't wait any longer. The blizzard was still troublesome, but not as severe as what they had encountered previously.

Kettleson and Mikkel, who had to return to the remainder of their herd at Golovin Bay, arose to say goodbye to their now "old friend." Jarvis, bent down beside his sled, was putting the finishing touches on tightening its cargo. Seeing Kettleson and Mikkel approach in the early morning gloom, he straightened up and faced his friends. "So, this is it."

"Yes, this is it," responded Mikkel, extending his hand. "You'll be fine, Lieutenant. You've learned a lot."

"I know," said Jarvis. There was no point in making jokes to lesson the sadness. These men had become closer than family in their struggles together, not unlike soldiers in a war.

"Yes, you've got good people," added Kettleson, nodding towards Charlie. It was an affirmation of his replacement. "And don't forget Ed," he added, trying to sound positive. Ed was a local guide who would come along for a small fee. These guides were necessary to help navigate the local terrain.

Mikkel and Kettleson had already voiced their opinion that Ed, this particular guide, couldn't be counted on, but Jarvis was in a difficult spot and decided he had to take a chance and use all the help they could get.

'Yes," Jarvis said now, "Ed will be particularly good for this mission because he's Inuit, he's had experience with a deer herd, and he's been a whaler at Herschel Island. I think he'll feel a kinship with the people we'll find on the trail as well as the men we're trying to rescue. Well, our paths will cross again," said Jarvis with a forced smile and a hug for both men. With that, Charlie and Jarvis went on their way with Ed as their guide.

The sleds pushed off into the snow, Ed in the lead, followed by Charlie. As before, Jarvis brought up the rear. The temperature was now minus 30 degrees, with a wind blowing hard out of the northeast. For four painful hours they slogged along, squinting to protect their eyes against the merciless, biting enemy.

Suddenly the lead sled stopped. Jarvis could barely make out Ed, who seemed to be agitatedly doing something with the cargo. When it looked as if Ed wouldn't start again, Jarvis approached the Inuit. It was painful enough to travel like this; they didn't want to stop and be punished by the wind any longer than they had to.

"What's going on?" asked Jarvis loudly above the wind.

"My rifle," responded Ed. "It must have fallen out along the trail." In the Arctic, where predators such as polar bears and wolves abounded, a gun was an absolute necessity. Jarvis knew that Ed wouldn't have two of such a precious commodity. While the team had enough guns to protect the group, such a valuable piece of personal wealth could certainly not be left behind.

"I have to go and find it," said Ed.

"All right, we'll turn around," said Jarvis, turning back to his sled.

"No," said Ed, jumping in his path. The suspicious movement surprised Jarvis. "No, I'll go alone and find it by myself."

Jarvis looked cautiously at Ed. After a long pause, he finally said slowly, "OK, we'll wait here."

"No, you go on; I'll catch up," said Ed, looking steadily at Jarvis. Fear instantly rose in Jarvis: something else was happening here.

"But you're our guide," said Jarvis.

"It's fine; just keep going in this direction," he said, pointing. "I'll be along."

Jarvis remained silent. He had to weigh the options quickly. Going ahead any distance without Ed would be unwise. They could easily become lost in the difficult terrain and lose valuable time. However, they could probably find their way to the next village. It was obvious that Ed wasn't going to allow them to return with him to get his rifle. Despite his suspicions, Jarvis seemed to have little choice but to see what Ed was planning to do.

The sled and dogs Ed used were his own. However, some of the cargo he carried belonged to the group—not enough to paralyze them if it were lost, but enough to hurt them. Every bit of supplies were important. Each man, especially a man of his experience, was badly needed. If he left now, their food supply would be that much more limited and the going that much more difficult.

"How long?" asked Jarvis finally.

"I'll catch up before nightfall."

Again Jarvis hesitated. He really didn't have much choice. "OK," he said finally. He knew not to argue. As with many of the Arctic men they'd encountered, confrontation was not a tool to be used. They were too tough for that—even dangerous. If it turned out that the negative opinion voiced by Kettleson and Mikkel about Ed the previous day was true, he'd abandon the group regardless. In fact, a confrontation would only make it worse.

Jarvis, now slightly shaken, walked slowly back and apprised Charlie of the situation. Although Charlie said nothing, it was obvious from his expression that he too had lacked confidence in Ed.

So Charlie and Jarvis climbed back onto their sleds and proceeded into the punishing wind as before. After two hours, they intermittently looked over their shoulders for Ed. But they knew he wouldn't return. Where they were going was dangerous, the trail punishing and the cold unforgiving. Ed would be crazy to go along. In fact, if they were smart, they'd turn back too.

They fought their way along the beach on the Arctic side of the Bering Strait. The going was slow and it was getting late. Charlie, now in the lead, stopped his sled. Jarvis looked on as his friend approached.

"We need to stop here," said Charlie.

Jarvis was tired and hungry; his foot still pained him. Without the doctor, he felt alone. He was angry at the obvious abandonment by Ed. Doubt crept in as Charlie pressed him to stop and camp.

"We have to keep going," said Jarvis. "It's only four."

"There's driftwood here on the beach. We can use that to build a fire against the blizzard."

"No, let's keep going." Charlie continued to press. "It's dangerous up ahead in the dark. The ice is crushed on the beach against the bluffs. We really need to stop here."

Jarvis looked angrily at Charlie. He already felt like a victim, having been abandoned by Ed. Now Charlie was talking about stopping; he seemed to exaggerate the danger and play upon Jarvis's fears.

"No," said Jarvis. Disgusted, tired, he clenched his fists and stared adamantly at Charlie. "We're going ahead."

Charlie stared back at the lieutenant. It was obvious that Jarvis wouldn't be persuaded. Charlie had to make a decision of his own. Finally after an uncomfortable silence, he shrugged and went back to his sled. They began again.

As the sleds moved forward, Jarvis watched Charlie's back with suspicion. Was Charlie second-guessing his own decision to leave his wife and go on such a dangerous mission? He must be. Now Jarvis was nervous. His anger gave way to fear at what would happen if Charlie left just as Ed had done.

They continued as darkness fell. Just as Charlie had predicted, the bluffs near Cape York came down to the sea, and the ice was crushed, creating an almost impossible trail in the dark. Each crush, higher than a man's head, had to be scaled like a small cliff. The sleds, which had to be dragged, pulled, and lifted, continually capsized in the jagged ice, and the men had to fight to right them and their heavy cargo. Each time, Jarvis and Charlie struggled in silence. Charlie was too big a man to say, "I told you so," and Jarvis was too embarrassed to express his mistake in judgment. He had learned not to underestimate Charlie or his determination in the future. At last they spoke and determined that Charlie should go slightly ahead on foot and try to find a trail through the ice crushes. After four more hours of this exhausting effort, they were near collapse.

Finally, Jarvis had had enough. "Charlie," he yelled.

Charlie, slightly ahead of Jarvis, hauling the sled up a crush, heard his name and stopped. Out of breath and slumped over, he tried to pull himself together.

Jarvis approached. "Charlie, can we camp here?" Asking rather than telling Charlie was Jarvis's way of saying, "You were right; I misjudged you and the situation."

Charlie seemed to understand the gesture and simply said, "I'm sorry, Jarvis, but we can't camp here."

"OK," replied Jarvis. This time he made sure not to ask for an explanation. His friend's simple word was enough on which to base his decision.

Charlie added, "The ice is unstable, there's no wood for a fire, and the temperature's dropping." So they pressed on, despite the blizzard's increasing severity. Unstable ice could break away from shore, leaving exposed, freezing water for the sleds and men to fall into.

Jarvis began to worry. How much longer could his body and the stamina of the dogs continue? He could barely lift his legs from exhaustion. He kept telling himself, "Just one more ice crush, David," but he knew he couldn't go on much longer.

Disaster struck just as Jarvis, Charlie, and the dogs were beginning to tackle the next ice crush. Jarvis felt the ice under his right leg give way. As he fell into the freezing water, he reached wildly into the air as if to grab an unseen railing. His leg instantly went numb as the frigid water soaked his pant leg.

They say that in an extreme moment—one that may be your last—your life passes before your eyes. This was certainly Jarvis's experience. As if in slow motion, he could see the ice surface rise toward his face as his body crashed down. He threw his body forward to keep on top of the ice as much of his bulk as possible, and the maneuver worked. In a panic, he pulled his right leg—now in the water to his hip—out of the frozen Arctic and in the same motion lurched away from the opening.

He had saved himself from immediate death. But now he must move quickly to save his leg—and his life—in the minus 40 degrees temperature.

Charlie looked back just as Jarvis lurched forward; then he saw the hole in the ice. "You all right?" he yelled above the wind. His voice was too loud for men now standing face to face, but Charlie's adrenaline was flowing.

"Yes," said Jarvis. "What do we do now?"

Charlie said nothing but looked rapidly around in all directions. Then he suddenly stopped, looking only at Jarvis. After a few seconds of silence, he said, "I remember an abandoned shack not far ahead. We can get you inside and dried out. There'll be driftwood nearby for a fire. But we have to hurry!" Charlie had made this trip before and knew the route to the Lopps', as well. He saw them each season and had even lived with them for a time.

The race was on. Jarvis' leg was already completely without feeling. He knew he was standing on it by looking at it, but he might as well have been leaning against a table leg.

They pushed and dragged the sleds and dogs over each ice crush. It seemed to go on forever. Hours passed and still they continued, now almost unable to drag the sleds. Jarvis almost lost hope of keeping his leg or ever building a fire. With the gale force winds, the minus 40 degrees seemed at least 20 degrees colder.

Finally at midnight there was a break.

"There!" yelled Charlie.

"Where?" responded Jarvis.

"There," Charlie repeated, pointing through the night to a barely recognizable outline—of a roof jutting out of the snow that buried it on each side.

"Charlie," Jarvis shouted, "you're amazing! If you hadn't spotted that thing, I'd have stumbled right on by it."

The two men pulled up the sleds, untethered the dogs, and grabbed their sleeping bags. Jarvis went first, dragging himself inside through a small opening in the snowdrift beside the shack, then crawling through a tunnel, to find himself in a cramped space only five feet high, ten feet wide, and ten feet deep . . . filled with people. Quickly surveying the room, he counted fifteen Eskimos crammed into the small area. They were obviously seeking shelter from the blizzard as well.

Jarvis hesitated for a few seconds to gather his senses. It was warm, maybe 50 degrees, from the body heat of all the people jammed inside. The Eskimos seemed aware of but undisturbed by his entrance. The nearest Inuit, only inches from him, silently adjusted his body to make room for the new arrival. Jarvis moved forward with Charlie right behind.

Jarvis was stunned at the abrupt change in circumstance. One minute ago he had been outside battling the blizzard, wondering if he'd survive. Now, suddenly, he was warm and all was serene. He wanted to share these thoughts with the group he'd just joined, but they couldn't speak the same language. This lack of communication and their seeming indifference to his arrival made him, again, keenly aware of his aloneness.

He continued to ponder all this as his leg regained its feeling. The warmth inside the shack soon thawed the ice covering his clothes. He knew he had to shed his now-damp clothing, but exhaustion suddenly caught up with him.

Somehow Jarvis managed to remove his wet garments and crawl into his sleeping bag before he fell unconscious. Once again he had barely averted disaster.

Chapter Eighteen

Jim. . .   *More Disputes*

Jim went outside to see the commotion, pulling his watch cap farther down over his ears to stem the cold. It was after 10:00 A.M. in January, so at least they had a late morning sunrise. At the end of the group of men he saw Jake, trying to stay out of the way.

"What's happening, Jake?"

"Mr. McIlhenny is mad at those men," he said over his shoulder, trying not to miss anything.

"Why?"

Jake just shrugged and continued to watch the commotion.

"You get out of here!" yelled McIlhenny, shaking his fist at a small group of crewmen. From Jim's vantage point, the men appeared to be looking quizzically at each other as if to say, "We don't know what you're talking about."

Just then, Jim was quietly pushed aside by two of the crew. They had Brower in tow.

"Hold it!" Brower snapped at the squabbling men. "What's going on?" he asked McIlhenny.

"I let these guys into the storehouse for their weekly ration of tobacco and they cleaned out half the shelves," McIlhenny said, waving his arms in exasperation.

"How'd they do that?"

"I don't know. They just swarmed in and grabbed the stuff when I was doling out the tobacco."

Disgusted, Brower turned to the accused. "It's one thing to steal from the dead," he said. "Now you're stealing from the living."

The crowd said nothing. To defend themselves was almost an admission of guilt.

Brower yelled back to the men watching out the station window. "Fred, get out here." Brower's assistant Fred Hopson scurried out and stood opposite him. "From now on, there will only be one man allowed in the storehouse at a time. I want you to carry an ax. If anyone tries to come in before his turn, you crack him in the head."

Fred just nodded and looked warily at the men. They were a hard bunch; he didn't relish being the enforcer of discipline on such a group. That might be enough to get him beaten up some night.

"Now you men," continued Brower, "I mean it. I've had enough of ship burnings, grave robbing, and now stealing from the storehouse."

Finally a bearded crewman spoke. "But Mr. Brower, we're dying in the Old Kelley House. The place is like a sewer. We're getting rotten meat for rations. We won't make it to spring like this."

It was partly true. When not enough meat came in from hunting parties, the men were forced to eat old, partially rotten meat from stock that had been around for more than one season. Most of it had thawed in the previous spring and refroze in the winter.

But Brower was in no mood to talk. He had to maintain some discipline among the unruly group or everything would be lost. It was easier to ignore their grievance and take a hard line. "Listen up. From now on you take orders from me alone. I'll crack heads if you don't obey my orders. If you got grievances, I'll listen to one man. That's it."

At about that time, an Eskimo approached with a reindeer carcass. That seemed to incite Brower even more.

"And I know that some of you are trying to make deals with Eskimos to get you food. Let me make this clear. I'm the only one that buys food here."

"But you'll get paid back for it. We're willing to pay from our own money," interjected one of the men. He was referring to the fact that Brower maintained a "profit-making" whaling station. Most times, the profit was illusory. Though Brower would submit a bill for anything he bought to maintain the men, in reality his getting paid would be another story.

Now Brower was really mad. This comment seemed to imply that he was keeping the men alive only for profit. "You listen. McIlhenny here's been giving his cotton, that he needed for packing specimens, to you men for blankets, free of charge. He's been hunting birds for food and managing all your rations. My assistants and I have been working round the clock to keep peace with the Eskimos and get food from their hunting teams. I got no guarantees that I'll ever see a penny. So you just do what I say, when I say it. If it weren't for me, you'd all be dead."

With that, he turned and stormed back to his office. McIlhenny and Fred took their cue and went after him.

Two days later, more conflict erupted in the Old Kelley house.

"Give me that blanket!" yelled one of the men.

"Why? You don't need it. You got two already."

"I don't care; it's mine."

"You settle down!" yelled Joiner. "Give him back his property."

The crewman just looked around the room. There seemed to be nobody coming to his aid so he tossed the coverlet back to its owner. "Before too long, there'll be plenty to choose from as we die off one by one."

Nobody said anything. They all knew he was probably right. Animals were running short; soon there would be even less food.

Jake suddenly tugged at Jim's sleeve and pointed to Ned Arey, who was pulling together his meager possessions.

"What's going on, Ned?" asked Jim.

Ned turned to Jim, his jaw firmly set. "I'm leaving."

"But where to?" asked Jim, incredulous.

"I'm going to go south," he said truculently. "You know things are going to get worse and worse."

Jim felt a surge of fear for Ned. "Ned, you can't go. You'll die out there."

Ned turned back and finished putting the last item in his satchel. "It's better to die trying to survive out there than slowly waste away in this filthy shit hole." With that he spun on his heel and left.

Jim sat stunned. It was one thing to try to survive here at Point Barrow, but another to try to walk south. Should Jim himself be thinking about going south with Ted? *Were* they all going to inevitably die? It was true that the food was beginning to run out and that conflicts among the men were becoming more frequent. Some of the Eskimos were even staying away out of fear. Would they turn on each other? Worse yet, would they kill each other for food?

Jim's mouth felt like cotton. New anxiety flooded him as he sat contemplating the grizzly future that may await. Should he follow Ned now? Maybe Ned, like Tilton and Walker, the messengers sent before him, had a better chance at survival than did the men remaining at the station.

Jim went back to his bunk and huddled under the covers. The one thing he had was time to think.

Chapter Nineteen

Lopp...   *The Missionary*

Tom Lopp watched his wife from a distance. How she handled the children was entertaining. She loved to laugh but had no problem taking control. He reflected on how much his life had changed since leaving Indiana. Just a few short years ago he was a young teacher in a farming community, and a good one at that. But his faith in Christianity was to bring him to a life he could not have imagined.

It started simply enough when he volunteered in the local Presbyterian Church, where he quickly rose to become an elder. At that point it occurred to him that he could make Church work a full-time vocation. One day he read an advertisement for a Christian teacher for a mission school in Alaska. Things moved quickly; just a few months later he found himself staring into the rigging of a steamer bound for Alaska.

The shock to his system both physically and mentally had been great. He didn't speak Inupik, the native language. The weather was colder than anything he'd ever experienced before, and the food was nothing like back home—instead of beef and pork, he ate seal, caribou, and whale. Nevertheless, with vigor he took up his post as one of two teachers in a one-room schoolhouse. He learned to speak the Inupiat dialect, survive in the bitter cold of Alaska, and teach the children English. A year later the other teacher, Harrison Thornton, decided to go home on furlough to find a wife and another missionary teacher to help them. A few months later Harrison ended up coming back with two women. One was Neda, his new wife; the other was a young teacher named Ellen Kittredge.

Lopp paused to chuckle as he recalled the first time he saw Ellen. She had come by ship from San Francisco with Neda and Harrison. Little had she known that his friend Harrison was looking for a woman to fill two roles: a teacher for the school and a wife for Tom. In Ellen, Harrison found the ideal person for both assignments. Ellen was a great teacher. She'd worked her way through Normal school and then moved to the heat of the southern states to take a teaching job. Luckily for Tom, she disliked the sweltering heat of North Carolina and answered the call to come to Alaska.

When Tom first saw Ellen, he was struck by her beauty. Petite, with an elegant form, she possessed beautiful piercing eyes that danced and sparkled, contrasting dramatically with her dark, tightly bound-back hair. He was instantly captured by her presence.

She, for her part, was drawn to the tall, masculine man with almost black eyes and neat short hair. He was what could only be characterized as a man's man. They hit it off quickly and a short two months later, they were married in a local ceremony. It was not exactly the typical church wedding he'd thought about as an elder of the Presbyterian Church, but he loved her.

"Papa," caroled Lucy, "are you coming?" Tom's five-year-old tugged on his parka and tried to draw him toward the schoolhouse.

"I'm sorry, honey, I have to help with the herd today," he said.

"Awww, are you sure?"

"Yes, I'm sure," he said. "You go off, now." Lucy skipped obediently off to school where her mother was teaching.

Lopp turned his attention to the deer herd, in his view the key to the Eskimos' future. As he worked he reflected on how far they had come. At one time there were no domesticated deer in Alaska; Siberia, on the other hand, had many. The Siberians lived off the reindeer much the way cattle ranchers lived off their cattle. The deer of the Chukchi people across the Strait of Alaska had caught the attention of Shelton Jackson, an American who traveled extensively on the *Bear* when visiting the missionary schools in his charge. Jackson was convinced that bringing reindeer to Alaska would provide an economic base for the Eskimos. He acquired private funding to buy deer in Siberia and ship them to the Aleutian Islands as an experiment. Successfully testing the concept, he arranged for additional funding to bring 171 deer to Port Clarence in 1892. Soon after, Lopp and his wife Ellen took on the task of learning reindeer herding.

The missionaries' efforts initially met resistance from Inupiat chiefs and white men alike. The chiefs didn't believe that the white man's government would turn over the deer to their care. Instead, they feared that they would simply be subjugated to laboring over the deer for the government's benefit.

The white bureaucrats likewise had little confidence in Eskimos in general. They saw them as a lazy, backward people incapable of ever managing a herd. They advocated the importation of Siberian and Norwegian herders for the task.

Tom and his wife Ellen fought this idea. They felt that the Eskimos *could* be trained to manage the herd. If Tom and Ellen went first to the government's reindeer station and received instruction in deer herding, upon their return they could pass these skills to the villagers. Thus as missionaries, they could not only teach the Inupiats English, but they could also demonstrate Christian love by improving the Eskimos' quality of life with a local economy based on the deer herd.

Tom soon demonstrated that he could use the new skills he acquired as an apprentice at the government's reindeer station. As a result, he was granted a small herd of deer for Cape Prince of Wales.

He selected a small group of teenage boys from the mission school and approached their parents, asking permission to train them as deer herders. His requests didn't sit entirely well. The Inupiat parents argued that they'd already sent their sons to the white man's school when they should be tending to their families. Now, when they should be learning to hunt and fish, they were being asked to tend the white man's deer.

Lopp explained that the deer would become the property of the Eskimos, to provide for their future so they wouldn't have to rely solely on hunting to survive. The Inupiats objected that they had heard other promises before from businesses and even some misguided missionaries. But finally they relented and granted Lopp's request.

Before long, the boys acquired skills beyond Lopp's wildest dreams.

They could adeptly move the deer from one area to another to find moss for food, they could take care of the young fawns, and they could see to the birthing mothers. Lopp and his "boys," as they became known, turned the small number of animals into a thriving herd of almost 300 in less than five years. In response, the villagers came to see the value of the deer for food and clothing. The village even attracted other Inupiats and grew to a small community of 500 people. Despite this success, racial prejudice still put obstacles in their path as many outside their community, both Eskimo and white, waited for them to fail.

Apart from the herding, Lopp marveled at the other skills acquired by his schoolchildren as they grew. Especially impressive was Sokweena, whose role in the Lopps' family life began humbly enough as a houseboy while he was a student. Sokweena assisted in maintaining the Lopp family by helping with the household chores after two Eskimo friends, Charlie Artisarlook and his wife Mary, left to manage their own mission. Quickly outgrowing that position, Sokweena soon went on to start a mission school of his own a few villages away. Now he was a respected headmaster, administrator, and pastor to a small community nearby.

Lopp was brought from his reverie by the approach of another of his boys. "Ootenna," said Lopp with a broad smile. He always enjoyed dealing with the young men. He treated them as if they were his own children, and they likewise treated him as another father.

"Hello," responded the young man with a smile. Just then a strong gust of wind hit them from the northwest. Lopp pulled tight the neck of his parka. "The elders say that winter has not come this early in many seasons," continued Ootenna. As a native Eskimo, he had strong ties to the chief of the village.

"I can feel it," said Lopp. "At least my house will be dry soon." They both laughed. Lopp and Ellen lived in a house of traditional American construction. Each winter the rafters froze with ice. As the spring and summer thaws came, the melting ice produced constant drips and mold. There was no solution to this problem—other than learning not to apply traditional American logic to the Eskimos. While winter this far north was brutal, at least it stopped the constant drips.

Lopp had learned to make light of his mistakes when trying to apply America's standards to Alaska. Unlike many missionaries, he had learned to embrace the native ways. In fact, he and his wife never found a moment alone, for guests from the village were constantly in their home.

"Men approach," advised Tautuk, another young herder arriving at Lopp's side.

"Inupiat?" asked Lopp.

"No, koblonas." It was unclear how Tautuk could tell from this distance with their hoods drawn around their faces. Perhaps it was how they handled the sleds or the manner in which they walked.

"That's strange," said Lopp, now talking to himself as much as to Ootenna and Tautuk.

"Yes, *Bear* isn't due for a long time," confirmed Tautuk. The *Bear* typically sent mail, visitors from the Education Department, and supplies. "The strait's frozen, anyway; *Bear* couldn't get this far north. It must be someone else." They didn't get many outside visitors, especially not in winter.

"I'd better see who they are," said Lopp, walking briskly back toward his home.

Chapter Twenty

Jarvis . . .   Christians on a Mission

For the next several days, Charlie guided Jarvis and the dog teams through a maze of ice crushes six to ten feet high. It was slow going as they dragged sleds and dogs alike up the crushes. At one point, Jarvis and his dog team fell off a ten-foot ice crush, barely avoiding serious injury.

Finally Jarvis and Charlie pulled into the village at Cape Prince of Wales. As Jarvis climbed off his sled in front of what appeared to be a small house or school, he saw a tall white man and a young Eskimo coming his way. Not far away clustered some deer from the herd he was seeking.

The white man approached, extending his hand. "I'm Tom Lopp," he said, reaching out to Jarvis.

"Mr. Lopp."

"My God," said Lopp with a start, now recognizing Jarvis, whom he had met previously during contact with the *Bear*. "What brings you here this time of year . . . and how did you get here?"

"It's a long story. I came overland from Tununak, near Cape Vancouver, Nelson Island."

"But that's nearly a thousand miles!"

"Yes, it took us almost two months." Jarvis almost couldn't believe the number as he said it.

"Almost two months! That's incredible," exclaimed Lopp. After pausing to reflect for a second he added, "But considering the terrain and the fact that it's winter, that makes sense."

Just then Charlie appeared from behind his sled. "Artisarlook!" said Lopp.

"Hello, Tom, good to see you," returned Charlie.

By now a small group of villagers had begun to gather around Lopp and Jarvis. It was unusual to get white visitors in the dead of winter.

"You must excuse me. Where are my manners?" said Lopp. "Come inside and warm up. My wife Ellen will want to meet you."

"Oh, let me get your mail," said Jarvis, turning quickly to the satchel in his sled.

"So *that's* why you're here. Those postal routes are getting longer and longer, aren't they?" Lopp said with a deep laugh.

Jarvis laughed at the joke. With that they went into Lopp's house. Attentive villagers crowded as best they could into the main room. Those who couldn't fit inside stood close by outside. It appeared perfectly natural for them to do so, for it was obvious that the Lopps and the villagers maintained a strong relationship, almost like a large family.

Jarvis and Charlie were met by a woman with one babe in arms and three others at her heels. Tom Lopp, putting his arm around the woman's shoulders, said, "Lieutenant Jarvis, I'd like you to meet Ellen and my children—Lucy, Dwight, Sarah, and Katherine."

Jarvis bent over to greet the children. Sarah turned her head, slightly shy at the moment.

"Glad to meet you," said Jarvis, straightening up and extending his hand to Ellen. Jarvis could tell that Ellen was no ordinary housewife; she had the bearing of a confident young woman.

"Welcome to our home," Ellen said, "and hello, Charlie. It's wonderful to see you again. Mr. Jarvis, Charlie and Mary used to work for us before they traveled south to establish their own mission and herd." With that she moved forward and hugged their old friend. Then, glancing at the room full of inquisitive guests, she added with a smile, "And of course you've met a few of our closest friends."

Jarvis chuckled. He received several smiles in return.

Introductions made, they sat and had tea while Jarvis told the Lopps of his travels. As this curiously well-attended event went on, the villagers listened intently for more than an hour. Those who weren't sitting, shuttled in and out of the room attending their sleds, feeding their dogs, and placing the cargo sleds on racks out of reach of animals. As villagers returned to the room, they were quickly brought up to date with the stories in whispered tones. Some left to continue their chores while others left to carry the news to those who hadn't fit into the main house. There were approximately 500 villagers in the community that surrounded the Lopps. Finally at the close of Jarvis's tale, everyone sat back in relative quiet.

"That's quite a story," said Lopp.

"But now it's your turn," said Jarvis, sitting back comfortably, having eaten more than he'd had for a long time. "Tell me about yourselves, please."

"Well, as you know, I'm a missionary," Lopp said, reaching over to touch Ellen, "as is my wife. I came here eight years ago as a teacher and later met my wife who came to do similar work. The people of many churches support our work to help the Eskimos. It's a responsibility we take seriously."

Jarvis listened intently. He could envision the many people back home who took out their coins and meager savings each week to help people they didn't know in a faraway land they'd never see. He thought how happy they would be to see the hard-working, entrepreneurial villagers who so carefully managed these deer.

Lopp, his wife, and the village elders went on to describe their functions and introduce their families. They explained how they had carefully managed the herd, increasing it to over 300 deer. They showed the clothing and food derived from the deer and the trading economy that had evolved to support them and others in the region.

After listening to their testimony, Jarvis felt part of something greater than himself. At the same time, an all-too-familiar knot developed in his stomach. He had not yet asked these people for their reindeer herd. Yet he knew that the Lopps were smart. They must have already figured out that the request would be coming. Jarvis had mentioned the number of deer that had been accumulated thus far and that Charlie had agreed to leave his wife to travel north with Jarvis.

It was Lopp who actually broached the subject. "It's been quite a trip for you, but I'm confident that you didn't come to our humble home to deliver the mail."

"Unfortunately, you're correct," said Jarvis softly, not quite bringing himself to meet his host's eyes. "I'm actually representing the U.S. Government with authority from President McKinley himself. In that capacity, I'm here to ask you for your deer with the promise that they and any supplies will be replaced by the U.S. Department of the Treasury." Jarvis paused to let the request sink in. It wasn't as if you could ask this missionary and the 500 villagers to give up their livelihood based on an obscure promise from a government agent on a sled.

"You realize that we and our friends rely on those deer to live?" asked Lopp. Obviously Jarvis was just a government representative without real knowledge of the intimate working of the missionaries and the Eskimos. Lopp had to make sure he knew the ramifications of what he was asking.

"I know. But you understand the gravity of the situation. With only the supply we have now, the whalers won't survive until spring."

There was a long pause during which the tension in the room became almost unbearable. Each person wore a look of deep foreboding. It was almost as if they were being told an army was approaching to begin a battle they wouldn't survive.

In the silence that followed, Lopp and his wife looked intently at each other and the people around them. Then she said, "Beyond the welfare of each family here, we also made a promise to the people that support us. They've scrimped, saved, and entrusted us to use their resources for this work. Would we be betraying that trust by giving to the government these deer that we don't own?" These questions were directed more at Charlie than anyone. As a missionary, he'd faced the same issues. What would be the right moral course of action in this situation?

"Yes, it's a difficult decision," responded Charlie. "But in the end, we were convinced of the sincerity of the government to pay us back."

"Yes, and it's not for any gain that the request is made; there are three hundred men whose lives depend on it," added Jarvis.

They sat in silence again. Looking slowly around the room, Jarvis was amazed that nobody was arguing against him. By their reaction, they showed that they were already prepared to give everything they had, including their livelihood, to help strangers they would never meet.

"Besides the very competent help of Charlie here, how do you plan to get the deer there?" asked Lopp. As a fellow herder, Lopp knew that a combined herd would require more men.

"We need you and your best men to drive them," said Jarvis. At this, Lopp shot a glance at his wife. She looked as if she had just been told she had a terminal disease.

"That's over 600 miles." He paused and added, "Over mountains that men would find difficult to cross, let alone a herd of deer." It was phrased not as a contrary argument, but as disbelief that Jarvis expected to carry out this plan.

"I know," said Jarvis. He had no more details to offer. It would be up to Lopp and Charlie to figure out how to make it happen.

"You need my husband to figure out a way," said Ellen, grasping the situation. With that she raised her gaze to meet her husband's eyes. Lopp was obviously shaken by the thought of leaving his wife while he traveled over mountains and ice. They held hands for a moment.

"Yes," responded Jarvis. "I've been advised by more than one person, from the lowest to highest levels, that he's the man for the job."

"And I'll be right there with him," added Charlie, trying to brighten the picture.

"Well, we'll need some time to talk between ourselves, and with my herders and the villagers. We rely on them as they rely on us. We have to decide together," said Lopp finally.

"Of course. You let us know." Jarvis and Charlie smiled and edged outside.

After what seemed an eternity, a villager summoned the pair. Anxiously they entered the room and sat facing the couple. Jarvis held his breath as Tom Lopp spoke.

"We've discussed your plight with the villagers and the boys. We've agreed unanimously to give you what you need."

"I'm grateful," said Jarvis with an exhalation of relief. Again he was amazed at the giving nature of these people.

Lopp put up his hand. "But I have personal concerns about the welfare of my family and the villagers. What is your plan for them?"

"Your wife can go to Port Clarence and stay with the missionaries, the Brevigs."

"I can't do that," objected Ellen. "My life is here with the villagers. I'll live as they live."

"You don't understand, Lieutenant," said Tom Lopp. "We have devoted our lives to our ministry and these people, and they to us. My family will remain here with them. They are our best hope." Some of the villagers smiled at this reference. It was obvious that the Lopps and the villagers had a strong mutual respect. These were not like other missionaries who had passed through this land before and maintained some distance from the people and their customs. This couple had truly become part of the people.

"But I will hold you personally responsible, Lieutenant," Lopp said firmly, "that you will make whole the villagers and insure that supplies are delivered for their welfare and that of my family."

"Without hesitation," responded Jarvis. "You have my word as a Revenue Cutter Service officer and my personal word on my family name. I promise that I won't rest until your family and the villagers are taken care of and their sacrifice repaid." It was true. The determination that had brought him this far was the same determination that would one day see his promises fulfilled.

"All right, then," said Lopp, "it's done." He rose and shook hands with Jarvis and Charlie, as did some of the Eskimos around him.

With that, the remainder of the deer were acquired. Lopp would lead the drive; his handpicked crew—Tautuk, Ootenna, Kivyearzruk, Sokweena, Keuk, and Ituk—would go along, seven herders in all, counting Charlie. These were smart, skilled young men that Lopp had learned he could count on. The party would need every bit of that skill. No one before had ever attempted to drive more than 300 reindeer almost 600 miles over the mountains in the roughest terrain in the world in subzero temperatures. This would be a first—if they made it.

In Lopp's village, work now began in earnest. The entire village pitched in, contributing their possessions, time, and skills. The men built the extra sleds required to carry cargo and provisions for the drivers. Women began

126

to fashion extra-warm suits and spare clothing for the rigorous trip. Furred sleeping bags had to be made for the sub-zero nights. Everyone who could do anything to help the cause was hard at work all day and into the night for the next five days.

They had to be ready soon. It was imperative that the herd reach the stranded whalers before April when the deer would begin to fawn, for at fawning, the mothers and the newborns would be unable to travel for a time. April also would find the whalers out of food.

There was another problem. Though the rescue party had new sleds, they needed trained sled deer to pull them. The deer had no natural ability to pull sleds, but like horses, had to be trained with fitted harnesses. At present there was one sled deer for each sled—but that wasn't enough. One reindeer couldn't pull a heavy sled day after day, but had to be relieved by another trained deer while the first recuperated from a long day's hauling. So the men had to train the deer as best they could before the trip, and even en route if need be.

To provision the travelers for the long trip, the villagers pitched in with what food they had, but there still wasn't enough. To secure more supplies, Ootenna, one of the young herders, took a sled to Port Clarence. Charlie accompanied Ootenna. He would prepare his deer and drive them back to merge with Lopp's herd.

At Port Clarence, Charlie met up with Dr. Call. After two days, Charlie and the doctor led the effort to drive the smaller herd. They left early in the morning to get a good start over the mountains. Ootenna left a few hours later after getting the last of the supplies and picking up Tautuk, who was staying in Port Clarence. That evening, Ootenna and Tautuk arrived back at Cape Prince of Wales.

"Glad to see you," said Jarvis.

"Me, also," responded Ootenna. "Where's Charlie and the other herd?"

"I don't know, I presume still back at Port Clarence."

"They left Port Clarence before I did!" said Ootenna. By this time, Lopp and two of the other herders had come to join the discussion.

"Did you pass them in the mountains?" asked Lopp, his face a study in concern.

"No, I never saw them. But the storms were bad up there. I guess I could have missed them, but I don't see how."

"Did they get lost?" asked Jarvis.

"That's possible, but I don't think so. Charlie knows the way, even with the storm."

"Could something have happened with the deer?" continued Jarvis, now addressing both Lopp and Ootenna.

"That's always possible," said Tautuk. "Driving deer is tricky business, especially over the mountains in a storm." All the men silently scanned the horizon; there was neither man nor deer in sight.

"What should we do?" asked Jarvis, turning first to Lopp and then the whole group, out of respect. He wanted to start his relationship with these young men by recognizing their skills and opinions in such matters.

"Wait," came the response from Lopp.

"Yes, wait is all we can do," came a couple of confirming words and nods from the men.

"Patience, Jarvis," continued Lopp. "The Arctic demands patience."

Jarvis and the villagers spent an uneasy night. They periodically left their huts to scan the distance for any sign of man or deer. There was nothing. No bells, nothing. Jarvis felt sick, powerless to do anything. It was one thing to be lost or stranded in a storm himself. But worrying about his men being lost or stranded was worse, especially since Charlie was involved. Jarvis acutely remembered his promise to take care of Charlie. But Charlie was experienced in these lands, Jarvis consoled himself. He knew what to do in an Arctic blizzard.

In the morning, Jarvis climbed out of his sleeping bag and hurried outside to check the dark horizon. He had already done so twice during the night. He stood and scanned the horizon. Still nothing. "How much damned patience should I have?" he muttered to himself.

Two of the young herders, Kivyearzruk and Sokweena, approached, also watching for any returnees.

"How long do we wait?" Jarvis asked the young men.

They looked at each other. "The snow in the mountains will be very deep," said Kivyearzruk. "It's difficult to say."

"Yes," added Sokweena, "It will be slow. If they had to camp in the night, it could be another day."

"So we wait until tomorrow?" asked Jarvis.

"Yes, tomorrow."

Jarvis returned to his work, as did the others. They completed packing the sleds in preparation for the journey; at least the delay was giving them time to make sure they had everything. Intermittently, they stopped to check the horizon.

Jarvis was working with Keuk, one of the young herders, when Sokweena, another herder, came running. "There!" he yelled, pointing back over his own tracks. "The deer."

Jarvis and Keuk jumped up and ran in the direction from which Sokweena had come. They could barely make out deer and the outline of two sleds in the distance. Jarvis quickly scanned the deer herd, trying to get a rough count. He knew the men were all right, given the sighting of two sleds, but he didn't know about the deer. There should be almost 150 to 200 animals. He could count maybe a hundred.

Finally Charlie and Dr. Call arrived. "Well, the lost tribe has returned," said Jarvis. "You don't know how worried we were!"

"Not as worried as we were," said Charlie. "It was touch and go there for a while."

"What happened?" asked Sokweena, now standing next to Jarvis.

"We got bogged down in the deep snow and ravines. We lost ten deer to falls. The first night we finally had to give up and camp, just hoping not to lose more deer in the night. In the morning we had to gather the deer that had wandered off. That took us half the day before we began again for the village."

"Well, we're glad to see you," added Kivyearzruk.

A large group of villagers now surrounded the men and their sleds. They hurried the travelers inside for warmth while the village men secured the sleds and cargo on racks for protection from scavengers. Both men were tired and hungry, so they were given food and their clothing was taken for mending. In the Arctic it was important to wear dry clothes with no tears or holes. Not minding your clothing could mean frostbite—even death.

Meanwhile, Kivyearzruk, Sokweena, and the other herders took care of the arriving deer. Driving them to an area were they could graze throughout the night in preparation for their long journey, the herders looked for injured deer that must be tended or removed before they made sure all were safe for the night.

The morning of February 3, almost two months into the overland rescue, everything was in place. Bertholf was farther east gathering deer and supplies, while Jarvis and the doctor had now acquired the main body of deer with the help of Charlie and Lopp. Last-minute preparations were made and supplies packed. The boys said goodbye to their families and prepared to go. They were about to travel a distance approaching the length of Lewis and Clark's journey from St. Louis to the mouth of the Columbia River—but over the ice.

Jarvis, like the rest, saw to last-minute plans. As the morning hours waned, he became frustrated by the delay. They were like men about to land on an enemy beach: They certainly weren't looking forward to the dangers ahead, but they were hyped up and ready to get moving.

Finally by late morning they were ready to start.

Jarvis inspected the men and sleds now assembled. Three sled trains were to haul supplies. The first train had five sleds. The lead sled, hauled by two deer, carried a standing driver responsible for navigation and steering—and most of the work. Behind this lead sled was tied a single deer pulling a single sled which carried a reclining driver. Three more such single deer/sled/driver combinations followed, each tied to the sled in front.

Two other sled trains, containing five and four sleds respectively, followed the lead train. Each train had the same linked configuration. Accompanying these three linked trains were three independent sleds driven respectively by Kivyearzruk, Sokweena, and Tautuk, with his small pet dog. These independent outriders would drive the deer and round up stragglers.

As the loaded sleds prepared to depart, villagers lined the sides of the trains. Everybody had turned out to support the group. Fathers, mothers, cousins, and friends stood close to their respective departing loved one, waiting for their last goodbye. As Jarvis glanced up and down the line of people, he had to swallow hard. They would never have made it this far without the sacrifice of these Eskimos and others they'd encountered on the trail. He stood in awe of their generosity.

"You ready?" Jarvis called to Lopp on his nearby sled.

"Let's go!" Lopp yelled back to Jarvis and the train.

Jarvis cast his fist forward and the trains instantly lurched into action as their deer jumped and broke into a fast trot. The families and other villagers waved garments, yelled, and cheered the men on, like spectators encouraging runners at the start of a race. But in this case, the departure was more serious and bittersweet. This wasn't a race: It was a dangerous mission at the cold, stark top of the world.

As the trains and herded deer picked up speed and the wind hit Jarvis's face, he thrilled to a strange mixture of fear and excitement. This was just the first step of a grueling trek across hundreds of miles of Arctic ice. Who knew what lay ahead?

The trains and herded deer sped through the snow for more than fifty miles before they camped for the night. This was no small feat, for the party numbered 438 deer in all.

That night in their tents, the men were quiet. As Jarvis looked around the bivouac, he realized that each man had just said goodbye to his family for what would be a long period, maybe months. He wondered what they were thinking. Were they suffering the loneliness of being separated from their wives? Were they worrying about what would happen to their families, forced to survive on less food and resources until these were ultimately replaced by the government? Or were they dreading the unknown dangers they faced in the weeks and months ahead on the frozen lands to the north? Whatever their thoughts, it was obvious that each man wanted to be alone with them.

Jarvis lay back and thought of his own family. Two years ago he had married a beautiful young woman. The thought of his stunning bride on their honeymoon in Newport, Rhode Island made his body ache. He would have given anything at that moment to have his naked body intertwined with hers. He chuckled to himself as he recalled how she had insisted on his getting a photograph of himself in his formal dark wedding suit. How he hated that heavily starched shirt with the high white collar and tie under that stiff, formal dress coat. She had said she needed a picture to remember him by while he was at sea. The image of that suit seemed an incredible contrast to the furred deerskin pants he wore now. The smile quickly left his face. Could that picture be the last image of him she'd ever see? He felt bitter that he was always cold, bitter that he was so far from home, bitter that he might never return alive. He forced the image from his mind and went to sleep.

The next day began with crisp, cold air entering the tent—the Arctic cold never seemed to rest. The men got an early start. As on the night before, there was little discussion. The reality of their mission had set in.

Although the village was comfortable and the people overwhelmingly friendly, Jarvis was glad that their camps from then on would be in the wilderness. Breaking camp and starting each day was less complicated and time-consuming. There would be no more long goodbyes.

Lopp and three herders drove the loose deer on lighter sleds, sweeping back and forth behind them. Tautuk's small dog worked with the sleds, keeping stragglers tight. The sled trains meandered along ahead of the herded deer most of the time, the lead sled in each train driving. It seemed like a simple system, but nothing ever worked that easily. The herded deer didn't like the arrangement. They would get nervous and excited when sleds came too close or took a turn. Such skittishness often created a jumbled mess of deer, sleds, and men.

After one such episode they determined something had to be done.

"These blasted deer," swore Charlie.

"What a mess," Jarvis agreed. "At this rate we'll never make it to Point Barrow before April."

"And we're slowing down," said Lopp, approaching from behind.

"Where'd you come from?" asked Jarvis. "I thought you were way back minding the deer."

"I was," he said, shaking his head from side to side, "but something has to be done."

"Like what?" asked Jarvis.

"The sled deer. They can't take this pace. They're completely played out. We have to lighten the sleds."

"How can we do that? We need every bit of this food to feed the men," Jarvis pointed out.

"Deer aren't like dogs," chimed in Charlie. "They don't have the endurance to haul these heavy supplies."

"Well, we can't mix dogs and deer, right?" asked Jarvis.

"Right," they chimed in unison.

"Then can we make it easier on the deer some other way?" asked Jarvis. Since the deer had to graze at night while the men slept, if the herders couldn't find moss by day's end, they often drove the deer back to the last known spot to graze. It added that many more miles to the work.

"How about a change in route so we don't have to backtrack for grazing?" Jarvis continued.

"No," said Lopp, "this is the best route."

"Yes," agreed Charlie, "but unfortunately, the grazing's going to become more difficult."

"How so?" asked Jarvis.

"The country ahead is going to be pretty barren; moss will be sporadic," said Charlie.

"Well, we'll just have to pray that things get better," said Lopp. At that, Charlie nodded. As fellow missionaries, they had the same belief in the power of prayer.

By this time, the boys had managed to get the train back together in some semblance of a line. The deer looked exhausted, but they plodded forward.

The winds, hard out of the northeast, were painful for the men and deer; however, the same biting hard winds packed the snow. Packed snow on the rolling hills meant that the sleds moved more quickly on the hard, sleek surface and the deer didn't break through. Firewood was not easy to come by, but moss, at least for the present, was found on the hilltops. So

133

apparently their prayers had been answered.

The conditions made it more comfortable for the deer. The men were a different story. Stoically they bundled up against the relentless wind, careful not to leave any skin exposed to be frostbitten.

By February 5, only days after they had begun, the train made a mere eight miles for the entire day. Even the favorable terrain was not enough to relieve the deer of their overwhelming loads. They were slowly grinding to a halt. Something had to be done.

That night, Jarvis and the men slumped by the fire, exhausted. They had just finished their rations of beans and tea. Everyone was silent except Kivyearzruk and Sokweena. It was obvious that Sokweena was trying to encourage Kivyearzruk to say something. Kivyearzruk, a naturally shy youth, was hesitant to speak. Finally, Kivyearzruk approached Jarvis and Lopp who, when together, shared command decisions, somewhat like the explorers Lewis and Clark.

"I've been thinking about this," said Kivyearzruk sheepishly. "You know, our problem with the deer?"

Everyone looked on in silence, too tired—or too dejected—to answer. "Yes, Kivyearzruk?" answered Lopp, ever the encouraging teacher.

"What if we split off the heavier cargo sleds?" the youth continued.

"I don't follow," responded Jarvis, still with an encouraging tone.

"I mean, what if we loaded some of the sleds to be heavier than the others. We split off these sleds to a village and get dogs to haul them. We travel ahead with these sleds to keep them away from the deer, and we leave behind the other lighter sleds with just enough food and gear to support driving the herd."

Jarvis stared. It was so simple, yet brilliant. He silently glanced at Lopp and Charlie to get their opinions. It seemed like such a perfect solution that there must be something wrong with the idea.

Lopp and Charlie studied each other's eyes. After a moment's silence, Charlie said, "I guess so."

"Yes," confirmed Lopp, "and that way you could also warn any Eskimos we encounter that the herd is coming. They've never seen domesticated deer north of Cape Prince of Wales before. They're liable to shoot first and ask questions later."

"Shoot?" asked Jarvis.

"Yes, shoot," responded Lopp. "They'll think it's a herd of wild deer, the easiest dinner they could hope for, a smorgasbord that would last for months."

Jarvis shuddered at the thought. Finally he said, "Well, if there's no objections, it looks like we have a plan." He patted Kivyearzruk on the back. Kivyearzruk grinned ear to ear, as did Sokweena, who had encouraged his friend. The other herders voiced their agreement. The young herder was the man of the hour. His triumph instantly lifted the spirits of the group. They were happy that the shy young man had had a victory, and that they hoped to turn things around.

Early the next day, the men began repacking the sleds. Six heavy sleds were put together in a separate train. Because Jarvis and Dr. Call had no experience with deer herding, they were the likely choice to take the cargo train to the coast, where they would find a village and acquire dogs to pull the heavy loads.

"So that's the plan; you'll get the dogs and go on to Kotzebue Sound," said Charlie.

"That's right," said Jarvis. He was a little nervous about the scheme. There were a lot of unknowns. What if they couldn't get any dogs? What if they got lost? Jarvis and Call were the least experienced of the group.

"Don't worry, you'll be fine, old boy," said Charlie, reading Jarvis's face. "Just think about how you got this far with less going for you than you have now. Your guardian angel is working overtime."

"Well, as long as that guardian angel continues to give me his undivided attention," said Jarvis with a laugh, "we'll be just fine."

"I think their guild allows for it," said Charlie, patting his friend on the back.

"I'll leave that to you," said Jarvis, referring to Charlie's occupation as a missionary. By this time they were encircled by Lopp and the other men.

"Well, let's send them off right, boys," added Lopp, linking arms with the herders. Lopp then delivered a prayer to protect the doctor, Jarvis, and his own men. He followed with thanks for having been given the opportunity to go on this mission and concluded with a prayer to help the whalers persevere. The prayer brought home to Jarvis the influence that the missionaries had on the people closest to them. Greatly moved, he added a silent prayer of his own, giving thanks for these men having been entrusted to him.

Chapter Twenty-One

Jim...   The Salvation Army

At the Old Kelley House, things continued from bad to worse. As the hunting season drew to an end, symptoms of scurvy were appearing more and more: weakness; joint pain; black and blue marks from internal hemorrhages; swollen, bleeding gums; and emotional instability. These signs, that had first appeared on *Belvedere*, were now prevalent among the men at Point Barrow as well as the whalers stranded on their icebound ships at Herschel Island and Smith Bay. The inadequate diet, deficient in vitamin C, deprived the men's bodies of collagen, the agent that binds ligaments, muscles, and bone; they were literally coming unglued. And from now on, food would become even more scarce. Now fear had become part of their daily lives. Its appearance caused daily arguments among the crew, who were now approaching lawlessness. To top it all off, the surface temperature plummeted to lower than −50 degrees.

But today, a little excitement broke the grim routine. At Jake's beckoning, Jim went outside to see what all the tumult was about. A small group of men huddled outside the station listening as Brower spoke to a man who had just arrived by dogsled.

Jim bobbed his head above the crowd and recognized Jim Wing, a mate from the *Belvedere*, and the old cook. He wondered why their arrival would be the cause of so much excitement.

"It's the box," said Jake, almost reading his thoughts.

"What's in the box?"

"Don't know. It's big, though. Mr. Wing had a terrible time lugging it all the way here. He says it weighs more than 150 pounds, and he don't know what's in it."

"They didn't tell him what was inside?" asked Jim in surprise.

"No. They says it would be worth his while to bring it from the *Belvedere*, and that it would make things better."

Now Jim was excited. They needed something to make things better. But what could it be? They didn't have long to wait.

"Lets see what treasure got you frostbit, Jim," said Brower, playing to the crowd.

With that, everyone lurched forward to witness the unveiling.

"Bibles?" said Brower, taken aback.

"Bibles?" exclaimed somebody in the crowd, obviously disappointed.

"Yes, bibles," laughed Brower.

Apparently, The Salvation Army had donated a case of bibles to the *Belvedere*. Obviously, Captain Millard felt that the men needed something to help them through these trying times and thought the bibles would do the trick.

Luckily, not all the men had Brower's cynical attitude toward the gesture. As he lifted them, about half the men eagerly grabbed one. Some could read, some needed the comfort of having one, and some just wanted something to do. Jake and Jim each grabbed one and headed back to the Old Kelley House.

Jake joined Jim on the edge of his bunk, excitedly turning the pages to illustrations that caught his attention.

"What's in here exactly, Jim?"

That was a difficult question to answer.

"Well, Jake. Some people think there's some truth in here. Some people think there's just a bunch of fables."

"But what do *you* think?"

Jim paused again. This question was harder than the last.

"Well, I think that God is in here and he is trying to talk to us."

"What do you mean, talk to us?"

"Well, things are pretty bad right now. He sent us the *Navarch* to keep us warm. He saved us from the *Orca* and *Freeman*. He sent the Eskimos to feed us. Now, I guess, he's sending these bibles to tell us why he did it."

"Do you think so?"

Jim pondered again. He was normally cynical himself, but he'd seen things over the past few months that were changing that attitude. Nothing makes you contemplate the divine like the prospect of imminent death.

"Yes, Jake, I think so."

"But where do I look? It's so big."

It was true: the book contained lots of print and difficult language.

"I don't know, Jake. Why don't you start with the drawings?"

So for the next several days, Jake and many of the crew occupied themselves with the books. Some were open to the messages, some just needed to break the monotony.

Periodically Jake came to Jim with questions, but Jim rarely had any answers. After a few days, Jake seemed to pull it all together by himself.

"So what do you think, Jake?"

Jake looked up from the picture he'd been studying for a long time. Jim recognized it as a particularly grizzly depiction of Jesus on the cross.

"This man seemed to be doing things for the people, but they treated him very bad-like. But he kept doing it anyway. He fed them when they were hungry and stuff like that. But he died."

"So what does that mean, Jake?"

"I guess, that he knows what we're going through here. Maybe he's the one that's been sending the food and the coal to us?"

Jim just stared in amazement. A simple child seemed to grasp what he'd been missing all along.

"I guess so, Jake. Maybe he's been sending it all along." Jim just hoped that he'd send some more. They needed all the help they could get if they hoped to survive until spring.

Chapter Twenty-Two

Jarvis...   Peninyuk

Jarvis and the doctor set off with the cargo train toward the coast. Their mission was to locate a village and acquire some sled dogs en route to Kotzebue Sound. The Sound was one of two major obstacles for the deer herd before Point Barrow, the other being the mountains. Eventually Lopp, Charlie, and the deer would have to cross its ice-covered surface. They needed to know the condition of the ice before they got there. If it was bad, they'd have to go another route that would take several days or weeks.

Since a southeast wind this time of year was known to break up the ice and leave an unstable surface, the condition of the Sound was always an unknown from one day to the next. If conditions were bad, Jarvis would send a letter via an Eskimo messenger, carrying word to reroute the herd. It would be pretty easy for Jarvis to detect unstable ice; he simply had to look for pools of open water, the legacy of a warm southeast wind. But the absence of any open pools was a good indication that the ice was probably safe.

The cargo train progressed toward its objective. On the way, they sporadically encountered villages and were able to acquire dogs to pull the heavy train. It appeared, at least thus far, that their plan was working.

Unfortunately, the dogs they acquired were somewhat problematic. Several of the dogs chewed through their harnesses at the first opportunity and ran back to their owners in the villages. Jarvis and Call had to constantly check the dogs to insure their bindings were secure.

Besides the dog problem, they had one almost insurmountable

obstacle before reaching Kotzebue Sound: they didn't know the way. They were heading into a relatively unknown part of the far northern Arctic. The men, including Eskimos, who could guide them to the region were few and far between. And because it was winter, even those who might know, feigned ignorance. At the last village, they had been told that there was only one Eskimo, named Perninyuk, who could lead them. Despite their best efforts, he could not be found. As a result, Jarvis and the doctor had no choice but to attempt to find Kotzebue Sound on their own.

"What are we going to do, Jarvis?" asked the doctor, sitting dejectedly on his sled. One thing they had learned from past drives was to take what rest they could, even if only for seconds at a time, to keep themselves going.

Jarvis paused and sat next to his friend for a moment. As an officer in the Cutter Service, he wasn't one to give up easily. Nor was he one to give any indication that he was afraid. But the doctor and he had been through a lot together. The doctor knew his triumphs and mistakes. He could trust him and owed him an honest answer.

"I don't know, Doc. The landscape around here is almost impossible to navigate, even if we had good maps, which we don't. But we have to keep going."

"What are the chances that we could find this Perninyuk, or whatever the hell his name is?" The doctor's frustration spoke. "Why can't they have regular names like Bill or Jim?"

Jarvis smiled wryly. "I guess they *are* regular names to them. They're probably sitting in their igloos and complaining about us, old what's their names."

With that, the doctor laughed. It wasn't much to temper his anxiety, but it was something.

"But really, Jarvis, can we take the time to wait here? You never know, he might show up."

"I don't see any other way. We have to determine the conditions at Kotzebue Sound before the herd makes it that far. Can you imagine what would happen if they got there before us and tried to make the crossing on bad ice?"

"Yes, I know; they could lose half the herd."

"Not to mention half the boys." Jarvis had formed an attachment to the young charges of the missionary. "Anyway, they say this Perninyuk's gone hunting. You know that could mean days or even weeks until he shows up."

The doctor was tired and frustrated. His exhaustion and the anxiety from not knowing the way made things even worse. On top of that it was cold, really cold.

"I'm sorry, Jarvis. I know we have to go," he said almost with a whine.

Jarvis sat silently beside his friend for a few moments, staring at the horizon, white with snow. It was *always* white with snow. His mood was not much better than the doctor's.

"It's OK, my old friend," Jarvis finally said. "I'm scared, too. I tell you what. We'll move slowly en route the best we can. Maybe Providence will smile on us and we'll find this, whatever the hell his name is."

So, hoping for the best, the two traveled throughout the day and into the evening, navigating by the stars. Then they broke for the night and camped. So far they were somewhat confident of their direction. However, they were bothered by the lingering doubt that they might be lost.

The next morning, as they prepared to leave camp, Providence did in fact smile on them. Jarvis was lashing the last of the cargo, preparing to leave for Sinrazat, the next village along the coast. As he looked up, he saw an Eskimo climbing down the hill behind their camp. The doctor followed Jarvis's gaze.

"You don't suppose that could be him?"

"We couldn't be that lucky."

As the man approached, Jarvis advanced to meet him. In these parts, it was best to be careful. Jarvis went alone, showing his hands to be empty, while the doctor stood back and prepared for anything.

"Hello!" called Jarvis.

"Hello," returned the man. "I not expect koblonas here."

"That's OK, we never expected to be here, either. I'm Lieutenant Jarvis, of the Revenue Cutter Service."

"Perninyuk," he said.

Jarvis was stunned.

"Did you hear that, doctor? It's Perninyuk!"

"I don't believe it!" called the doctor from twenty yards to the rear.

The Eskimo looked perplexed. He wasn't sure whether to be insulted because they might be making fun of him or happy at the reception.

By the look on his face Jarvis realized that the Eskimo didn't know they were looking for him. It would obviously seem that they were playing a joke at claiming to know his name. He quickly tried to backtrack and explain their reception.

"We were told that you are the only man who can take us to Kotzebue Sound," said Jarvis.

Perninyuk was silent. Jarvis uncomfortably cleared his throat and continued, "I assumed that you came after us and found our camp."

Perninyuk, still silent, peered intently at Jarvis. It wasn't unusual for men to be bushwhacked and left for dead in the wilderness. Finally Perninyuk answered, "Was hunting."

Jarvis was astonished that the very man they were most hoping to see in this vast wilderness had tripped over their camp quite by accident. Hell, he couldn't believe it himself. Jarvis thought that a quick description of his travels and mission might allay Perninyuk's fears, so he told the Eskimo guide of the stranded whalers, the villages they'd seen, and the deer they'd amassed. He mentioned as many names as he could, hoping that Perninyuk would recognize one. Perninyuk thoughtfully listened, occasionally shaking his head.

When Jarvis was finished he quietly looked at the prospective guide. Surely after they'd just stumbled across 500 square miles of wilderness, he wouldn't just walk back to his village.

Finally Perninyuk spoke.

"Tornak is guiding us."

Jarvis thought for a second. Tornak was a term he'd heard before, but in a different way. Then suddenly he remembered; Tornak was a short variation of Torngarsuk. It was a name that shamans, or Eskimo medicine men, referred to as a helping spirit.

"Yes, I believe so," said Jarvis. At first he felt a little guilty for attempting to play on shaman Perninyuk's faith to his own benefit. But then he thought, who was he to say what form of divine help they were receiving? It seemed obvious that something beyond themselves was responsible. God went by many names to many people.

Perninyuk smiled. "I'll take you to Kotzebue Sound."

Jarvis grinned and turned to the doctor.

"Bless my eyes!" exclaimed the doctor, clapping his hands.

They couldn't believe their luck . . . or maybe it was more. For now it didn't matter. All they knew was that Perninyuk, the only man for miles and miles in any direction, had stumbled upon their camp right when they needed him. It couldn't have been better.

They completed their packing with the help of the shaman Perninyuk, and went on their way. Once again, Jarvis was amazed at the giving spirit of the Eskimo. He couldn't imagine anywhere else that a man would, virtually in an instant, abandon his activity and lead them through dangerous terrain to their destination on a journey that would take days or even weeks to complete.

Their next destination was Sinrazat, a village on the coast partway to Kotzebue Sound. To get there, they traversed a series of lagoons that reached back to Cape Prince of Wales. It was a strange journey.

First they came upon a series of abandoned shacks. Passing the first and second, they stopped briefly at the third deserted village. They found no sign of life.

"This is really weird," said the doctor, walking back from an empty shack. "It's like an old deserted mining town I once saw."

"It's strange," agreed Jarvis. "This is the third abandoned village we've been through today. You almost feel that the world has disappeared and somebody forgot to tell us."

"They moved," said Perninyuk.

"Why?" asked Jarvis.

"Because it was time," said Perninyuk, wondering why they were asking. It must have seemed an odd question: in his world, such behavior was normal.

"What time was that?" asked the doctor with a small chuckle.

"It was time to make another home," replied Perninyuk matter-of-factly. Jarvis and the doctor stared at him blankly. Obviously something wasn't connecting. He tried again. "When your home has been used too much, you move."

Jarvis glanced at the dilapidated shack, strewn inside and out with remnants of animal and human discharge. Then it finally struck him: When your home became too full of waste, it was easier to move than attempt to clean it. It made eminent sense. With several feet of snow outside, burying the waste was impractical; even if you could get to the ground below, it was frozen hard as a rock. Therefore, when the ice melted, the waste remained. It was easy to see why, season permitting, they simply built new homes at another location.

After taking a break for tea and resting the dogs, the group continued. At last they arrived at the village of Sinrazat. Here the villagers came out to see the strange travelers. It was unusual for people to travel in the winter unless to hunt or fish.

The villagers of Sinrazat looked beleaguered, poorer than those encountered previously. Nevertheless, they kindly assisted with putting the sleds high on fish racks to protect the provisions from the animals. They also helped to feed the now-ravenous dogs.

In reciprocation, Jarvis shared with the appreciative Eskimos what tea and food they could spare. When they had a private moment, the doctor and Jarvis asked their shaman guide why these Eskimos were in such poor condition. He explained that the sealing was unusually thin this year. For whatever reason, the seal population was down. Since the main source of food for all Eskimos along the coast was seals, these people were starving.

As they prepared for sleep, the doctor turned to Jarvis. "I wish there were something we could do for these people," he said.

"I know, but we barely have enough to sustain ourselves and the guides we pick up along the way," answered Jarvis. He could tell that the doctor wasn't satisfied. Why should he be? Jarvis didn't feel good about it either.

Seeing their discomfort, Perninyuk interjected, "You are good men. Not worry. These people will survive better than you."

Jarvis's brow furrowed. The shaman's words had been meant to assuage their feelings of guilt. But they seemed to have a quite different effect. Coming from a medicine man, the statement that "They'll survive better than you," almost seemed like a deadly prediction of the two men's future. Jarvis and Call glanced at each other with the same worried frown.

Knowing he had to be strong and control his thoughts, Jarvis forced himself to shake off such negative feelings. Given the length of the journey yet ahead and the fatigue they'd be experiencing, obsessing about risks would be devastating. If nothing else, he'd treat the comments as a chilling reminder that they'd better be careful while traversing the next 600 miles. The terrain would take them across a mountain range and dangers worse than anything they'd yet encountered. Every ounce of their energy—physical and psychic—would be needed.

Jarvis, the doctor, and Perninyuk proceeded along the coast, their destination Kotzebue Sound. It was one of the two critical points remaining along their 600-mile trek to Point Barrow. Either critical point could end the journey—or their lives.

On this leg of their trip, at approximately twenty-mile intervals they found a series of small villages consisting of one or more families. At some of these villages they were able to acquire replacements for their exhausted dogs, but unfortunately, more than once the dogs chewed through their harnesses and returned home. Sled dogs were like family pets in that respect: they didn't want to leave their homes and owners.

Perninyuk knew the way in general and proved an excellent and reliable companion. However, they still needed local guides for help traversing local obstacles, much as a ship needs a harbor pilot to guide her into port. Unfortunately, these guides usually proved to be as much of a hindrance as a help.

After a long day's travel pushing and running with the sleds, the men finally halted and made camp. They were exhausted and running out of food. Gathering driftwood, they broke out the crackers and beans that constituted their typical dinner.

146

Two of the local guides sat in prime spots next to the fire. The doctor and Jarvis watched them in silence. They needed these men to guide them through a difficult area. The guides filled their plates, while the three travelers ate little. They had to stretch their provisions partly because they had underestimated what the dogs would eat, but more because they had miscalculated the guides' appetites. These last guides had no such compulsion to conserve food. They'd be gone soon, anyway.

"Watch them," whispered the doctor as the two men laughed and filled their bellies. "Why do we have to let them take all our food? Isn't it enough that we're paying for their services?"

"They are bad men," said Perninyuk.

"Thank God for you, Perninyuk," said Jarvis, looking appreciatively at their new friend. "I don't know what would happen if we lost you, too."

"Not worry, Perninyuk stay with you to Kotzebue Sound like promised."

"Are you sure we need them, Jarvis?" asked the doctor. He knew the answer, but hope led him to ask. Maybe the answer would change.

"They know the local area. Perninyuk can get us the rest of the way if they can get us through here," said Jarvis. There was more laughter from the two guides.

"Why are they this way?" the doctor asked Perninyuk.

"It's not so much them; it's the white men," answered Perninyuk.

"What do you mean?"

"The other koblonas that come through here. They only pay what they have to. They use Eskimos to get to the gold. They don't care if Eskimo dies."

"So they're using us like some other white men have used them?"

"Yes, and they think you will die."

There it came again, some sort of premonition of death for the doctor and Jarvis. They both waited for an explanation, but none came. Finally Jarvis spoke.

"Why do they think we're going to die?"

"They can see you have no food left. No beans. No meat. They think you are like the other white men. You not know how to live in Arctic."

"I see. So they think we're about to die anyway; why not take what they can get while we're still living?"

"Yes, like other koblonas treat them."

So there it was. These Eskimos thought Jarvis and Call were going to die. And since the other koblonas they'd encountered hadn't considered their lives of any value, why should they care about Jarvis and the doctor? The rescue team was at the mercy of men who had been used and abused by previous travelers.

Jarvis sat and thought about the contrast. The Eskimos exposed to the missionaries, Artisarlook (Charlie) and Lopp, were willing to give everything they had to follow the men and help them in their cause. Other Eskimos in the interior were likewise willing to sacrifice; the less they had, the more they gave. Each was the product of his environment. The men treated with love and respect returned the same; these men had not been, and therefore they did not.

Like the others, these guides abandoned the group in the night, taking their dogs with them. Jarvis, the doctor, and Perninyuk were left to fend for themselves. But they made it to Toatut at Cape Espenburg, near Kotzebue Sound. At that point they only had a few crackers, enough beans for a day, and some tea.

On the opposite side of Kotzebue Sound, forty miles distant, was Cape Blossom. There, if the ice proved solid enough to cross, they hoped to meet with Lieutenant Bertholf and his cargo of food. If he couldn't make it, they would run out of food, get continually weaker, and possibly die.

"God, I hope he's there," said the doctor, looking at his last ration of beans and crackers.

"I hope so, too."

"When was the last time we saw him?"

"December 20th, before Christmas."

"That's almost two months ago."

"I know."

"And he had to have gotten our note."

"I know!" responded Jarvis, beginning to feel irritated. He, too, was

148

filled with anxiety. They'd parted with Bertholf, who was assigned to get a small group of deer and provisions for the trip by himself. He went a different route that took him to St. Michael, where he was supposed to originally meet with the doctor and Jarvis. They'd arrived sooner than anticipated and left a letter for him saying to go on to meet them at Cape Blossom. That had been a long time ago. And if Bertholf had had the same difficulty with the local guides as Jarvis and the doctor had, there was slim chance of finding him at Cape Blossom.

"I'm sorry, Jarvis," said the doctor.

"I'm sorry, too," said Jarvis. "I know we're near the end of our rope. The chances that he's there are slim to none, especially given the date." It was true. Jarvis had said in the letter that they anticipated being at Cape Blossom a week earlier. If Bertholf was as efficient as Jarvis knew him to be, he would already have struck out for Point Barrow. He was driven by the same need to feed the starving men as Jarvis.

"Well, we beat the odds before. Just look at Perninyuk!" Both men glanced at the medicine man, who seemed to be deep in thought. Maybe he was in some sort of trance, or maybe he was starving, as they were, and was just trying to bear it the best way he knew how. They were silent for a minute. The talk of Bertholf reminded Jarvis of the difficulty of his route.

"Bertholf would have had almost no villages on his route, as we did. He had to live entirely on his provisions collected earlier. He had no way to replenish his stock or dogs as we did," said Jarvis in low tones. He wanted to be truthful to his friend, to make him fully aware of the odds against success in finding Bertholf and his food waiting for them.

"So what does that mean, exactly?"

"Well, it could have taken him longer because he couldn't get fresh dogs and has just gotten there, or maybe not. He could have run out of food because he couldn't get more. Or maybe he has more because he didn't lose his food to greedy guides. I'm not really sure. I was just making you aware of his situation."

The doctor sat in pensive silence. Perninyuk now was rolled up in his sleeping bag. He was the smart one. They say that the Arctic teaches patience.

Well, it was foolish to waste precious energy worrying about their chances.

Finally the doctor spoke. "It looks like we have to leave it in the hands of the man upstairs." Maybe he was right. So far the missionaries had proved to be a godsend; maybe Bertholf would, as well.

Chapter Twenty-Three

Jarvis . . .   *The Crossing*

Morning came, and with it the departure for the rest of their journey. With their food virtually gone, it was imperative they reach Cape Blossom and Bertholf, if he was there.

Jarvis turned to the north. He shuddered as the wind hit his face. It was minus 20 degrees, but that was good. If the wind had been warmer and out of the south, that would have meant that Kotzebue Sound would have unstable ice. Southerly winds for a week or longer would thaw some of the ice, making it impassable for the deer and herders. Such ice could collapse, sending the men and deer to a frigid death. At Arctic temperatures, a man would die within four minutes of hitting the water. Usually, the body was in such shock from the temperature that it instantly shut down and the victim lost consciousness, slipping below the surface. It was small consolation that an Arctic drowning victim's last four minutes were spent in relative peace. To avoid such a fate, if open water was visible to Jarvis, they'd have to travel around Kotzebue Sound, adding several weeks to their journey.

As they traveled, the weather started to turn. It began to snow hard, reducing visibility to little more than a few feet. They had to stop many times to get their bearings, trying to read the local topography. The wind began to pound them, making exhaustion even worse. Finally, after a hard day's travel, they arrived at Kotzebue Sound with a blizzard in full force. There was no way they would be able to determine the condition of the Sound.

At the ice's edge, they found two huts. Jarvis chose one and dragged himself inside. Quickly looking around, he counted up to thirty Eskimos squeezed into every available cranny. The Eskimos, undisturbed by his entrance, said nothing as the three men crawled into the small space. Jarvis had learned enough about the culture at this point to accept everything as it was. He and Call simply used what space was available to slip into their sleeping bags and go to sleep. To the Eskimos these were just three more people trying to survive the winter. All were welcome, no questions asked.

In the morning, Jarvis awoke to an almost suffocating stench. As he climbed out of his bag, the foul air of the tiny room made him gag. This many people in this small a hut made conditions almost unbearable. As he scanned the faces of the people around him, Jarvis realized that the hut's inhabitants were covered in dirt and other objectionable material. Understandably, they couldn't check into a hotel for a hot bath.

The men were famished and the inhabitants had a small amount of food to offer, but despite himself, Jarvis had to refuse. Hungry as he was, he couldn't have stomached it. As he and the other two men stepped out into the open, the blizzard hit them. Diminished from the day before, it was nevertheless a formidable force.

"Those people are unclean," said Perninyuk, the shaman guide.

"Are they always like that?" said the doctor.

"I not know," said Perninyuk. "Many people, many different ways."

Jarvis realized he was saying that not all Eskimos are the same. As with any other ethnic group, each was an individual. Likewise, every family or community had different habits. They discussed this idea for a moment, and then the conversation turned to their mission.

"We need to cross the ice," said Jarvis, partly driven by the mission to determine the ice's strength and partly by the need to find Bertholf and get food.

"Storm is strong," said Perninyuk.

"Do you mean we can't go?"

"We need people of hut to guide us. We not see danger."

Perninyuk was referring to the fact that they had to traverse a sixty-mile stretch of ice. The locals would know the safest route and where the ice was weaker because of the subsurface terrain. The men themselves wouldn't know when they were entering dangerous areas.

"Can you ask them for help?" asked Jarvis. Each area had a different dialect. Since they were now farther north than the miners ever traveled, the locals up here had no command of English.

"Yes."

Jarvis entered the hut with Perninyuk while the doctor remained behind. Though he stood in a blizzard, at the moment he preferred it to being inside the hut.

As Jarvis and Perninyuk entered, the Eskimos paid little attention. Perninyuk spoke in Inupik. In response one man pointed to another. Perninyuk redirected his comments to the second man, who said nothing but shook his head. Perninyuk repeated the question. The second man finally answered. Even not knowing the language, Jarvis knew they had been turned down.

Jarvis turned to the shaman guide and asked, "What did they say?"

"Too dangerous."

"Too dangerous, how do they know that? They haven't looked at the ice."

"Too dangerous to look!" Apparently they considered the act of even going on the ice to be too perilous. This, Jarvis hadn't anticipated.

"Offer them something. We have money and some gear to give."

"No, it not change them."

"Please try," said Jarvis.

Perninyuk turned once again to the men. From the look on his face, Jarvis knew it was futile. The men listened and shook their heads once again. Perninyuk persisted, but to no avail. Finally, one said something in response.

"What did he say?"

"He said too dangerous. But maybe not too dangerous tomorrow."

At least that was something. The reluctance wasn't permanent; it was linked to the storm. They needed better visibility before going across the ice, or maybe they needed colder temperatures. With the snow had come slightly warmer air. Jarvis didn't know the details, but he knew enough to wait another day.

153

The next day came and went. Jarvis sat inside the hut, miserable and hungry. It had been two days since he had consumed enough food. The air was foul and he was anxious to get moving. The storm continued to pound the hut and the Sound. The people prepared to go to sleep again.

To pass the time, Jarvis had spent the day studying each person. There were twelve men, eight women, and four children. Of the men, eight appeared to be married and four single. The eight women, as far as Jarvis could tell, were married to the eight men. In Eskimo society, polygamy was a common practice. As long as a man could hunt and fish to support the family, all was fine. The sailors talked of the Eskimo customs as they knew them with some awe. It was said that a man could share his wife with another. It was also rumored that Eskimo youths were tutored in the ways of love by the community's widows, thus making happy the young men, the widowed women, and the future brides of the now-experienced young men.

As they prepared for bed, Jarvis was drawn to a husband and wife. He was an old man and his wife appeared to be suffering. You could tell by her pained expression and intermittent moaning that she had bad headaches. As Jarvis watched in silence, the man looped a cord around his wife's neck and put a stick through the loop at the base of her skull. Jarvis suddenly concluded that he was about to witness a murder by strangulation. He jumped to his feet and yelled for the man to stop. All the people of the hut jolted alert.

"Stop!" said Jarvis again. The old man, startled, said something back in his native language, then again began securing the cord.

"Stop!" yelled Jarvis again and began moving forward. "Don't kill her. I don't care what's wrong with her!"

As he continued forward, two Eskimo men moved to restrain him. As they moved toward his arms, the doctor angled into position. He wasn't going to sit back while Jarvis was restrained. They would take on the twelve men of the hut by themselves if they had to.

Jarvis looked behind him; Perninyuk was gone. Jarvis and the doctor didn't speak Inupik, the native language, and Perninyuk was their only translator.

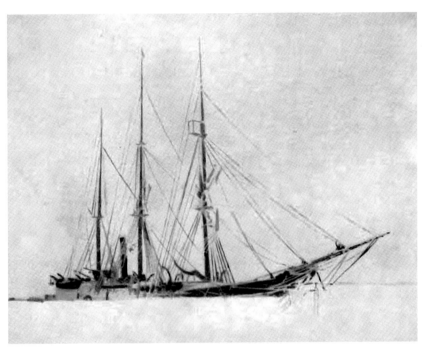

THE WHALER BELVEDERE
AT POINT FRANKLIN

WHALERS NEWPORT AND FEARLESS
IN THE ICE EAST OF POINT BARROW

A

WHALER JEANIE IN THE ICE

WHALER ROSARIO
CRUSHED IN THE ICE

OLD GOVERNMENT REFUGE STATION
POINT BARROW

OLD KELLEY HOUSE AT POINT BARROW
WHERE WRECKED CREWS LIVED BEFORE EXPEDITION ARRIVED

C

CHARLIE BROWER'S HOUSE AT POINT BARROW
THE MOST NORTHERN HABITATION OF A WHITE MAN IN ALASKA

NATIVE HOUSES AT POINT BARROW VILLAGE

BEAR

FORECASTLE OF THE BEAR AND VIEW AHEAD
SHIP WAS HEADED SOUTH ON ACCOUNT OF ICE

E

DUTCH HARBOR, ALASKA
WHERE THE BEAR SPENT THE WINTER OF 1897-98
THE BEAR LIES AT THE END OF THE WHARF

OFFICERS OF THE BEAR

F

BEAR OFFICERS COMPOSING OVERLAND EXPEDITION
(LEFT TO RIGHT)
2ND LIEUTENANT E. P. BERTHOLF
SURGEON S. J. CALL
1ST LIEUTENANT D. H. JARVIS, COMMANDING

G

ALEXIS KALENIN'S HOUSE
AT TUNUNAK

ESKIMO DOGS AND LOADED SLED

H

FEEDING THE DOGS

NATIVE HUT, SNOW ENTRANCE

SNOW HOUSES

HARBOR OF ST. MICHAEL

J

STARTING FROM GOLOVIN BAY

ICE CRUSHES ALONG SHORE

K

LAST COAL FROM NAVARCH

TILTON'S CAMP
ON THE SHORE OF NORTON SOUND

ON THE KOYUK RIVER

DEER TRAIN
SHOWING SLEDS AND HARNESS

M

SEAL HARVEST

RETURNING FROM A SEAL HUNT

N

GOING OUT FOR WHALES

CUTTING UP WHALES

O

TENT CAMP AT ICY CAPE

MIDDAY HALT FOR TEA AND HARD BREAD

P

PART OF CHARLIE ARTISARLOOK'S DEER HERD

NATIVE VILLAGE
YUKON DELTA, WINTER

Q

TOM LOPP
CHRISTIAN MISSIONARY

NATIVE MAN AND WOMAN
FROM POINT HOPE VILLAGE

NATIVES OF GOLOVIN BAY

PRESBYTERIAN MISSION
POINT BARROW

T

WHALERS HAULING ICE

HAULING SUPPLIES
FROM THE BEAR TO THE WHALING SHIPS

U

RETURNING FROM A DUCK HUNT
POINT BARROW

V

REINDEER FAWNS

ESKIMO GRAVE
KOTZEBUE SOUND

W

AN OLD GRAVE AT POINT HOPE

ESKIMO GRAVE AT POINT HOPE

WHALING STATION
POINT HOPE, ALASKA, SPRING

WHALING STATION
POINT HOPE, ALASKA, WINTER

Y

SLED WITH SAIL
HERSCHEL ISLAND

HAULING MEAT
TO THE VESSELS EAST OF POINT BARROW

Z

BLASTING OLD WRECK FOR FIREWOOD
NEAR THE ROSARIO

REINDEER HERD IN SUMMER
POINT BARROW

AA

KILLING DEER FOR THE WHALERS
AT POINT BARROW

SKINNING REINDEER
POINT BARROW

AB

SOME OF THE SHIPWRECKED MEN

TEARING DOWN THE OLD KELLEY HOUSE FOR FUEL

AC

MIDNIGHT SUN

BREAKING UP OF THE ICE
POINT BARROW, SUMMER

AD

PRYING OFF ICE AFTER A BLAST
POINT BARROW, AUGUST 7TH, 1898

BEAR GETTING FREE FROM THE ICE PACK
AUGUST 16TH, 1898

AE

MISSION ACCOMPLISHED

HOMEWARD BOUND

AF

One of the Eskimo women ran out of the hut. As Jarvis struggled to get free, the Eskimos moved between him and his target to protect the old man. They spoke to Jarvis in loud tones as if he had gone crazy from being confined in the hut too long during the storm.

Finally, the woman appeared with Perninyuk in tow. "Jarvis!" said the exasperated shaman. Everyone in the hut looked and began speaking at once. They were all pointing at Jarvis and the doctor as if to say they were insane.

Jarvis protested. Turning to face Perninyuk, he said, "The old man's killing the woman! See how he's strangling her? He doesn't want to care for her any longer."

Now that he understood Jarvis' motivation, Perninyuk turned to the Eskimos. Each looked at the old man to explain his actions. The old man spoke rapidly in Inupik; he appeared to be angry with Jarvis for the accusation. Finally, Perninyuk turned back to Jarvis and the doctor.

"He not kill her; he heal her."

"How can tying a cord around her neck do that!" interjected the doctor. Obviously it wasn't something he'd ever seen in medical school.

"She is possessed of demon shaped like dog. It making headache. They tie like dog to drive out evil spirit." As a *unatkook*, or shaman, Perninyuk was well acquainted with the spiritual ceremonies involved in healing.

Jarvis and the doctor were dumbfounded at this strange development. There were many aspects of Eskimo beliefs that were confusing to the outside world. Among them was Piploktog, or Arctic hysteria, as it was called by the whites. In this condition, natives would suddenly run, screaming unintelligible words, in any dialect, and rip off their clothing. Academics attributed these attacks to various causes ranging from the harshness of the climate to a lack of potassium in the Eskimo diet, with its general shortage of fresh fruits and vegetables. The Eskimos themselves attributed Piploktog to the supernatural. Although this old woman was not suffering from this Piploktog, the supernatural still apparently applied.

Possibly because of his training, the doctor couldn't give up that easily. "Jarvis, that's wrong. Maybe I can help."

Jarvis intently queried Perninyuk. "Can the koblona's medicine man help?"

The shaman turned to the group and explained the offer. They let the old man respond; he instantly rejected the help. He obviously had no confidence in white man's medicine.

As they looked on, the old man completed tying up his wife in a rough fashion akin to hog tying, only with the arms and legs constrained in front of the body instead of behind. He then began repeating what appeared to be medicinal incantations.

"Jarvis?" said the doctor, looking at him. "Can we do nothing?" Seeing his face, Perninyuk said to both, "Worry no, his song is good medicine."

Jarvis acknowledged the effort with a slight nod. He looked at the doctor and said, "These people have a right to their own practices. We can't interfere. Besides, how many times have the Eskimos bailed us out and not condemned our ways."

The doctor began to speak, but then decided to say nothing. Having served in Unalaska for several years, he knew something of Eskimo customs.

The Eskimos released Jarvis and the doctor and returned to their previous positions. They finally fell off to sleep. The incantations continued long into the night.

The following morning the men once again conferred. None was willing to guide the travelers across the Sound and determine the safety of the crossing. Without this expert guidance, the team could unknowingly wander into a more dangerous area and fall through thin ice. They would have to wait yet another day.

As they sat another day in the odorous hut, Perninyuk took it upon himself to entertain with a demonstration of native chants and dances. After a highly impassioned recital of native chants, Perninyuk shifted to entertainment and did magic tricks.

In the afternoon, a local guide went out and checked the ice conditions deep on the Sound. He agreed to guide the men to the village of Kikiktaruk at Cape Blossom, based on a promise of food as payment at the other side. This promise assumed, of course, that Bertholf would be waiting with ample supplies, a long shot at best. Normally Jarvis wouldn't have made such a promise, knowing that he might not be able to produce the food, but now he was desperate. If Bertholf wasn't there, they'd be in worse shape than today, *and* be in the company of one irate guide. Nevertheless, they'd set out across the Sound in the morning.

The doctor and Jarvis awoke in the still-dark morning and quickly dressed. They crawled through the opening in the hut and found Perninyuk outside, wearing a disturbed look. Jarvis looked around for the volunteer guide. Suddenly he feared the worst.

"Where's our guide?" asked the doctor, whose line of thoughts matched Jarvis's.

"Not here," replied Perninyuk.

"Is he gone? Will he be back?" asked Jarvis.

"No, his dogs gone," answered Perninyuk.

Jarvis and the doctor didn't need a further explanation. They knew that the guide had been highly skeptical of their promise of food at the other end. Obviously, past travelers had cheated the natives more than once. This man had little reason to trust a group of koblonas, desperate and without food, so he left.

"What do we do, Jarvis?" asked the doctor.

Jarvis stood in silence. Now almost six months into their trip, he was more than accustomed to bad news and making desperate decisions. In this case, he had an agonizing decision to make: either risk a crossing without a guide, or wait longer to find another. Since they could feed neither man nor dog, he could easily justify the risk. On the other hand, they'd come through a lot just to chance it all this close to Point Barrow.

After a long pause, Jarvis said, "We have to wait to find another guide." The doctor quietly groaned, but knew it was the right decision.

At this point they approached each man of the village with the offer of food and supplies. Disbelieving them, none was willing to make the sixty-mile trip across the Sound. Even if it were pronounced safe, that was a relative rating. Men were still known to die crossing the ice as unseen hazards masked the freezing water below. Finally they turned to a teenage boy, their last hope.

As the doctor and Jarvis looked on, Perninyuk spoke to the young man. He seemed to be resisting. But unlike the older men, he wasn't as definite. Jarvis resisted the urge to break into the conversation between Perninyuk and the young man to get a translation. Finally Perninyuk turned to Jarvis and said, "He will guide us."

"Great!" rejoiced Jarvis.

"But we must trade," responded Perninyuk.

"Yes," said Jarvis slowly, "we can trade. What does he want?" Jarvis looked anxious. Given their situation, he had little to trade and no bargaining power.

"He wants us to buy his dogs and his other stock once we get to Cape Blossom."

"Sure, of course," said Jarvis with great relief. After a pause he added, "How will he get back?"

"He not come back," said Perninyuk. "He go to friends." Apparently the young man wanted to visit friends on the other side of the Sound.

"He's going to live with friends?" confirmed Jarvis.

"Yes, and trade."

Jarvis was slightly dumbfounded. How could he trade if he had just sold his dogs and other stock to Jarvis? Then Jarvis realized that he needed the cash or other items from Jarvis to trade. They'd fetch a higher price than his current possessions.

"It's a deal," agreed Jarvis.

With that they quickly prepared to leave and cross the Sound. They finished securing the sleds and sled dogs, then drove down the banks of the shoreline and hit the ice.

While the ice may have been safe, it was anything but easy to travel on. The ice had piled upon itself, creating six-foot crushes. It was like trying to weave and climb your way through the rubble of scattered rail cars piled one upon another after a bad accident—only this time, the accident seemed to go on for miles.

They spent more time carrying and lifting the sleds over the ice crushes than being pulled by the dogs. They would barely find a smooth patch that lasted at most a hundred yards, before encountering another range of ice crushes. Unfortunately, the smooth ice meant that only days before, it had been a patch of open water. While it was easier to travel on such patches, the danger of crashing through was continually present.

After a full day's travel, the other side didn't seem any closer.

Perninyuk and the young guide looked at Jarvis. "We need stop for night."

"No, we need to keep going," returned Jarvis. He was concerned that they had no food. If they stopped for the night, the young guide might abandon them like some of the others.

"We should stop," they reiterated.

"No, we must keep going. Food and heat is on the other side," said Jarvis. It was as much a hope as a promise.

Perninyuk translated to the young man. After conversing he said, "He not know way in dark."

Jarvis hesitated. He was desperate. Given the ice crushes and the youth of the guide, he surely must be rethinking his decision. "We must keep going; we can go by the stars." As a sailor, Jarvis could keep their group going in the right direction to the other side—or at least avoid going in circles.

Perninyuk translated to the young guide, who looked up for a moment, then down at the horizon. It was as if he were thinking through the logic. Could he look at the ice formations to avoid danger while the sailor looked at the stars?

He hesitated and seemed to come to a decision. He said something barely more than a single word to Perninyuk, who turned to Jarvis.

"We go."

Jarvis heaved a sigh of relief. His desperate logic had worked for the moment, but they had better get to the other side soon.

So they pressed on, sometimes pulled by the dogs and sometimes dragging the sleds over the huge crushes themselves. Each was tired to the point of exhaustion. Even the dogs had to be beaten to continue.

Finally at 10:30 P.M. they reached land, but it was strange. Jarvis looked at the unusual formations. Perninyuk came to his side and whispered, "Graveyard."

"Graveyard?" said Jarvis.

"Yes," quietly responded Perninyuk. "We near." His response was a strange mixture of reverence and happiness. The Eskimos treated all graveyards with reverence, but this one was special: Since Eskimo graveyards were always located near dwellings, finding this one meant that they had hit their target, almost dead on the village of Kikiktaruk at Cape Blossom.

They dragged themselves up the bank to what appeared to be a large cabin. It was either the communal lodge or another important dwelling for the village. Unlike the others, this one had a standard door such as could be found on a New England home. Jarvis knocked.

He was slightly taken aback when a young woman came to the door, wearing a long wool dress and shawl. For a moment he felt as if he were back home.

"Good evening, I'm Lieutenant Jarvis of the Revenue Cutter Service," he said with a slight bow.

"Oh, good heavens," replied the young woman, "come in, come in; we've been expecting you."

Again, Jarvis was astonished. How could they have possibly known he was coming? As the lieutenant entered, he saw three people sitting near the fire with their backs to the door. Before Jarvis's eyes adjusted to the dim light, a male voice called, "Lieutenant Jarvis!"

"Lieutenant Bertholf! My God, man, you made it!" It was a miracle. There *would* be food and supplies, after all.

"Thank God. I thought I'd missed you," said Bertholf.

"Sorry we're late; we got stuck in the blizzard, among other things," returned Jarvis. "We thought you'd come and gone."

Bertholf began to laugh. "I just got here late yesterday. I was sure *I'd* missed *you!*"

"I don't believe it!" said the doctor, coming up from behind. "After two months apart, we arrive at precisely the same time. A New York train conductor couldn't have done it better."

They greeted each other with hugs uncharacteristic of Cutter Service Officers. After a few moments' revelry, they settled down to introductions with their hosts and traveling companions. A Quaker missionary named Robert Samms and his wife owned the house. The young woman greeting them at the door was Miss Hunnicutt, who'd recently arrived to take her post as a teacher in the village.

Jarvis and Bertholf described their trips thus far to the amazed missionaries, who provided dinner for their companions, including Perninyuk and the young guide. The men ate ravenously at first, until, hunger abated, they were able to describe their recruitment of Lopp and Artisarlook, who were driving the deer toward the Sound.

Bertholf described his travels and the difficulties he'd encountered after a trader at Unalaklik had failed to keep his part of the agreement and furnish teams for the trip. He recounted his unplanned trip to another deer camp where he had acquired seven deer and sleds. Unfortunately, the drivers he'd recruited proved to be somewhat unscrupulous, causing a great degree of hardship and complications. But thanks to his characteristic resourcefulness, he made it around Kotzebue Sound with supplies and deer in tow. There was no doubt that he was not the loose cannon that had left the naval academy in his youth.

Despite the exciting recollections, they finally succumbed to sleep again. The next morning they attended to their gear and rested up for the remainder of the trip. They agreed that the Sound, with its large ice crushes, would be too difficult for the deer herd to cross. With the tough climbs and lack of a straight path, the deer would become scattered and lost. Unfortunately, Lopp, Artisarlook, and the boys would have to take an alternate route around the Sound that would take ten days or more.

They still had to determine *which* route to take around the Sound. And it wouldn't be just a matter of following the shoreline; the possible routes were more complex. Luckily, Lieutenant Bertholf had just come over one of these routes to arrive at Cape Blossom. After a lengthy discussion examining all options, they decided to choose his path. A volunteer messenger was sent with a letter to the village of Toatut, which lay at the end of Lopp's route before he reached the Sound. The letter told him that crossing the ice was not advisable, and recommended the alternate route around the north shore.

Bertholf remained behind with the Quaker missionary Robert Samms, to wait for Lopp with provisions. Jarvis and the doctor got ready to go on to Point Hope to prepare the way for the herd. They began again by crossing Hotham Inlet in the direction of Cape Kruzenstern, making the village of Anyok the first night's stop. This would be the end point for the herd if they followed the route described by Lopp.

The weather was turning ever colder, but at least there were no harassing gales or blinding snow, just the ever-present, relentless, bitter cold. Upon their arrival at Anyok, they were once again treated to the generous nature of the Eskimo inhabitants, who gave Jarvis and the doctor the lion's share of what little food they had, reserving the best place in the huts for the travelers. Once again, it seemed that the less the Eskimos had, the more they gave. Listening intently to the rescuers' mission, they offered items they thought helpful for the whalers.

The next day Jarvis and Call began again en route to Point Hope by way of Hotham Inlet. In the successive days, they went from village to village, each time encountering the same hospitality and assistance. But they would soon encounter the unexpected.

Chapter Twenty-Four

Jim . . .   *Deprivation*

Jim looked on respectfully as Brower spoke to three Eskimo hunters. They had caught no game; it was late in the season and the caribou were leaving. When Jim first came to Point Barrow, there had been a relatively steady, albeit meager, supply of food from Eskimo hunters. That was drawing to a close, leaving the men to rely on half-rotten meat stored many seasons. At least two years of freezing and thawing had taken their toll on the stores before the men even arrived. The men on the outlying ships were no better off, despite attempts to share food among themselves.

"How's it look, Mr. Brower?" Jim asked the approaching manager. Brower had made a Herculean effort to keep the whalers alive, working with the Eskimos to find food for them. He was respected as honest and forthright by both the white and Eskimo side. That's what made the system work.

Brower pushed his hands along either side of his face from the front to the back, as if to wipe away the anxiety and frustration. The weight of these many lives was beginning to show on his face.

"It's becoming harder, Jim," said Brower, frowning. Now that Brower was the only person the men would take orders from, they had developed a relationship in which he knew each by name. He ordered work parties and settled disputes.

"Is there anything we can do?"

"No, just try to stay warm and keep out of trouble. I know you will," said Brower, smiling. Brower had more than his share of disputes to settle lately. As the food supply diminished and the men's health deteriorated, the stranded whalers became more and more restless. Many blamed the ship captains for their current situation; others found fault with their shipmates for every deprivation. Arguments grew more frequent as their suffering increased. It was a wonder that they hadn't broken down into total lawlessness. If the food supply stopped, they certainly would.

"A man inside is looking real bad," said Jake, stepping to Jim's side. He could often be found there, partly out of friendship, partly out of the need for safety. With things degenerating, it was better to pair off with friends to avoid trouble.

"How bad?"

"He's all swelled up and breathing real hard."

"I'd better take a look."

Brower, Jake, and Jim went back into the Old Kelley House, which was now almost totally uninhabitable. The air was heavy with a strange mixture of filth, moisture, and soot from seal oil lamps in the men's berths. Anyone unaccustomed to the smell would almost certainly have run out of the room vomiting. At the very least, he'd have a roaring headache within minutes of entering. Brower, Jake, and Jim made their way through the crowded berths, to the sounds of considerable hacking and wheezing.

Along the way they passed other men in various stages of affliction with scurvy and dropsy. Without a decent diet of healthy meat, the men were beginning to degenerate. Most now didn't even bother to leave their berths.

Two other crewmen were sitting by the dying crewman's side as the three finally reached him. He had been sicker than the rest for more than a week. Crewmen took turns sitting with him to bolster his spirits, but in the last few hours he had really started to decline.

"How you doing?" asked Brower.

The crewman tried to speak but broke into violent coughing, spewing blood and fluid. His body was swollen, his stomach bloated. His face was pasty and pale.

"Well, don't try to talk," consoled Brower. "I've got a little seal fat to make you some soup."

"Don't waste it on him, he'll be dead soon anyway!" snarled one of the men from a nearby bunk.

Brower turned and glared. He didn't bother to answer. With the mood of the men, you didn't go out of your way to start an argument, but the man continued.

"Really, he's just the first. Soon we'll all be that way!"

"Just you shut up," yelled Joiner. "It's bad enough in here without having to listen to you bellyaching."

"Why don't you come over here and try to shut me up, you bastard!"

Now Brower intervened. "Stop! It's hard enough to stay alive without wasting our energy killing each other. I'll get the missionary doctor. You two just hush up."

With that they both grumbled quietly, but stopped their verbal assault. Brower was the hand that fed them; they knew not to bite it.

Jim and Jake waited as Brower left to fetch the doctor. Now the crewman's breathing was becoming more labored. His breaths came rapid and shallow as he tried to draw in breath that fluid-filled lungs could no longer accommodate. Finally his anguished breath stopped altogether.

The room was silent for a moment.

"Maybe he wouldn't have died if he had had a decent place to live!" a crewman yelled at Brower, now entering the room.

"You shut up!" said Brower. "You're lucky to have this!"

Brower sat on the dead crewman's bunk for a moment in silence, his head in his hands. The room quieted again.

Brower looked up. Now many of the eighty sets of eyes in the room watched him through cracks in blankets, wood, and clothing piled to keep berths warm in the frigid cold.

"We was talking, Mr. Brower," said Joiner. "We was thinking that we got maybe a month or two. If we don't starve, we'll be dead from sickness."

"Don't worry. I've got it under control," said Brower.

"You've been good by us," said Joiner.

"Yes, we wouldn't have made it this far without you," affirmed a few other voices from around the room.

165

Most of the men just lay in their bunks. They had begun to resign themselves to their fate and simply curled up to keep warm. Their bodies were sore, weak, and cold.

Chapter Twenty-Five

Lopp...   *The Boys*

Lopp shaded his eyes and gazed at the mountains in the distance. The snow-capped giants were towers of strength and grace, immovable by man or time, a monument to the God that created them. The wind carried clouds along the peaks, enveloping the mountaintops. It was a bittersweet sight. The mountains, while beautiful, represented one of two major obstacles for the herd to cross; the other was Kotzebue Sound. Since the mountains banked to the north of the Sound on the backside of Cape Kruzenstern, they signaled the approach of the first major test.

As his eyes moved down to the mountains' base, Lopp could see Kivyearzruk, one of his boys, approaching in the distance. Bright-eyed, smiling young Kivyearzruk had a good heart. As he and his sled approached on an intercept course, Lopp brought his own sled deer to a halt. Since he hadn't heard from Jarvis, he had sent Kivyearzruk ahead to check out the ice conditions at Kotzebue Sound.

The young man approached. "Kivyearzruk," said Lopp with a smile.

The young man smiled back, recognizing his teacher. "Mr. Lopp," he said, still out of breath, addressing him as he had as a pupil. Old habits die hard.

"You made it back quickly. Are you well?" Having recruited the young man for the trip, Lopp felt responsible for his welfare.

"I'm fine; the ice is not," said Kivyearzruk. Lopp's face fell. "The ice is not good. An offshore wind has made it weak," he continued.

This was devastating news. The delay could mean many lives.

"But I have more," continued Kivyearzruk. "Lieutenant Jarvis and

Surgeon Call are stranded with no food."

"What do you mean, stranded?" asked Lopp.

By this time the other boys had arrived. They too had seen Kivyearzruk from a distance and were anxious to hear the news.

"They have run out of food. They are trying to hire a guide to take them across to Espenburg, but have nothing with which to pay," said Kivyearzruk. The other boys mumbled at the news. Lopp frowned at the young men in an effort to quiet the group.

"We need to help them," interjected Sokweena.

"Yes, we can't go on and just leave them."

Turning to Kivyearzruk, Lopp asked, "Did you see them?"

"No, I was told this by a villager out hunting, before I reached the Sound. I rushed right back to tell you."

"Message received," said Lopp. "Did he say anything more about the ice?"

Kivyearzruk shrugged. "It's bad. There are holes and bad ice crushes the height of a house in places." With this added detail, the picture looked even worse.

"We should go anyway," Sokweena urged. "We can give supplies to Jarvis and the doctor, and look at the ice again. If it's still bad, we can turn around."

Lopp was proud of his boys. They were as exhausted and dejected from the news as he was. But still they instantly moved to make a decision favoring the aid of two strangers, even if it lengthened their trip. Lopp nodded toward the other boys. "And what do you think?"

"We have to go," said Ituk.

"Yes, let's go," said Tautuk.

He looked at the remaining boys; they simply nodded their agreement. He then turned to Charlie, his second in command. Charlie must agree— and he did.

"All right then, it's unanimous," said Lopp. "But what route?"

The boys conferred for a moment.

Sokweena answered first. "We should go east from here and up the coast to the bay on the south side of Kotzebue Sound. That's the fastest."

"I don't think the deer can handle the terrain," said Charlie. "It's longer, but up the coast would be better for the deer and might be faster still."

Lopp listened. He had two alternate recommendations. Turning to Kivyearzruk, he said, "And which do you prefer?" Lopp was sensitive to the fact that Kivyearzruk, who had just returned from there, was hearing his recommendation about the ice conditions ignored for the moment. By inviting Kivyearzruk's input, Lopp would be showing the young man the respect he needed.

Kivyearzruk stood pondering the alternatives. The boys waited patiently. Having had Lopp as their childhood teacher meant that classroom rules still somewhat applied, and Kivyearzruk had been asked the question.

"I think that we should go up the coast," he finally declared.

Lopp looked at the other boys, who were nodding their heads in agreement. "All right then, let's go!" he said, slapping his hands. Each knew his position and moved quickly. With no food, Jarvis and the doctor would need their help now.

While the boys hastily prepared to drive the deer up the coast to Espenburg, Lopp hit the trail ahead of them, driving a dog sled and team he'd hired from some other Eskimos along the way. He would go on with food for Jarvis and the doctor, more than ten miles ahead.

Despite its name, imposing Espenburg was little more than two or three igloos. About nine miles before his destination, Lopp encountered a handful of natives, including Knunk, whom he'd met before. They informed him that Jarvis and the doctor had started to cross Kotzebue Sound with a young guide the previous day.

That was both good and bad news. The good news was that the ice must have been safe enough for the two to travel on, with a guide to lead them. The bad news was that Lopp was too late to help his friends. Lopp prayed that Jarvis had enough strength to reach Cape Blossom on the other side. There he would at least find Robert Samms, a missionary who Lopp was sure would help.

With the herd moving toward Espenburg, Lopp decided to continue on his present course. He reached the village at the end of the Sound the same day and received a warm welcome from its inhabitants.

The next morning Lopp woke up to the stiff, frigid wind of the Arctic. Like Jarvis and the doctor before him, he was cramped into a small, partially buried snow house. He crawled out through the tunnel and shuddered. It was teeth-chattering cold. A crisp gale was blowing from the southwest. The thermometer he'd brought read −28.

With the help of a local boy, Lopp followed the sled tracks left by Jarvis the day before. The ice seemed safe, but crushes were piled high, with no breaks anywhere to weave through. Lopp went farther onto the ice to one of the higher ridges. There it was as if a million homes had been strewn about by a horrendous storm. From this vantage point, all he could see were ice crushes similarly piled high in all directions. The sleds and the deer could never make it over such obstacles. It appeared that their gamble hadn't paid off. They'd have to travel around the Sound and lose up to ten days.

Disheartened, Lopp walked back to the village and was met by the boys. They'd left the herd two miles back to graze.

"How does it look?" Charlie asked. His face looked hopeful, like the boys standing near. Lopp dreaded having to tell them.

"Bad," Lopp replied, shaking his head.

The boys looked at each other. They could tell by his tone that it was very definitive and that they'd have to take the alternate route.

"Let us look," said Sokweena.

"Yes. We've come this far; it's worth an extra look," added Kivyearzruk. Lopp didn't answer. He didn't want to keep the boys' hopes up.

One of the villagers chimed in. "Sometimes the ice is better to the northeast."

There was silence again as the boy herders looked at Lopp. With the opinion of the local inhabitant thrown in, he had no choice. After another pause, Lopp simply nodded yes. After this long a journey and such hard work, he owed it to the boys to investigate every avenue rather than take the long way around.

Two of the boys went with the villager to examine the Sound to the northeast. In the meantime, the rest unpacked the camp sleds and began preparing dinner. Lopp tended the fire and talked to them about the day's drive.

About three hours later the boys returned from their reconnoiter. The others, tending to various chores, moved toward the fire to hear the news.

"We think we can make it," said Sokweena.

"Make it? How?" asked Lopp in disbelief. He knew from his own inspection that there was no way to weave deer through the continuous crushes.

"The crushes are still bad to the northeast, but not totally impassible; we think we can pick our way through."

"I don't see how," continued Lopp. "The sleds will break apart, and the deer will be impossible to drive." Lopp had the most experience and could best estimate how well the deer could be driven over various landscapes. He'd apprenticed as a herder at the government reindeer station upon their first introduction to Alaska and had subsequently trained the boys.

"We think we can do it," said Kivyearzruk, but Lopp raised his hand to interrupt.

"Boys, I know you're anxious to avoid going around the Sound, but we've come too far to risk the herd now."

"I think they can handle the herd," said Charlie, trying to help the boys. He'd been personally astonished at the handling abilities of the boys, and he, too, had the experience to judge herding.

Lopp stood back for a moment and tried to be introspective. He had been their teacher since they were kids. Like a parent, it was difficult for him to see that they'd grown into adulthood.

The standoff continued for a moment. Finally Lopp broke the silence. "All right, you've all come a long way and deserve a say. What do you think?" he asked.

"Let's go," said Keuk and Ituk.

"Yes, we can do it. Two weeks is too long for the whalers," added Ootenna. Each of the boys likewise advocated going across the Sound.

Lopp smiled. While he was concerned with the decision, he was proud of his boys and their unanimous vote. He knew that if any herders in the world could do it, these boys could. They'd already driven the deer in record time through terrain never tried before.

"All right then, but we can't turn back. We have to make it no matter what. The deer won't survive too long on the ice," cautioned Lopp.

The boys shook hands in celebration. To help them in their efforts, Lopp hired two dog teams with the intention of going ahead to find a route through the ice crushes. They planned to load the dogsleds with moss to sustain the sled deer during the days they expected to be on the ice. The herd deer, which only had themselves to move, would have to go with no food until the other side. For the rest of the day, the boys set out to gather moss.

They rose on the morning of February 15th to a strong wind out of the north with a surface temperature of −34 degrees. It was colder than some of the boys could ever remember. They set out across the Sound with fourteen deer sleds, while the two hired dog sleds went ahead. They went due east to pick a way through the rough ice with Tradlook, an old man from the village, acting as a guide. The going was slow. Picking through the ice crushes turned into a zigzag tour that went in so many directions that by the end of the day they had no idea how far they'd traveled. It was late at night when they finally stopped.

Lopp walked up to the old man, who was now sitting and out of breath from the hard day's travel. "Are we far from the north side?"

"Not far, I think." As he said this he gazed at the mountains. The mountains were on the other side of the Sound, but mountains can be deceiving. "Tomorrow, maybe."

Lopp looked over at the boys who now were walking up for instructions. "Let the deer roam. Maybe they'll keep going to the other side to find moss in their hunger." It was a natural ability of the animals to search for food. If moss was near, they could find it.

They made camp, ate, and fed moss to the sled deer and then tied them to the ice hummocks, or crushes. Sleep came easily, for they were exhausted.

At 3:00 A.M., Lopp was roused from his sleep.

"The deer are gone!" said Charlie, shaking Lopp's shoulders.

"What do you mean? We tied them up."

"No, not the sled deer, the deer herd."

Lopp quickly rose and went with Charlie to look at the deer tracks. They went north a short ways. Since the deer seemed to be following their instinct to find moss, the men's stress was somewhat relieved. They roused the boys from their sleep and pulled food from the grub box for a quick breakfast. Since the deer were going north, they could take their time before beginning another long day. When they finished breakfast, the boys followed the tracks while Lopp and Charlie broke camp.

Ituk came running back. Lopp looked up, concerned, as he saw the young Eskimo rapidly coming his way.

"What is it?" called Lopp.

"The deer; they went south!"

"How can that be?" asked Lopp. He himself had seen the tracks that went north.

"They started north, but within 200 yards they turned south again. They're going in the direction we came!"

Lopp stood stunned for a moment. "Well, considering how long it took us to weave our way here, they couldn't have gone far. Take Sokweena, Ootenna, and Kivyearzruk south to collect them. We'll continue picking our way through the hummocks. We'll go slow and you should be able to overtake us in a couple of hours."

Ituk nodded in agreement and went quickly on his way. The boys got their sleds together and went after the deer.

Lopp, Charlie, and the rest continued slowly on their way, weaving a path through the mountains of ice crushes. After six hours, Lopp stopped once again. Three of the sled deer—Tutpan, Healy, and Moses—unable to pull their sleds another step, had collapsed on the ice. Unlike the nameless herd deer, the sled deer were individuals well known to Lopp and the boys, who had personally trained them. Trainers and sled deer had developed a master/pet relationship.

Lopp knew there was nothing he could do. He knelt in front of Moses, his personal deer, and cupped the creature's muzzle in his hands.

"I'm sorry, my old friend," he muttered through his tears. "You've hauled and hauled without complaint, and now it's come to this. We can't even take you along; to save ourselves and the whalers, we have to just leave you here. It isn't fair, it isn't right, but it's all we can do." A single sob escaped him. He blinked and looked away from the deer quietly expiring on the ice. There was still no sign of the boys and the herd. Ahead there was nothing but ice.

Charlie had kept a respectful distance, but now he approached Lopp. "Where can they be?" Charlie said, referring to the boys.

"I don't know; the deer must have gone farther than we thought."

"The boys don't have any food."

"Well, since we have to leave behind the deer," said Lopp, "let's also leave the sled with some hardtack. They'll pick it up on the way back while following our tracks."

He and Charlie unhooked Moses and left the sled beside his body. Removing the weight from some of the other sleds to relieve the exhausted beasts, they pushed off again. As the hours passed, both men periodically looked back until the night sky enveloped them. Despite two days' travel, they were still in the middle of the Sound without the deer herd. Thirteen sled deer were near collapse. It seemed that their gamble was turning into a nightmare.

Now convinced that the boys were in some kind of trouble, they made camp and waited. Over a fire made from driftwood they'd previously collected—wood was a rare resource they grabbed when they could—they cooked a meal large enough for themselves and those who were coming behind them. Lopp had great confidence in his boys. He knew that they'd use good judgment and work themselves out of any difficulty.

As Lopp and Charlie ate in silence, they heard something. It was faint. It might be hooves, or just wishful thinking. Unable to resist checking, they sprang to their feet and clambered up an ice crush. Charlie reached the top first.

"The herd!" said Charlie. "It's the herd!"

Just then a deer sled rounded a crush. Sokweena was driving.

"Woo-hoo!" yelled Lopp, pumping his fist in the air. Then the other four appeared.

"What happened?" asked Charlie.

"The deer went all the way back to Espenburg. We caught them only a couple hundred yards from the beach. God knows what would have happened if they'd made it to land," explained Sokweena.

The thought was frightening. They could have scattered along the landscape looking for food and fallen prey to hunters, or just scattered for miles.

"Praise God you found them in time," said Charlie.

The men continued to rejoice for a few more minutes before Lopp pulled them down to earth. "OK, we can't stay here any longer. I know you're tired, but we have to keep moving. The deer haven't eaten for two days; they'll take off again in the night. We have to press on. If we linger, we could lose everything."

The boys were silent. Though they were exhausted, they knew he was right; they'd already lost three deer. After gobbling down some dinner, they packed up the campsite and moved on.

Now the sled deer could barely keep up with the herd. Burdened and famished, strained to the limit by the daunting ice crushes, they weren't far from the fate of Moses.

Lopp and the boys regretted having to push the deer beyond their limits, but if they didn't, everyone might die on the ice. To make matters worse, the rough ice took its toll on the sleds, which at intervals would break down and need to be jury-rigged. Finally the party found a stretch of new level ice that went on for several miles. This was both a Godsend and a curse. On the positive side, it was fast and easy. On the negative side, it was newer ice and thus more dangerous.

On this flat trail, the drivers occasionally leaned forward on their sleds and fell asleep from exhaustion. The bitter cold, now -35 degrees, woke them as their limbs became numb. They then had to beat these body parts to keep from losing them to frostbite.

At one point, Lopp saw a fawn struggling on the ice to get to its feet and catch up to its mother. As with Moses, he had no choice but to leave it to its fate. He was bitter as he thought of the animals being tortured in

175

their drive to be sacrificed to save the whalers stranded in their pursuit of wealth. Distracted by these angry thoughts, he nearly slid into the sled in front of him. He scolded himself for his inattention.

As the sleds began again, he tried to think more positively. He gazed up at the auroral displays, which seemed like a multicolored, frozen heavenly flame. A student had once told him to do the "whispering whistle" when the aurora danced, for it would call closer the spirits of the departed. Invoking that Inupiat belief, he whistled softly now, wondering if Moses would hear.

For hours he endured, until, semiconscious from exhaustion, he saw the deer as phantoms gliding on top of the ice and periodically disappearing in the abyss of an ice ridge. The trains pushed on through the night.

At last, at daybreak they saw in the distance a long black streak in the ice. As they approached, the streak turned out to be a gash separating the new drift ice from the grounded ice. That meant that land wasn't far away. But it also meant that the connecting thinner ice was unstable.

The boys stopped the deer in front of the large cleft in the ice. They had to determine which way to go.

As Lopp looked on, he suddenly heard a crash. Before his eyes, the herd started to fall into the water as the ice collapsed beneath them. Because they were bunched up in such a small area, the new ice couldn't support their combined weight.

He heard a frantic "No!" shrill as the scream of a madman. As he ran toward the drowning deer, he realized it was his own voice. To his crazed mind, time slowed; he watched one deer after another fall as if in slow motion.

The boys, themselves only feet away from the frigid waters, tried to drive the surviving deer away from the collapsing ice. Just seconds after the initial crack, over 150 deer were in the water; the others were frantically moving away. The entire drive was about to fail.

Lopp could hear himself yelling something unintelligible again. As he ran he watched the deer struggle, desperately trying to keep their heads above water.

Finally he stopped. He realized there was nothing he could do for them. Falling to his knees, he called, "Oh, God, please help us. We've come so far!"

Then something strange began to happen. The first deer that had fallen into the water reached the other side . . . and crawled out. It shook the water from its fur as a dog would shake after a bath. A second deer, then a third did the same. As the boys watched in awe, the remaining deer followed, climbing onto the firm ice on the other side. The deer acted as if nothing unusual had happened; they almost seemed to have enjoyed the swim.

The herders were speechless.

"What just happened?" said Lopp, looking at Charlie.

Charlie gaped. Finally he squeaked, "That's the strangest thing I've ever seen. I didn't even know deer could swim in the ocean."

"Neither did I!"

"They don't even seem to be cold," said Lopp in disbelief. "Is that a miracle or just my ignorance of deer?" Lopp and Charlie both laughed at the joke.

"Well, let's get the rest of the deer across before something else happens!" said Charlie, striding toward the sled.

They quickly gathered the other deer and followed the crack until it was sufficiently narrow to cross. They couldn't help but think that either they had just seen a miracle, or else the deer somehow knew a better plan all along.

Despite wanting to recover from the emergency, they quickly moved on. They drove the herd the now-short way to the shore. Villagers who had seen them coming, rushed out to meet them.

Here the men and reindeer were the objects of great curiosity. Never had the villagers seen a domesticated deer, let alone so many. The villagers directed the boys to moss for the deer, who happily grazed for the first time in days, while Lopp marveled at their experience. Just as they had thought the mission was lost, they were delivered to the proverbial Promised Land.

"What a great sight," said Sokweena.

"Yes, I don't believe we made it," said Charlie.

"We have to give thanks for this," said Lopp, looking at his two friends. They quickly joined hands.

"Sokweena, do you want to do the honors?" asked Lopp.

Sokweena smiled brightly in response. It was a sign of recognition to the young pastor from the older missionaries. He bowed his head and prayed. "Dear Heavenly Father. We love You and we praise You. Just as You parted the Red Sea for Moses, You carried us across the Sound to the Promised Land. We pray Your blessings on these people and the whalers we're attempting to reach. May all come to know Your love and glory. In Jesus' name we pray. Amen."

They would need this help with the mountains yet to come.

Chapter Twenty-Six

Jarvis and the doctor continued up the coast to the Point Hope Whaling Station. There they met Nelson, the station manager, and Ned Arey. Ned had traveled over 500 miles from Point Barrow, in the process damaging his feet and hands with frostbite. From Ned, Jarvis learned that scurvy and dropsy were affecting the men. One death had occurred from dropsy and two from freezing.

The next morning Jarvis received a letter from an Eskimo messenger, sent by Lopp, saying that he wasn't far behind. Obviously, Lopp had not received the Jarvis letter warning that the Sound was too unstable for the deer to cross. Instead, in his innocence he crossed the Sound and saved almost a week from his time.

After some quick planning, Nelson and a friend, acting as guides, went with Jarvis to gather more supplies and start down the coast to meet Lopp. The doctor remained behind at Point Hope, the meeting point for Bertholf. According to Lopp's letter, they were to make for the Kivalena River, which they would follow until they intercepted Charlie, Lopp, and the herd at a village hut that would be relatively easily spotted from the frozen river.

Compared to their recent experience traveling the sixty miles across the Sound, the going was relatively easy to the coast. They stayed the night at Cape Seppings and the next day made the remainder of the distance to the Kivalena River. But the hostility of the Arctic once again caught up with the group. Upon their arrival at the Kivalena River, a blizzard hit.

Jarvis had difficulty seeing ahead of the sled. The bitter wind pounded the sleds; ice particles pelted his eyes.

The three sleds stopped at the base of a large bank. "We have to find shelter!" yelled Nelson only inches from Jarvis's face.

"Where?" returned Jarvis, yelling to be heard above the howling wind.

"I think there's an old hunting hut near here!"

"Make for it as fast as you can; it seems to be our only hope!"

Nelson returned to his sled and mushed the dogs. They traveled along the bank for another hour until Nelson suddenly stopped. "There!" he pointed.

Jarvis could barely make out the outline of a hut in the pounding wind and snow. They quickly secured the dogs and sleds. As before, they crawled through a small opening into a hut. This time there were no Eskimos to greet them, and unfortunately the hut was also open to the elements. They quickly patched holes as best they could, to shield against the wind and snow, then they prepared some beans, crackers, and tea over a small driftwood fire.

Jarvis munched on his ration of crackers. "Nelson, how long do you think the storm will last?" He knew that Nelson had little or no more experience than himself, but he was making conversation with the hope that his companion might have some special knowledge.

As Nelson chewed he looked up and replied, "Don't rightly know. Maybe the night, maybe another day."

Jarvis and the doctor were more than accustomed to having to wait out a storm. From their journey's beginning they had learned why experience and patience are the chief virtues of Arctic survivors.

The group was silent for a moment, then Nelson peered curiously at Jarvis. "What made you do this, anyway?"

Jarvis looked slightly stunned. He'd not been asked that before. He hesitated.

"I mean, you got a wife and all. What made you risk it all to come out here?" continued Nelson.

Again Jarvis hesitated. How could he explain the myriad conflicting emotions that go into a decision like this? On one hand, he was a Revenue

Cutter Service Officer. Search and rescue was the primary mission of his service. He was physically fit, with Arctic experience from his time on the *Bear*. It was his life's work. On the other hand, he had a young wife and plans for a family. As with many in the Cutter Service, the sense of duty and lengthy time at sea would always compete with family. This conflict often led to depression and anguish.

Finally Jarvis simply said, "There was no one else." It seemed easier than exploring the inner conflict between duty and family.

Nelson nodded his head in acknowledgment. He knew it was a much deeper question, but left Jarvis with his privacy. They finished their meal and tucked into their deerskin sleeping bags for the night. Outside, the dogs covered themselves with snow, instinctively seeking insulation against the freezing wind.

Next day brought no reduction in the severity of the blizzard. They were forced to weather the storm in the hut for another day. Finally, on the succeeding morning they were able to travel once again.

After a short distance they entered a large valley that cut a path through the mountains. This was both a good and bad omen. Because of its sheer size and virgin white snow, it was an awe-inspiring sight. But on the darker side, it served as a cruel reminder of the mountain range yet to come. That range would have to be conquered by Lopp, Charlie, and the boys—not an insurmountable task alone, but almost impossible while driving a herd of deer.

They continued through the valley and then began winding their way along the Kivalena River. Finally they spotted the hut where they were to meet the herd. It was abandoned and in too much disrepair to inhabit, so they set up their tents around a small driftwood fire.

As they warmed themselves, they noticed an Eskimo boy running toward them along the river. The men watched with interest; it was obvious that he saw them and that they were the object of his race.

"That's strange," said Jarvis.

"I wonder what he wants," added Nelson.

The youth drew closer. The three stood, partly out of courtesy to their visitor, partly because they wanted to learn the reason for his haste.

"Hello," Jarvis greeted the boy, who now stood bent over, chest heaving, trying to catch his breath. Finally he gasped out a single word.

"Deer!" he wheezed.

Jarvis smiled and looked at the other men.

"Deer. Are there a lot of them?" he asked the lad in a gently jovial voice.

"Yes, many, many, many deer. More than I've ever seen!" It was true; domesticated deer were located much farther south. Nobody this far north would ever have seen anything more than a rare wild deer. It must have been the sight of a lifetime for the youngster—or anybody else, for that matter.

"Can you guide the man leading the deer to us for two bits?" asked Jarvis, knowing the probable answer.

"Yes!" exclaimed the young man. With that affirmative, the boy and Nelson's friend left to guide Lopp to Jarvis. Since Jarvis's team had dog sleds, it wasn't safe to bring the deer the whole way to the shack. They would have to get Lopp himself and bring him in.

Chapter Twenty-Seven

Jim . . .   Scurvy Gets Worse

Jim looked down at the tooth staring back at him from the confines of his lap. He had been chewing Eskimo gum when the tooth came out by its roots. This was the type of gum you'd find only in the Arctic, boiled down from seal oil until it was hard and black. Jim wasn't driven to take the gum as a tasty treat, but more as basic food, for like everyone else, he was feeling the effects of malnutrition. In fact, the tooth in his lap, like all his teeth, had been loose to begin with. Spongy, bleeding gums were just one of the symptoms of scurvy suffered by all the men. Lacking proper vitamins and minerals, at this point their diet was anything but adequate.

"How you faring?" asked Joiner, spotting Jim's languishing tooth. Joiner had made his way from the other corner of the Old Kelley House. Just as on the ship, the foremast hands occupied one area while the cook, carpenter, sailmaker, and the other "half sailors" occupied the rest.

"I'm OK, I guess," said Jim, trying to sound strong.

Just then Jake stirred a couple of berths away.

"So he finally went to sleep?" chuckled Joiner.

Jake, the youngest, full of energy, seemed always to be nearby observing some activity. For him to nap was unusual. The effects of malnutrition were showing even on him.

"Yes," replied Jim. "He was out yesterday watching some Eskimos prepare to hunt. He asked them a million questions. Lucky for them they didn't speak English; otherwise they'd have had to answer them all."

They both chuckled quietly. It served as a distraction from what they were about to do.

"Should we wake him?" asked Joiner.

Jim simply shook his head.

Joiner didn't ask any questions. He knew that Jake was barely more than a boy. It was bad enough that he'd probably die before the age of thirteen in the Arctic. He didn't have to preside over the death of another.

All the men were fading from slow starvation. The two worst off, the eldest members of the crew, died first, with long, hard lives behind them.

Upon hearing that two of the whalers were gone, the Eskimos offered to take care of the funeral. The survivors quickly agreed.

The preceding day, the whalers had watched from a short distance as the Eskimos gathered the bodies and placed them in small plank coffins, then covered the boxes with bark and raised the deceased on four posts. The Eskimos had painstakingly adorned each box with a scene of ships hunting their whale prey. Such funeral art honored the deceased by depicting their hunting skills. The whalers themselves, most being Christian, had little familiarity with Eskimo customs, but most appreciated the gesture all the same.

Now that preparations were complete, the Eskimos gathered what little food they had for an earnest, albeit skimpy "feast." They asked that the closest friend of each man place near the body a staff bearing a small carving of a spear. Mr. Brower explained that the staff was intended to summon to the grave the spirits of those deceased. A ritual lamp was lit for each of the dead, to honor them in preparation for the feast, which insured that the men's souls didn't suffer in the land of the dead.

At the prearranged time, Jim and the men stepped out of the Old Kelley House, braced against the frigid wind. Jim's breath instantly came in short spurts. The survivors filed out to the funeral platforms a few hundred yards from the building. As Jim scanned the horizon, all he could see was endless white. It reminded him of the scenery as they left the *Orca* months before. He remembered how he had found it so amazingly beautiful. Now he had no such feelings.

Solemnly, silently, over eighty whalers approached the graves to stand behind the four or five Eskimo families already present. Ahead of them, Brower stood next to an Inupiat elder who seemed to be in charge. Seeing that all were assembled, Brower nodded to the older man, who said a few words in Inupiaq with his hands raised to the sky, then chanted to another Inupiat's drumbeat.

As Jim watched the Eskimos, he was struck by their demeanor. The whalers just observed the ceremony as if it were the afternoon's entertainment, but the Inupiat frequently looked to the sky and closed their eyes, seeming to feel the presence of the departed spirits.

The drum abruptly stopped, bringing Jim back to reality. As the ceremony ended, the Eskimos remained standing in silence as if waiting to see if the koblonas had something to contribute.

Joiner felt compelled to take action. "Mr. Brower," he said in a hushed voice.

"Yes."

"Would you say a few words for us?"

Nearly from the outset, the whalers had looked to Mr. Brower as their leader, for he settled disputes and worked desperately to obtain food for the men. Though he had no official rank, he was now for all practical purposes the captain for all crews. Since it would have been customary for the captain to speak at a seagoing funeral, Brower was the logical choice for this occasion.

Brower cleared his throat and took a few steps forward. He paused for a few seconds to collect his thoughts. Then, hands folded, he began.

"These were two good men. They worked hard and tried to survive as best they could. When the time came to see God, they went without hesitation. We know that God will accept them in the pearly gates." He hesitated again, realizing that these were empty words that provided little comfort for the men.

He began again. "In heaven there are only warm tropical breezes and plenty of food all the time." The men looked up. Now he was making it real to each in his present situation.

"There is no loneliness or fear. There are no night watches or bad gales." The men began to smile; they now felt that this was truly the ceremony their friends would understand.

"The mail satchel is always full and every letter finds its mark. We salute our friends and commit their souls to God through Jesus Christ, who can truly understand their struggles before death. Amen."

As he finished, each whaler looked at Brower with warm eyes, the way a child looks at a parent when he's received the Christmas gift he's been hoping for—a look of pure respect and gratitude.

Now the ceremony was complete. As they filed past the Eskimos on the way to their cabin, they each spoke a thank you with a smile. While the Inupiat Eskimos didn't understand the words, the smile was a natural translator.

The exhausted men filed back into the Old Kelley House and crawled back into their berths without discussion. Just standing to watch the ceremony had been a great feat of physical exertion. Their bodies, struggling to remain warm in the Arctic cold, burned what calories were available—and there weren't many. The despairing men could only assume that more deaths would follow as they continued their slow starvation at the top of the world. Each thought, *I should have gone with Ned.*

Chapter Twenty-Eight

Lopp...   First Casualty

It had now been almost a week's hard travel for Lopp and the boys. Despite strong winds from the north gusting against their faces with −40 degree temperatures, they'd managed to go through Cape Blossom en route to the mountains. Here they met with Lieutenant Bertholf, who'd managed to acquire seven good sled deer, already trained. Since Lopp had lost six sled deer to exhaustion and the rest were in similarly bad shape, this acquisition was critical. With these deer they continued to their next big obstacle, the mountains, and said goodbye to Bertholf, who went on to Point Hope to acquire badly needed supplies and catch up with Jarvis along the coast. After getting more supplies and additional instructions, he planned to meet Lopp at the mouth of the Kivalena River for the last legs of the journey.

On the 20th of February, exhausted, Lopp, Charlie and the boys were positioned to begin what no one had ever tried, summer or winter: a reindeer drive over the mountains. Ideally, they should have been in good physical shape to make the attempt, but they weren't.

Lopp and Charlie broke to make camp while some of the boys drove the herd back for moss. It had become a routine: Drive the deer as long as you can, taking note of moss along the way; if by nightfall you don't find additional moss, you must backtrack with the deer to the last-known food source, where they'll graze throughout the night.

Upon the boys' returning, they all sat around the fire, mentally and physically spent. Lopp scanned the faces of the tired boys, who gazed into the fire as if in a trance. Suddenly, he realized that one was missing.

"Where's Ituk?"

The other boys quickly looked at each other, half expecting Ituk to answer from the group.

"I don't know," said Sokweena.

"He was with the deer a while ago," said Keok.

"Do you think he got lost coming back to camp?" asked Lopp.

"He could have. He was cutting across the ice," said Keok. It was easy enough to lose your way in the dark on ice with no landmarks. It was useless to search; they would risk having more men wandering and lost.

"Shoot a rifle," said Charlie.

With that Keok got to his feet, grabbed a gun, checked to be sure the action wasn't frozen, and fired. The shot reverberated into the night; hopefully, it would help Ituk find his way to camp.

"There's nothing we can do in the dark," said Lopp in anguish. "We'll just have to wait until first light."

Throughout the night, they rose and fired a shot. Each time there was nobody in sight. Finally as day broke they saw Ituk limping into camp. They ran to meet him and help him the rest of the way to camp, where they seated him in front of the fire. Shaking badly, he had obviously suffered damage in the frigid night.

"What happened, Ituk?"

"I got lost. I finally got too tired and slept on the ice."

They pulled off his boots and saw the frostbite. It was clear that he would lose at least one toe, maybe a few: they would turn black and eventually fall off as dead appendages.

The men worked quickly to warm Ituk as best they could. Such damage was severe enough to send him home; he couldn't travel any farther. Lopp shook his head sadly. The boys had come to be like his own children, and he'd convinced them to make this trip. He was responsible.

Lopp surveyed the situation. He'd acquired two more men in the last village, Sekupseezruk and Ookweeruk, who had agreed to go along as guides. They weren't experienced herders, but they would help to guide the group through the endless maze of frozen streams through the mountains. He could send two of the boys back with Ituk. While he logically shouldn't lose two experienced herders, he would not entrust Ituk's welfare with anyone else. Sokweena's wife was expecting a child, and Keok was a close friend of Ituk. He'd send them.

Lopp walked back to Ituk. "How are you, old friend?"

Ituk looked up. He smiled gamely despite his extreme discomfort. "I'll be ready to push on, just give me a few minutes."

Lopp gazed at him with great affection. His boys were remarkable. They didn't deserve the prejudice they'd received from bureaucrats convinced that Eskimos didn't have the character to manage deer.

"Sorry, my friend. You've done well and we couldn't have made it this far without you. But now you're going home."

"No, I can make it, see!"

Two of the boys stopped him from getting up by placing their hands on his shoulders.

"No, you have to prepare the next *Eskimo Bulletin* for me," said Lopp. As a missionary dealing with both the whites and the native Eskimos, Lopp had realized early the prejudice the Eskimos were up against. He knew that they needed a common voice through which the world could understand their accomplishments. He had therefore created the first newspaper for the natives, by the natives. Even though the *Eskimo Bulletin* was published just once a year, it was instantly a hit and broadly requested.

"I'll do it," said Ituk with tears in his eyes. Lopp couldn't speak any more. He couldn't believe that that timid young boy sent to school by his parents had turned into such a fine man. He wished that the detractors who had fought to bring Siberians to Alaska instead of letting the Eskimos manage the herds could see the sacrifices these Eskimo herders were making to save the white whalers.

"Don't worry," said Sokweena. "We'll have you back chasing girls before you know it."

"Yeah, you should have had this happen sooner, Ituk," laughed Keok. "You could have saved us a lot of cold nights." The group joined in to cheer up and chide their young friend. The three would depart for Cape Prince of Wales the same day, outfitted with enough supplies to last the trip. It was a tearful goodbye.

Finally, Lopp and the rest of the boys continued on their way. For almost five days they battled frigid winds pounding from the north. At night, the tent would strain, flapping under the beating. They had to dig a hole with snow walls to act as a barricade just to erect the tent and hold it in place long enough to pound the stakes. By the morning of the 23rd, a month after Lopp and the boys began, they arose, now barely able to walk from their grueling travels, and dug out the sleds. The day before, they'd caught up to Bertholf, who was also fighting against the wind to get more resources for the herd, per earlier instructions. Bertholf had become adept at improvising his route.

Lopp stood next to the lieutenant, both men slightly bent against the gale. "I'm off once again," said Bertholf. "Maybe this time I'll shake you guys."

"I don't know, sailor. Maybe at sea, but not here," said Lopp with a laugh. As they spoke, Sekupseezruk and Ookweeruk approached from behind. The two guides acquired at the most recent village didn't have the prized furred reindeer clothing that the boys had been given by the villagers back in Cape Prince of Wales. As a result, they were suffering from the frigid cold in the open country. They looked more haggard than the rest.

"Mr. Lopp," said Ookweeruk.

Bertholf whispered, "Those poor fellows; this can't be good."

Lopp simply nodded.

"We're going back."

Lopp said nothing at first. He had known this was probably coming, but didn't want to lose his guides through the mountains. "Are you sure?"

"Yes. You gain little with us. We taken you as far as we know." He was telling the truth. Few living men had ever made the journey entirely through the mountains; these two certainly hadn't. "And besides, we not prepared." This was true, too. Their route could take them farther north where few Eskimos were well prepared for survival in the unrelieved cold.

Lopp was silent again. He knew these two should return to their village, but the mission was in desperate straits. They would have a bad time of it finding their way through the mountains. He'd already sent three of his own boys home. Finally he said, "All right, then. God bless you for your help." With that the men turned and gathered their sleds.

"Should I stay?" asked Bertholf.

Lopp thought for a moment. Bertholf had acquired some skills with deer. Finally he said, "No, you go on and get us supplies. You've developed an uncanny ability to get us what we need from the most unusual places."

"Are you saying that I should have been a thief, preacher?" laughed Bertholf.

"We're all called to serve in our own way," rejoined Lopp with a smile.

"All right, missionary, that's enough. I'll leave while I've still got some dignity."

"God will protect your path, my friend."

"He'd better."

With that Bertholf was off once again. Lopp and the remaining group set off themselves.

For another three days they continued along the frozen river through the mountains. It was a difficult uphill battle. And then, as they peered up the steep side of the timbered mountains, out of nowhere came an Eskimo boy.

"Mr. Lopp! Mr. Lopp!" he yelled.

Lopp recognized the boy as yet another of his former students. "Mitlik?"

"Yes!" he shrieked.

"How are you?" said the surprised teacher, giving the lad a hug.

"I'm good. I saw your deer coming through the valley and told the white men up the river. They paid me to bring you to them."

"White men, what white men?"

"Three men. One Eskimo, two white. One is from far away with the government. His name is Jarvis."

"Jarvis!" cried Lopp. "Yes, take me to Jarvis."

"We can walk, it's not far."

"OK."

Knowing that Jarvis would have dogs, they decided to leave the deer where they were and make camp. Here there was sporadic moss and the deer needed to rest and graze. Lopp's heart beat faster at the prospect of the upcoming reunion. It had been many weeks since Lopp had seen Jarvis, and he had no clue that he would ever find him. He'd just hoped that he was ahead preparing the way and not lost or injured.

Chapter Twenty-Nine

Jarvis...   The Reunion

In the distance, Jarvis could see the small boy walking with Lopp. They seemed to be carrying on a conversation as if they knew each other. After a few more minutes, they finally climbed up the banks of the river to the camp. Jarvis saw the signs of frostbite on Lopp's cheeks and nose.

"Well, hello, my friend!" said Lopp. Despite the damage to his face, Lopp still carried a broad smile. The dark eyes that added to his well-favored features seemed to brighten at seeing his friends.

"Hello, Mr. Lopp," said Jarvis, with an equally large smile. It was like a homecoming for old friends who had been through the same trials and tribulations. They obviously had a lot to talk about.

Jarvis stared at Lopp's face. "You see my reminders of the Sound," said Lopp.

"Yes," said Jarvis, who took this as an invitation to step forward for a closer examination. "You've gotten some damage from frostbite."

"Yes, the journey across the Sound was miserable."

"I'm sorry about that. You didn't get our letter?" asked Jarvis, distressed. The main reason for his rushing to the Sound had been to save Lopp from that kind of hardship and danger if the conditions were bad.

"You sent a letter?" asked Lopp. "I knew it. I couldn't believe you'd have us try to make that crossing with the ice in that condition."

"You're right. We almost didn't make it ourselves and had a hard time getting a guide to take us," answered Jarvis.

"Well, we made it with most of the deer, and cut two weeks from our time. That's what matters," said Lopp.

"Agreed," said Jarvis, still wearing a frown of consternation. He'd done his best to avoid having Lopp make that crossing.

"We assumed you had friends in high places," added the doctor, referring to their survival and to Lopp's vocation as a Christian missionary.

Lopp chuckled at the gesture. Then he quieted and replied sincerely, "My savior in death is also my savior in life."

With that, the men quietly sat down for dinner and tea. It had been a long, hard trip for all and they were glad to make it this far. They exchanged pleasantries; Nelson and his guide also told stories about their journey to date. Finally they had to turn to the difficult decisions at hand.

"The hardest part of the journey still lies ahead—over 400 miles of it," said Lopp.

"Yes," agreed Jarvis and Nelson.

"We need to examine all the routes carefully. There are several," said Lopp. With that the group discussed the pros and cons of each.

"Which do you recommend?" Jarvis finally asked. While he knew which route he liked, he wanted Lopp to choose. He owed him that, given the sacrifice he'd made of his herd and his family.

"Well, I think that going up the Kivalina River and then crossing the mountains to the north at the headwaters of the Pitmegea River would be the shortest route away from the shore," said Lopp. "But at the same time, it keeps us as close to the coast as possible."

Jarvis looked at the other members of the party, both white and Eskimo alike. Each nodded in agreement. "All right then, I'll go back to Point Hope with Nelson, collect the doctor and Bertholf with their supplies, and go up the coast past Lisburne. If we time it right, I should get there to meet you and the boys at the Pitmegea River," said Jarvis.

"That should be just about right," agreed Lopp.

But the longer they spoke, the more the weather worsened. The tent, battered by the wind, strained against its pegs. Heavy snow had been falling continually, creating almost zero visibility. Lopp watched the deteriorating conditions, unable to do anything to help the exposed deer herd a few miles away.

Ultimately, the men had to wait helplessly for two days. During that strained time, some of the conversations turned uncomfortable as Lopp and Nelson disagreed over the Eskimos. Nelson saw them as worthless deadbeats; Lopp obviously did not.

Finally, late in the morning of the third day, the sun broke through the clouds, the snow stopped, and the wind came down to a manageable level. It was now March 2nd, three months since they began. March brought sunrises before 9:00 A.M.; the long, dark days were finally over.

Jarvis pushed his way through a drift blocking the front of his tent. The air was crisp, but not unbearable. Remnants of the blizzard were everywhere. The sleds lay covered by drifts a foot deep. Nelson helped Jarvis dig out their precious cargo while the dogs, that for warmth had let snow cover them, now shook the white blankets from their bodies—a little was insulation, too much could suffocate, so the dogs would dig out periodically, to repeat the process as the snow continued.

As Jarvis and Nelson began to hook their dogs up to the sleds, they realized that two were missing. Jarvis instantly feared the worst.

"We're two dogs short!" he yelled at Lopp.

"Oh no! Where are they?" demanded Nelson in a panic.

"I don't see them!"

"We'd better hurry!" yelled Lopp. While they had kept the deer downwind so the dogs could not raise their scent, changing wind conditions must have alerted the two loose dogs to their presence, even at a distance. Two ravenous dogs could wreak havoc among a domesticated herd.

The men raced toward the deer herd. When they arrived, the boys were already frantically chasing the dogs, with no success. They had their rifles out but were unable to shoot because of the density of the deer herd. They couldn't risk killing the deer and scattering the herd more than the dogs were already doing.

"There they go!" yelled Jarvis. The deer, in a panic to keep away from the lunging dogs, began to stampede. Lopp yelled instructions on the move.

"Kivyearzruk, Tautuk, Ituk, and Ootennago, after the dogs! Everyone else stay with the deer!"

The deer ran frantically in huge circles as the dogs lunged at their necks and hooves. Already the marauders had managed to draw blood from two deer.

As they came near again, everyone yelled and tried to spot the dogs among the herd. Just as they had them spotted, the herd would turn and the boys had to race out of the way or be trampled. The two dogs continued on their rampage. In a mountainous region, the dogs could easily drive the unsuspecting deer off a cliff or into a ravine. Then all the hard work and over a thousand miles of travel would be for naught—and all because of two uncontrolled canines. At last the deer ran straight ahead for five miles, only to become trapped by the looming mountain. It would mean death to the cornered deer. But luck intervened.

As the dogs chased after the deer careening straight toward the mountain, they became bogged down in drifts from the previous two days' blizzard. Finally, both dogs collapsed from exhaustion in the deep snow. Thus, in a wonderful irony, the same snow that had trapped the group for two days, saved them from the predators.

Jarvis looked on as the boys guided the deer back to camp.

"Good job!" said Jarvis, patting the weary, breathless young men.

"Nice job," added Lopp.

"How do they look, Kivyearzruk?" asked Jarvis.

"They all survived well, except for two cows," returned Kivyearzruk with a distraught look.

As soon as a clear shot was to be had, the two rogue dogs met an outlaw's fate.

The snow was covered with blood from the two pregnant deer that had fallen victims to the dog attack. The dogs, as predators do, had gone after the weakest animals—that usually included the very old, very young, and pregnant. Two pregnant cows, unable to keep up with the herd and fight off the attackers, now lay collapsed in the snow, their lungs heaving. Intermittently they struggled to rise, but couldn't lift their frames off the ground.

"Can we save them?" asked Jarvis. He already knew the answer, but couldn't help asking. It was difficult to see nature in action: the survival of the fittest.

196

Kivyearzruk looked at Lopp, not to get an answer, but just to share his pain with a man who would understand. Lopp turned to Jarvis, who agonized but said, "No. We'll have to leave them. We don't have time to dress them and can't carry the carcasses. It's a pity, losing two deer that are about to calve. It's like losing four deer a month from now."

After they stabilized the herd, Jarvis had to say goodbye once again to Lopp, Charlie, and the boys. This time the pain of the killings added to the pain of saying farewell to friends about to continue on a dangerous mission. Jarvis knew that all precautions had been taken to separate the dogs from the herd, but he still felt angry and hurt at the loss.

"See you at the Pitmegea River," said Lopp. "And don't stop for any stage shows." He could see the pain on his friend's face and wanted to lighten the mood.

"Well, since you didn't get an invitation, I won't go either," returned Jarvis with a smile. With that they parted company once again.

Jarvis, Nelson, and the guide returned to the coast, where they made for Point Hope. They had stopped for a rest and food break at a village known as Cape Seppings, when they saw a Caucasian man standing right in their path. It was very unusual to see a white man this far north in an area without a whaling station. As they came closer the man yelled.

"Jarvis!"

Jarvis was surprised for a moment, but was getting used to hearing his name yelled in the strangest places. The man removed his hood and Jarvis recognized Bertholf.

"My God, Bertholf, what are you doing here, of all places?" said Jarvis. Bertholf was supposed to be at or en route to Point Hope with supplies for the journey. He folded his arms and laughed at the situation.

"I was en route to Point Hope as planned when the blizzard hit. It was all I could do to get here. The villagers told me that you'd just passed going south and would probably return this way. I decided to wait for a day after the blizzard."

They both sat on a sled and talked about their travels. Jarvis briefed Bertholf about the dogs attacking the deer and his happiness at seeing

Lopp, Charlie, and the boys. So much of their lives and attitudes had changed since the journey began.

"I feel like I've aged about twenty years since we began," said Bertholf, the younger of the two.

"I know. Do you believe that we've traveled about twelve hundred miles?" said Jarvis. He looked at Bertholf and saw his slightly dejected look as he faced the horizon, contemplating the tougher 400-plus miles to come.

"You know there won't be any villages to help us after Point Hope," said Bertholf. After they dropped off Nelson at the Point Hope Whaling Station, they were truly going to be in a frozen wasteland. There would be no Eskimo villages at all.

"Well, at least we've acquired skills up to this point that'll help us," replied Jarvis.

Bertholf thought back to the experiences he'd had and the close calls he'd survived. Then breaking with his normal military discipline he asked, "David, do you think we'll make it?"

Jarvis was taken aback. Everyone, including himself, harbored fears born of the desperate risks they were taking, but nobody verbalized them. It was even more shocking because Jarvis had given Bertholf incredibly difficult assignments requiring him to travel without the rest of the team. Despite the hardship, he'd managed to acquire guides, supplies, and deer by virtue of his own determination and resourcefulness. Up to this point he had somehow seemed fearless compared to other men. Still, it was comforting to Jarvis to know that he wasn't alone in his anxieties.

After a few moments, Jarvis finally responded. "The Vikings that traveled the Arctic seas long before us used to say a man cannot control the time or place of his death, but he can control how he is to be remembered."

Both men fell silent again. Since they both knew where they were going and the deprivation they were to face, there were no words of comfort Jarvis could give. Instead he added, "But with this behind you, you'll be in charge of the Cutter Service one day." With that he pushed his young friend in an act of jovial playfulness.

Bertholf smiled and laughed at being chided. It was an unattainable dream for most men. Little could he have known that Jarvis's remark would prove prophetic in later years, as Bertholf would rise to be commandant of the entire United States Coast Guard.

After more days of hard travel, they finally arrived once again at Nelson's station on March 3rd, two and a half months into the overland expedition. They had now made it three-quarters of the way to the whalers.

As they pulled into Point Hope, Nelson's assistants were waiting. They didn't have the happy faces of welcoming friends. Nelson took one look and said, "What's happened?"

"Washok has died." Washok was a young villager known by Nelson.

"What happened?"

"He was murdered."

"Murdered?" responded Nelson. "How, why?"

"Whiskey dispute," said Nelson's assistant.

"Damn!" swore Nelson. "Do we know who?"

"Avulik and Shugunera, we think."

Nelson looked at Jarvis. As the ranking officer in the Revenue Cutter Service, Jarvis was responsible for the enforcement of territorial law. There were no other lawmen this far north.

Jarvis suddenly realized what Nelson was thinking. "I can't."

Nelson's assistant interjected, "We're confident we know they did it; we just have to get them."

"But after that we have to have a trial, with a jury of their peers. It could take days, maybe longer. We don't have that kind of time."

Suddenly Bertholf interjected, "I can do it."

Jarvis just looked at him. There was an uncomfortable silence as Jarvis started to think through the ramifications of Bertholf's staying behind, but Bertholf intercepted his train of thought by addressing Jarvis's possible concerns. "I've gotten deer and supplies. You have enough dogs and food to make for Point Barrow. Whether I go with you or follow in a few days, the outcome is the same. We have nothing to gain by my going with you straightaway."

They continued their discussion as Jarvis weighed the options.

"All right," Jarvis finally relented. "But come as soon as you possibly can."

"I'll make it fast," said Bertholf.

So they decided that Bertholf would stay and tend to Cutter Service business, investigating the murder, while the doctor and Jarvis would continue to Point Barrow with a guide. When Bertholf's investigation was concluded, he would follow after them but leave 500 pounds of flour, tea, bread, and other foodstuffs at the mouth of the Pitmegea River about halfway to Point Barrow. In the event that all the ships were crushed and Point Barrow could not accommodate all 300 men, they could attempt to transport the men by sled and on foot south to Point Hope. Since that journey would be almost 400 miles, they would need food to sustain them along the way.

It would be a difficult journey if it came to that, but at least the wind would be at their backs. Everyone agreed that this was a last resort that would most likely claim the lives of many debilitated whalers. But given the circumstances that would drive them to this desperate pass, it was better than the sure starvation they'd face by remaining at Point Barrow.

Chapter Thirty

Lopp...   *The Mountains*

It had been almost a week since Lopp left Jarvis, the doctor, and Nelson. Since that time, he and the boys had acquired two new guides, Omrok and Avaluk, who agreed to take the group through the mountains to the Pitmegea Divide. After two days, Avaluk came down with severe diarrhea and had to turn back. Before leaving he drew a map in the snow for Lopp and the other guide to follow.

The group struggled along the Pitmegea River, which led to the Pitmegea Valley and onto the Imikilly River. Here the moss was very poor and the deer were becoming weak. Considering their debilitated condition, Lopp decided he had to make it through the mountains to the ocean in less than a week or risk losing the deer.

As they progressed to the sea, they came upon a route Jarvis and the doctor were expected to follow. Finding no trace of their having yet been through, Lopp left a wooden cross made from a box of crackers, placing a note between its boards.

Lopp's party was now mostly through the mountain region. They'd made their way along frozen streams and rivers without major incident. The danger didn't seem to lie in the mountains as they'd expected. They pressed on for another week along the edge of the range, leaving two more notes for Jarvis with supplies buried at the base of wooden markers.

On March 12th they began to see signs of the last major mountain challenge. Lopp watched the boys from his sled. They continued to drive the deer with great efficiency. Then out of the corner of his eye he spied Omrok mushing toward him. Lopp stopped.

"Mr. Lopp, we've got trouble."

"What kind of trouble?"

"Wolves."

Lopp frowned. Wolves could attack the deer and easily cause a stampede. Given enough wolves, they could potentially lose a majority of the deer before reaching Point Barrow.

"How many?" asked Lopp.

Omruk just shrugged. "One pack, maybe more. I saw the tracks, that's all."

Lopp hesitated for no more than a moment. "OK, boys, get your rifles ready. Make sure the actions aren't frozen, and be on the lookout. We'll camp soon."

As they continued, Lopp began to pray. Their present course was eerie. They passed a series of abandoned shacks as he scanned for wolves, expecting them to lunge at every turn.

They stayed on their present course, but each herder scanned the horizon with a rifle ready for anything. Thus they moved past the mouth of the Kukpowruk River, their nerves frazzled by the relentless cold, now minus 50 degrees.

Finally the abandoned shacks gave way to an inhabited igloo in the distance. Omruk went ahead to warn the people to hide their dogs. After a lengthy discussion with the woman inhabiting the snow house, Omruk came back laughing. The woman couldn't understand why she wasn't allowed to kill the deer. She didn't understand the concept of a domesticated animal. Her husband was due back from seal hunting. Maybe they'd have better luck explaining it to him.

"She was the stupidest person I ever met," laughed Omruk. The other boys joined in the fun as he used his face to mimic her confusion. "I swear I told her ten times, maybe more."

Lopp chuckled, too. They needed a break from their tension and exhaustion.

"Well, we'll see if the story goes better with him," laughed Charlie.

"OK, let's make camp," said Lopp. The boys began breaking out the tent and camp gear.

Suddenly, Omruk spotted someone in the distance. "There he is, the husband," he called. The boys stopped their work and looked.

"What's he doing?" asked Tautuk.

"He's crawling, I think," said Charlie. Everyone squinted to make him out against the bright white background.

"Now he's up again," said Omruk, pausing. "No, he's crawling again."

Suddenly Charlie saw the gun. "He's hunting, and he's got a rifle!"

The group was frantic. His wife had reported that he was seal hunting; that usually meant that he would be carrying a spear, not a gun.

"Quick, Omruk, run and tell him they're domesticated!"

"Me? He'll probably shoot me!"

"No, he won't," said Charlie.

"No, really! If he's as dumb as his wife, he will."

Lopp grabbed a red Siberian snow shirt and put it on a pole. He ran back and forth in front of the deer, waving the shirt trying to get the man's attention. It was no use; the hunter was too intent on his prey.

In desperation Lopp turned to Omruk. "Run with this and wave it."

Omruk hesitated.

"Go! Go! You're the only one who's talked to his wife and can convince him."

Omruk grabbed the pole and began running down the hill to the hunter.

Lopp muttered to himself, "Come on, those are not caribou; they're deer."

As the group watched spellbound, the man finally noticed Omruk running directly at him. He raised his rifle to his shoulder. Omruk hesitated. The man lowered the gun. Omruk settled to a walk, dropped the shirt, and raised his hands above his head to show he had no weapon.

As Omruk walked toward the hunter, they seemed to argue. After a few tense moments, Omruk stepped forward and placed his hand on the man's shoulder as if consoling him. He had just lost the opportunity to kill enough food for the entire season. The two walked toward camp.

As they arrived, the man extended his hand in greeting. Lopp was surprised, but he took it. Shaking hands was not an original Eskimo tradition; the custom had been adopted only after exposure to Christian missionaries. Generally, any Eskimo that used the custom acknowledged his conversion. It was a surprise to find a Christian native this far north, away from the mines and whaling stations.

The Eskimo explained that he had no sight on his gun; otherwise, he would have begun shooting before they could have reached him. He invited Omruk to stay in his igloo and gave excellent directions to assist the remaining guide in finding moss along the frozen lagoon. So the near disaster once again turned into a blessing.

Lopp and the boys remained in camp throughout the night. But again the weather worsened. In the morning, frigid wind pounded the tent. Lopp turned to the guide for a recommendation.

"What do you think, can we go?" By this time the thermometer read −50 degrees. To make matters worse, snow was coming down hard. Typically in states such as Washington and the Dakotas, snow means that there is cloud cover and some warmth to moderate the cold. But in the Arctic, things are different; there, extreme cold and snow can coexist.

"No," responded the guide, "weather is too bad." There was almost zero visibility with the gusting wind and snow. The ice and snow particles combined with the frigid temperatures made any exposed skin hurt.

"So we can't go because of the cold, but could we make our way?"

"You can survive, but I not go."

"But we need you to show us the way," said Lopp above the wind.

"Just go four or five miles up the lagoon," pointed the agitated guide.

Lopp said nothing. He faced a critical decision. The clock was ticking on the whalers, who he presumed were starving. "How long can the storm last?"

"Maybe day, maybe week," the guide answered. Lopp scanned the faces of the boys, who were now circled around the two.

"We can try!" yelled Omruk above the wind.

"Yes, let's go," confirmed Tautuk.

As always, Lopp was proud of his boys. It seemed as if nothing could deter them. He wished the bureaucrats who argued that Eskimos were good-for-nothings could see this. These boys had already done the impossible in driving the deer across Kotzebue Sound and now the mountains.

"OK, let's go!" said Lopp. So the boys struck camp and went. Lopp donned his fourth parka. He now wore four coats: two of furred reindeer skin and two of squirrel fur. The frigid wind pounded the herders as they tried to stop any exposure—even the smallest bit of skin would be instantly frostbitten. Such a wind exploits any opening and fills clothing like a balloon.

Finally finding moss, Lopp and the boys stopped and camped. The blizzard continued the following day; they retreated into their tents and let the deer rest.

Finally on March 17th, two months into Lopp's journey, the blizzard subsided. While the wind continued with less force, the temperature remained at −50 degrees. As the boys came out of their tents at first light, they could see that they were virtually on the beach. A village lay just two miles ahead on the open landscape. Providence once again played a hand, for they emerged just in time to see another danger about to strike.

"There!" yelled Tautuk. "Hunters!"

Lopp scrambled from behind the boys to see. Seven men armed with rifles were approaching the deer; it was a safe bet the guns were already loaded. Since domesticated deer are trained not to bolt at the sound of gunshots, the seven men could virtually wipe out the herd before the survivors scattered.

Charlie and Omruk instantly took up the challenge and ran along the beach waving shirts, putting themselves between the men and the deer as a human shield. Two of the men were poised to begin the slaughter.

One old man stood next to the group, armed only with a spear. Since he couldn't shoot from any distance, he seemed less preoccupied with the deer and thus spotted the frantic herders. He raised his hand in the air, whereupon the hunters stopped.

Charlie and Omruk were winded as they ran, yet they couldn't stop and rest, lest they push the men's patience. Lopp and the boys watched anxiously as the emissaries approached the hunters.

"What are they doing?" Tautuk asked nobody in particular.

"I can't tell if they're arguing or just confused."

As they watched, the men pointed animatedly at the deer, then at Charlie and Omruk. Finally they all turned and began walking toward the herd. Luckily, the hunters lowered their weapons; Charlie and Omruk had succeeded.

"God in heaven," exclaimed Lopp.

Once again they had averted disaster. While they had been praying for safety from the wolves, God was protecting them from a much deadlier hunter.

The Eskimos from the village were desperately disappointed. Nevertheless, they drew a map for the group to help with the trek north and to help find moss.

As the boys began to break camp to continue their journey, Charlie spotted a lone sled rider speeding in their direction. He seemed to be trying to get their attention.

Now what? thought Lopp.

Chapter Thirty-One

Jarvis... No Help For The Last Miles

With Bertholf assigned to take care of official Cutter Service business back at Point Hope, Jarvis set out to find a guide for the remaining distance to Point Barrow. It was a difficult task for several reasons. First, very few people had ever made an overland journey that far north. Second, if anyone *had* attempted the trip, it would have been in the spring or summer; nobody in his right mind would attempt it now, in the dead of winter. Third, no Eskimo wanted to enter a starvation camp. Men in that situation represented a significant danger. They would be desperate enough to steal dogs for food, or worse yet, eat other humans to survive.

Jarvis went from one prospective guide to another. Not one was willing to make the trip. Beyond the reasons just mentioned, each had a family to take care of. The Arctic winter was a time for survival, not travel. A man had to hunt and fish or see his family perish.

Nelson and Jarvis trudged through the snow following sled tracks to an outlying hut. Standing away from the others, it was the home of an Eskimo named Nekowrah. As they approached, Nelson prepared Jarvis for virtually their last hope. "Nekowrah's not a young man, but he might be the most sympathetic to our cause."

"How so?" asked Jarvis.

"Well, Nekowrah and his wife once lived at the village near Point Barrow."

"Yes? Then he'll know the way?"

"No. He's never attempted the trip overland," Nelson said. "For that matter, few living men have. But he came to know some whalers from the ships putting in at the station."

"So he might go with us because he likes whalers?" asked Jarvis almost sarcastically. Frustrated from their rejections thus far, he was getting impatient.

"Yes."

"But what good does that do us if he doesn't know the way overland?" continued Jarvis.

"He's lived and traveled in the Arctic his whole life. He knows enough about survival, even in the mountains, to help you. If you travel along the coast as much as you can, not knowing the route may not matter," said Nelson. He couldn't say more because they had arrived at the hut. Jarvis sighed; it was a bad choice, but they were out of options, and they had to get moving.

They slowly entered the long descending entrance to the room below. Like all Eskimo homes, this one was built mainly underground for heat retention and protection from the frigid Arctic winter. Inside were Nekowrah and his wife. Nekowrah invited them in and shared what little food they had with their visitors.

They engaged in small talk and introductions before Nelson finally revealed the main reason for their visit.

"Nekowrah, Jarvis is on a mission to Point Barrow. He has to save three hundred stranded sailors. You are his last hope to get there."

Nekowrah was silent. He looked at his wife, who gave no indication of emotion. Either she already knew his answer or she was subservient to him.

Because Nekowrah had learned some English from the whalers, he responded directly to Jarvis.

"I know from what others say of your mission." Apparently Nekowrah and his wife had already heard of the mission.

Neither Nelson nor Jarvis responded. Instead they patiently waited for more to come. Nekowrah paused for several seconds. He seemed to be attempting to recall the right words for a language he seldom used.

Finally he said, "Other guides know your mission and know you need them to take you. They ready to say no." He paused again, "I not young man. I need to hunt and fish for my wife to live."

With this, Jarvis cringed; it seemed to be the beginning of another rejection.

Nekowrah continued, "So she must go with me."

Stunned, Jarvis looked disbelievingly at Nelson. The man had actually said yes!

Nevertheless, Jarvis had concerns at the prospect of taking Nekowrah's elderly wife. "It will be a difficult journey for your wife. We can make arrangements for her care from Nelson."

Nekowrah looked again at his wife. This time she did show emotion. Rather than keep silent, she said something in their native language to her husband. He responded. She smiled.

"She good woman. She know things. She can do things. We stay together now like we stay together before."

Jarvis looked at Nelson once again. He simply shrugged. Obviously Nekowrah and his wife had a strong bond. He wouldn't go without her and she wouldn't stay behind without him. Jarvis had no choice.

"We go tomorrow," said Jarvis. Nekowrah and his wife smiled. They had come to a deal. The one thing missing from the discussion was payment. Like many of the other Eskimos Jarvis had encountered en route, Nekowrah and his wife gave out of compassion for people in need. They sought no personal gain, nor did they even ask to be repaid for their efforts and possessions. Jarvis was grateful to the man and his wife who would lead them the difficult remainder of their journey.

Jarvis, the doctor, Nekowrah, and his wife began their trek to Point Barrow the next day. It was rough going, as always. The snow was deep, and the dogs had difficulty fighting through it. Ideally, Jarvis or Nekowrah would have run ahead of the dogs to check out the trail. But after two hard days, they were too tired.

On March 7, the next day, things became progressively more difficult. The wind blew hard out of the northeast, and the ice and snow were heavy along the shore of Cape Lisburne. In most spots, the snow built up in drifts. They had to literally dig passageways so the heavy cargo sleds could be pulled through.   At one point Jarvis stopped shoveling to catch his breath. Nekowrah likewise stopped.

"We can't keep going this way. At this rate, we'll have to dig a tunnel all the way to Point Barrow," said Jarvis wryly.

Nekowrah studied Jarvis. "We go inland. Snow not so deep."

Jarvis appraised the guide. He remembered Nelson's warning that Nekowrah had never been to Point Barrow overland. They were to stay to the shore to avoid getting lost or running into unanticipated dangers. But on the other hand, they were making almost no progress. At this rate, they couldn't make Point Barrow in months, if ever. This was another of those command decisions that seemed to have no good outcome.

"We go inland," concurred Jarvis.

They finished digging through the drift far enough to get the sleds through, and then turned inland. They hadn't gone far when they ran into the steep grade at the base of the mountain. Jarvis looked up the cliffs; their angle was almost 70 degrees. They would have to put wings on the dogs to go any farther.

It seemed like a no-win situation. On the left was impassable snow, on the right a steep mountain wall. Making matters worse, strong winds were known to blow rocks and ice off the cliffs to the ice below. The group constantly watched boulders ahead and behind come raining down. If they stayed here, odds were that eventually they'd be hit.

Jarvis stopped to confer with Nekowrah. He had to yell because the wind ran along the cliffs, creating a wind tunnel, yet one more force pushing against them. It was almost as if something didn't want them to get to Point Barrow.

"Nekowrah, we can't stay here!"

"It dangerous," agreed Nekowrah.

"Can we go out beyond the shore to the ice over the sea?"

"No, ice break away, go out to sea," responded Nekowrah.

"Can we take that chance?" yelled Jarvis, looking up the cliffs as more rocks hit the ice ahead.

"No, I do that long ago. I float in ocean three days trying get back!" yelled Nekowrah.

Once before Jarvis had ignored the advice of a guide and followed his own judgment. It had proved to be a mistake. Now he knew better. "OK, we go your way!" he yelled.

For a while they crept along, hugging the cliffs for protection from the cascading ice and rocks. Finally they had to stop, for the rain of debris was increasing as the wind strengthened.

Securing the dogs, they made camp under a shelf of the cliff. There they huddled in their tent, listening to the crash of rocks around them. With each crash came a vibration, like a sudden, short earthquake.

Nekowrah's wife began to prepare the food. They had managed to collect a small amount of driftwood for a fire to heat their dinner and themselves.

"Jarvis, what are we going to do?" said the doctor.

Once again, things were out of their control. There seemed to be no way to avoid disaster. Jarvis looked at Nekowrah, then at the doctor. "We must wait," he said. "We have some protection here. We'll have to wait for the wind to die down."

Nekowrah said, "We not have much longer before cliffs end." Seeing that Jarvis and the doctor didn't understand, he continued, "We go around cape."

Jarvis saw his logic and translated. "The mountain range will stop crowding the beach once we round the cape ahead. At that point we can gain some distance from the cliffs and the falling rocks and ice."

The doctor shook his head. It seemed as though they were in a battle, with enemy bombs falling around them. Their only protection was a small stretch of cliff that jutted out, forming a small shelf. They stayed below it, hoping that *it* wouldn't fall.

Finally, exhausted, they fell asleep. Even the crashing rain of rocks couldn't keep them or the dogs awake.

The next morning, Jarvis began to stir in his sleeping bag. As he drifted toward consciousness, he thought something was wrong. Cautiously he lay and listened. Then he realized that something wasn't wrong; something was missing. It was quiet. Not entirely quiet—he could still hear the

211

wind—but it was much calmer. It appeared that timing had once again come to their aid.

Jarvis quickly roused the other travelers. Hastily they packed the tent and tied the dogs to the sled. Then as fast as they could mush, they moved along the cliffs, racing toward the cape and relative safety.

After a long, suspenseful day, they finally made their goal. Reaching the cape, they pulled into a small village named Wevuk, one of the last before their final march to Point Barrow. Though Wevuk was called a village, there were only two huts, containing one family each. After a brief stay, during which they obtained extra food from one of the charitable families, they were off again.

The northeast wind continued in force. It never seemed to falter, but blew relentlessly, as a trade wind does in the south. But the snow was packed hard, so the sleds glided along quickly. For the first time, they seemed to be moving well. Jarvis started to get excited. The journey that had seemed so endless, now might actually come to an end—and soon.

His euphoria quickly turned to frustration as the snow started falling again. The wind, while consistent, wasn't strong enough to blow the snow from the trail. Deep drifts built up, once again making slow, heavy toil for the dogs. By evening they camped in an abandoned shack. Much of its wooden walls had been taken by Eskimos to build fires. Nevertheless, it offered some shelter.

The next morning they began again in the soft snow and rough ice. As difficult as things had been the day before, this day they became worse. Deep hollows seemed to swallow the sleds and dogs as they tried to move forward. The ice became rougher, like the crushes in the Sound. It was almost as if the Arctic didn't want them to reach Point Barrow and was throwing every possible hindrance in their way.

Jarvis reached a hollow that seemed impassable. The wall of ice on either side created a passageway too narrow to travel through. Dejected and tired, he stopped to rest. The doctor approached and slumped against the sled.

"I'm very tired."

"Yes, I am too. It just seems to get worse and worse."

They both stared into the cavern facing them.

Nokowrah drew up to Jarvis and Call. Jarvis was amazed at the stamina of the old man.

"We have fill it," he said cryptically.

"What do you mean?" asked Jarvis.

"Take ice from bad ice and fill hole for sled," he explained.

Jarvis took a deep breath and nodded. Laboriously they chipped ice and filled the hollow until they had a surface over which the sled could pass. For the next several hours they had to repeat the same routine many times. Finally, near the point of total exhaustion, they reached the mouth of the Pitmegea River. Here they were supposed to meet Lopp and the deer herd.

Jarvis slumped against his sled, almost unable to move.

"I can't believe we had to build the road," said the doctor, laughing. In their exhaustion, it suddenly seemed like a hilarious joke. They broke into gales of laughter. Nekowrah's wife, looking on, must have thought they had cracked from the strain.

Nekowrah sat silently next to Jarvis. He didn't understand all the words, but he clearly understood the sentiment. Then Nekowrah spoke. "You see herd?"

"No."

They squinted at the horizon but found nothing.

"Over there," said Nekowrah.

"What, the herd?" Jarvis couldn't see anything.

"No, over there. That not from Eskimo. That from koblonas," said Nekowrah, pointing to a cross made of two pieces of a breadbox. As they drew near they could see writing: "Letter between boards." Inside was a note from Tom Lopp.

"What does it say?" asked the doctor.

Jarvis quickly read the letter. "It says that they arrived on the seventh, three days ago. They crossed the mountains. The sled deer were exhausted. They waited a day to let the deer recuperate and went on again."

A grin spread over Jarvis's face, then he suddenly gave the doctor a high-spirited shove. "They made it! They made it! They made it through the mountains. I don't believe it." Jarvis, normally sedate and disciplined, was almost giddy. Nekowrah smiled. Nekowrah's wife approached, and Jarvis grabbed her arm to swing her about. He clapped his hands.

Suddenly infused with new energy, they climbed back on their sleds. They had to catch Lopp.

It had been three days of hard travel. The deep snow still made it slow going for the dogs. Just beyond the end of the mountain range, Jarvis and his little party stopped at a camp where it appeared that Lopp had stayed the night before. As Jarvis sat, he looked at the thermometer he'd brought. The temperate was −20 degrees; oddly enough, Jarvis found it almost uncomfortably warm. It was interesting how his body had changed with the environment over the months.

Early the next morning they began again, traveling along a lagoon that paralleled the coast for about a hundred miles. As they camped that night, a strong gale rose and pounded the tent, which started to pull from its stakes; they crawled deeper into their sleeping bags.

Finally Jarvis had to roust the doctor and Nekowrah. "The tent is going to blow away. We have to do something."

"But what?" asked the doctor.

Both men turned to Nekowrah. He had the most experience.

"We build wall," he said in his characteristically few words. With that they began to pull on their coats to go out in the gale.

"Great," exclaimed the doctor, "more building."

Jarvis just smiled.

Following Nekowrah's instruction, the men cut blocks of compacted snow and placed them alongside the abandoned hut. Most of its walls were already gone, so they pulled off the roof to reach the hard snow beneath, then they built a wall in the same manner as Eskimos build an igloo. Finally, after over an hour, they crawled back into their tent, exhausted. They only had a couple of hours to sleep before they had to rise again in the morning.

The next morning they started and pressed on for two more days, fighting the blizzard every step. Blowing snow made it almost impossible to follow the deer tracks left by Lopp's herd, but they pressed on. Finally on March 17th, just over three months into the overland expedition, they entered a small village, the first they had found since traveling this far north. Now they were almost to the polar rim at the top of the world.

As they pulled next to the igloos with their sleds, an Eskimo emerged. He said something to Nekowrah in their native dialect, then produced a letter. Nekowrah delivered the letter to Jarvis; he didn't have to ask whom it was from.

Jarvis quickly opened the note. "It says that Lopp passed through here yesterday. He's traveling quickly and into the night to make up for time lost during the blizzard."

"Well, let's go; we can try to catch him," said the doctor. Jarvis checked with Nekowrah, who nodded his agreement.

They quickly clambered on their sleds and went on. Before long, through the falling snow they could barely make out in the distance a large black form. "There!" yelled the doctor above the wind. Jarvis mushed his dog team, pressing them as fast as they could go.

As Jarvis looked ahead, it appeared that the black mass wasn't moving. They were going to catch Lopp at last.

Jarvis, out of breath, stopped his sled to the south of the herd. Lopp walked toward him. "Well, I wondered when you'd show up," he said.

"We stopped for a couple of floor shows," laughed Jarvis, referring to Lopp's joke months earlier. "You're well, I see."

"We've had a bit of trouble with the blizzard and wolves."

Jarvis' face fell. "How much trouble?"

"We've managed. Only one loss. By the grace of God they simply left."

"What do you mean?" asked Jarvis, puzzled.

"We haven't seen any signs since we drove them off. They seemed to just give up after only one attack and go south." Once again, they had received an inexplicable gift.

They weren't far from Point Barrow now. As hard as they had worked, their rewards would be even greater. There were no major obstacles left, only a clear trail to Point Barrow. Hopefully, the men were still alive.

Chapter Thirty-Two

Jim... Dying Men's Letters

Jim thought this was the end of the line. He was feeling the effects of scurvy. All the men were. Their food supply was diminishing. They were cold and totally demoralized. After a heroic effort from the Eskimos, the caribou season had come to an end. Most, fearing that they would never see home again, had written letters to their families including parting words for their children in neatly scribed hands. Men who couldn't write got help from those who could. That was what Jim was doing now for Joiner, his old friend.

"Go ahead, Joiner," said Jim tenderly. "I'm ready."

"To my dearest son," said Joiner, speaking slowly and carefully. "You might wonder why I was always gone while you grew. It was not because I didn't love you."

It seemed strange for Jim to hear tender words from his burly friend. But when you have advance warning of your death, you have the rare opportunity to say what you might not otherwise.

"I came to sea to earn money so you could have a future. I think of you every day. I think of your mom." Joiner choked on the words. Unable to continue, he ended on a simple note that said it all. "Be a good man and take care of your mom. Love, Dad."

Jim paused for a moment and left his friend to his thoughts. It was a short letter but nobody could have said it more from the heart. Jim folded the note and wrote Joiner's name and hometown on the back. Like the rest, Joiner planned to have it on his person, hoping that after his death, somebody would find and deliver the letter.

Like Joiner, many of the men had great regrets. While they were at sea, they had thought only of their families at home. With each shore leave, they planned to stay home and get a regular job that would bring them home to their families each night. Yet after just a few short weeks, their minds turned to the sea again and the life and death struggles with their prey and the ocean. Within a month, they usually found themselves on the docks searching for a ship. And all for a tiny fraction of the proceeds from each barrel of whale oil.

Jim left his friend to go outside. This was the end of the line; he had no desire to be with other people. He'd rather feel the bite of frigid air than watch the end coming to each man inside.

As he stood gazing across the barren landscape, he saw several dogsleds coming toward the station. They didn't look like Eskimos; their configuration was different.

Jim, mesmerized, watched the dogsleds skim swiftly closer. He stood motionless, breathless, as the driver pulled the dogs to a halt. Then the white man dismounted, pulled back his parka hood, and strode up to Jim.

Jim was speechless. The man slowly removed his mittens and extended his hand.

"I'm David Jarvis from the Revenue Cutter Service."

Epilogue

The rescue party reached the stranded whalers at the Point Barrow Whaling Station, located nine miles south of Point Barrow at Cape Smythe, on March 29, 1898. Many were so astonished by their arrival that they asked if the travelers had come by balloon. Dr. Call found four cases of severe scurvy, one suicide, and lesser symptoms of scurvy in the remaining crew. Up to this point, many of the men, refusing any authority, had reverted to lawlessness. Jarvis quickly asserted his leadership and established control of the men.

Jarvis and Dr. Call determined that the housing conditions were unsanitary and almost intolerable. With the aid of Charlie Brower, they converted an old storehouse to maintain twenty-eight men. An additional twenty-eight were placed in a Presbyterian Mission schoolroom with the blessing of Dr. March, a missionary doctor who had previously assisted Brower with the medical needs of the crew. The remaining sixteen were added to the officers' quarters at the old refuge station with McIlhenny. All new quarters were light, dry, and warm. Jarvis instituted daily inspections to maintain the sanitary conditions of the men and housing until the arrival of spring.

Of the 448 deer driven north from the combined herds and Lieutenant Bertholf's acquisitions, 382 survived the trip. The remainder were sacrificed for food or lost to wolves, dogs, or other mishaps. With the delivery of the deer, each man's fresh meat ration was increased to 2.5 pounds per man, per week. This change in diet quickly eliminated all signs of scurvy. Likewise, the deer and other supplies were shared with the crews on the ice-bound ships through a series of supply deliveries.

Epilogue

The *Bear* fought through breaking ice to arrive on July 28, 1898, four months later. Seaworthy whaling ships were freed from the ice, while the 98 men from destroyed ships were loaded on *Bear* for the voyage home.

Upon arrival in the United States, First Lieutenant David Jarvis, Second Lieutenant Ellsworth Bertholf, and Surgeon S. J. Call became national heroes. They were awarded specially created congressional gold medals. Thomas Lopp, Charlie Artisarlook, Charlie Brower, Edward McIlhenny, Tom Gordon, Fred Hopson, Dr. Marsh, Dr. Kettleson, and others were recognized as being instrumental in saving the lives of the men.

Lieutenant David Jarvis

During the expedition, the Jarvis family received a daughter, Anna T. Jarvis. In the years following the expedition, two additional children were born. David Jarvis went on to achieve the rank of captain and served in that capacity as the Collector of Customs for Alaska. He later resigned his position in the Revenue Cutter Service (United States Coast Guard) to become a senior executive for the Northwest Fisheries Company, rising to become secretary of the parent syndicate. He died in 1911.

Second Lieutenant E. P. Bertholf

Ellsworth Bertholf went on to become captain of the *Bear* and later, commandant of the Revenue Cutter Service. In that position he oversaw the merger of the Revenue Cutter Service with the Life Saving Service to form the United States Coast Guard in 1915. In this capacity, he guided the Coast Guard as Commodore Commandant to distinguished service throughout WWI. Upon retirement, Bertholf became a vice-president for the American Bureau of Shipping. He died at the age of 55 in his hotel residence in New York, New York.

219

Doctor S. J. Call

The year following the expedition, Dr. Call left the Revenue Cutter Service to establish a private medical practice in Nome, Alaska, where he served the 25,000 member Gold Rush town. At that time, Nome was badly in need of medical help because of unsanitary conditions and disease. He later returned to the Cutter Service in 1903, where he served on two more ships before he retired in 1908. In 1909 he died in California, where he lived with his sister.

The Whalers

Nothing is known of James Lee (Jim) other than his having been a general seaman on the *Orca* and witness to all events described in the journals of others.

Tom Lopp

Tom Lopp remains a pivotal figure in Alaskan history. He was instrumental in the initiation of reindeer herds and an outspoken proponent of Eskimo rights. In this capacity, he created the first newspaper devoted to Eskimo issues, the *Eskimo Bulletin*. After leaving a long career in Alaska, he continued in missionary service and spread the gospel until his death. He and his wife had a total of eight children. Kathleen Lopp Smith and Verbeck Smith faithfully preserved and published family letters in the book *Ice Window*, University of Alaska Press.

Charlie Brower

Charlie Brower stayed a lifetime in Alaska. Through two Eskimo wives, he is the patriarch of many present-day Point Barrow residents by the same name. His family maintained a restaurant at the site of the station for multiple generations. In 1945, Brower published his memoirs in the best-selling book, *Fifty Years Below Zero*, no longer in print. Charlie Brower was probably the single most instrumental agent in saving the lives of the crewmen.

Charlie Artisarlook and the "Boys"

Charlie and his wife Mary continued as missionaries. Little is known about the boys: Tautuk, Ootenna, Kivyearzruk, Sokweena, Keuk, and Ituk. Besides being instrumental in the success of the overland expedition, they proved to many detractors that Eskimos were capable of maintaining deer herds. Their feats in driving the deer through mountains and impossible terrain are still unmatched in the world today.

E. A. McIlhenny

Edward Avery McIlhenny became widely known as a naturalist, conservationist, world explorer, and author of several books, including *Autobiography of an Egret*. As a naturalist, McIlhenny is credited with saving the snowy egret from extinction. His willingness to help, and his uncanny hunting skills, were invaluable in the assistance of Charlie Brower.

Those Amazing People Called the Eskimos

Most importantly, countless numbers of unnamed Eskimos were instrumental in the survival of the stranded crewmen and the rescue party. The particular Eskimo tribes providing assistance were the Inuit, along most of the rescue route, and the Inupiat of the far north in and around Point Barrow.

Unfortunately, no Eskimo journals were found. However, Perninyuk, the guide who traveled longest with the rescue team, exemplified the sacrifice and bravery of these amazing people. Without the help of multiple guides, villagers, and hunters like Perninyuk, all would have perished.

Detractors

Some people questioned the value of the overland expedition, pointing out that the men may have survived until spring without the arrival of the malnourished, underweight deer. Upon their arrival in Washington, it took two months of hard lobbying by David Jarvis and Charlie Brower to convince the government to pay for expenditures, including those made by Brower to feed the men. However, Congress finally repaid Charlie Brower and awarded him a $3,000 bonus for his efforts.

Notes

Chapter One
Jim . . . It Begins

All individuals named in the book were actual participants in the event. James Lee, a crewman on the *Orca*, was the only whaler known to have participated in the span of events ranging from the destruction of the *Orca* to the long stay at Point Barrow. Therefore, he was selected as the story's main character to witness events involving the whalers. Joiner was created as a nickname for a sailmaker, and Jake was later referenced as an unknown cabin boy. There were no historical references to their actual names.

Dialogue among the whalers was built from references to actual whalers' diaries (Creighton, 1995) and sailors' diaries (Dana, 1946).

No historical references were found on the actual method used by the *Freeman*, *Belvedere*, and *Orca* to blast through the ice, other than the use of "gunpowder." Laura Pereira at the New Bedford Whaling Museum provided a special opinion as to the probable method used.

Descriptions of the fate of earlier expeditions were created from a historical brief written by Bertholf (1899).

Chapter 2
Jim ... Trapped

The destruction of the *Orca* and *Jesse H. Freeman*, and subsequent rescue of the *Belvedere*, were built primarily from a brief reference in *The Journal of the National Archives* (Bockstoce, 1977) as well as an excerpt from the *San Francisco Call* that stated,

> *Orca*...was caught between two immense ice floes and crushed with such force as to take the stern post and steering gear completely out of her and hurl the wheel through the pilot house. Her officers and crew jumped for the ice immediately.

Bockstoce derived additional information from the journal of Edward McIlhenny and went on to say:

> The *Belvedere* and the *Freeman* were able to get within three-quarters of a mile of the *Orca* and rescued all her men.... The *Belvedere* under steam and sail succeeded in forcing her way through thickening ice; however, two hours later the *Freeman* was caught and crushed. The *Belvedere*, safe behind heavy ground ice at the Sea Horse Islands, took the *Freeman's* crew aboard as well."

Compensation for the whaling crews consisted of a percentage of the profit from cargo sales, distributed according to the skill level of the sailor. A cabin boy would have earned as little as $1/400^{th}$ of the proceeds. James Lee, a foremast hand, would have received only a small percentage of the profit from cargo sales, amounting to anywhere from a $1/150^{th}$ share to $1/190^{th}$, depending on his skill level. Among the officers, lesser mates would earn from $1/40^{th}$ to $1/70^{th}$, while the first mate would earn $1/24^{th}$. The captain would generally earn $1/15^{th}$.

Chapter 3
Jim . . . Belvedere

Daily lives of general crewmen on *Belvedere,* including crewmen's hobbies, were built from Creighton (1995). Preparations for survival on *Belvedere* were taken from Jarvis's recollections (Tuttle, 1899). Jarvis's actual words were:

> A house had been built on the sand beach, and all the provisions and coal stored there . . . a line stretched from the vessel to the shore . . . in case the vessel should have to be abandoned.

Chapter 4
Jim . . . *Orca's* Graveyard

Dramatization of the attempts to gather food from the wrecked *Orca* was built from very brief references in Bockstoce (1977) and excerpts taken by Bockstoce from a *Belvedere* Log (*Belvedere,* 1898). Bockstoce wrote:

> Meanwhile, George Fred Tilton, third mate of the *Belvedere,* and Charles Walker, fourth mate of the *Orca,* had been hard at work salvaging supplies from the *Orca....* Charles Walker, the fifth mate, and James Lee, a sailor, were sent out to her to see what could be saved.

In point of fact, Jim Lee and the mate Charlie Walker had been to the wreck several days before this described return to *Orca.* With the help of natives from Point Belcher, they retrieved some supplies and some whalebone (worth about $20,000). Using a sail from *Orca,* they created a tent for storage and for protection from the wind. Sitting in the tent, they dreamed of holding the whalebone until it could be sold in the spring to compensate for lost wages. This plan would never come to fruition. (Bockstoce, 1986)

Given the volume of provisions extracted from the wreck and based on probable techniques employed, a proportionate number of other crewmen were used in this telling of the second return to *Orca*.

Although we don't know the name of the ship's cook from the *Orca*, he was described as being a rotund African American. Whaling, although a risky occupation, provided employment for many disenfranchised men in the nineteenth century. Asiatics and blacks found it relatively easy to obtain a berth on a ship bound for whaling waters.

Superstitions evoked upon the sailors' entering the wrecked ship were drawn from other whaling works, including Creighton (1995).

Chapter 5
Jim ... Time to Leave

Little is known about the actual move from the *Belvedere* to Point Barrow, other than the distance traveled, time, and condition of the men upon arrival. Information was drawn from Brower (1942), who said:

> On October 5 the house was ready, and on that day the first party from the ships arrived, having been two days on route... Many of the men were unfit and were unable to walk...The captains could bunk with us – officers in the Rescue Station – most of the men in Kelley's old place – double rows of makeshift bunks – a wood stove in the center – no end of details.

Other background information was derived from the journal of David Jarvis, found in the Congressional report submitted by Captain Tuttle (Tuttle, 1899).

Chapter 6
Jim . . . Life in the Old Kelley House

The dank and dismal conditions of the Old Kelley House were primarily built from vivid descriptions recorded by Jarvis upon the arrival of the rescue team (Tuttle, 1899).

> They were all in a horrible state...One window gave feeble light (Old Kelley House), and there was little or no ventilation except through the door and cracks....lower down on the walls ice formed 3 or 4 inches thick and the drippings and meltings ran down over this into the berths....soot and smoke from these lamps (seal oil) covered everything, their clothes and bodies, with a black greasy coating, so they were scarcely recognizable as men....filth and vermin were everywhere.

Upon his arrival, Jarvis moved the men to new quarters and instituted daily health inspections to insure sanitary conditions.

The conflict at Point Barrow was built from general references in multiple sources. While the actual participants were not known, the basic causes were noted as:

1) General neglect by the officers, who felt they had no obligation to care for the men, since their ships had been destroyed (paraphrased from the Jarvis journal).

2) The feeling that the masters of the *Orca*, *Belvedere*, and *Freeman* had stayed "several crucial days" at Point Barrow before attempting an escape south while they "drunkenly caroused together," as reported by Bockstoce (1986), quoting Jim Allen, engineer of the *Freeman*.

3) One captain's delay in moving south was attributed to his waiting to drop off his Eskimo girlfriend before traveling on. This was reported to Lopp by an unnamed crewman and recorded in Lopp's private journal. Lopp (1898).

4) The failure to house the men in the whaling station built by the government for just such an emergency.

... the house had been built to accommodate
100 men in an emergency, and this was
about the number to be provided for, but Mr.
McIlhenny refused to allow anyone but the
officers in his house, and these represented but
a small part of the whole number ... (Tuttle,
1899)

Other sources referencing conflict included:

Jarvis settled all grievances and ruled that, by maritime law,
the masters of the wrecked vessels were obligated to provide
for their crewmen until they could be returned to a proper
U.S. Port of Call. (Tuttle, 1899)

Brower and the Eskimo hunters would have encountered
predominantly caribou, which are part of the deer family (and look just
like reindeer). Traditionally, reindeer herders have problems when caribou
herds come through and their domesticated reindeer leave the herd to
accompany the caribou. Caribou and reindeer do mate and produce
offspring that are generally weaker than either animal. Caribou are the
only deer species where both male and female deer have antlers. They were
referred to in various rescue documents as wild deer in general, or more
specifically caribou (as the species).

Regarding Tilton and Walker, the two messengers whom Brower sent
south, Bockstoce (1986) reported:

The men set out in October on an arduous trek of more than
1,700 miles; they arrived in the United States only a few
weeks apart. . . . It was thought that Walker, had he pressed
on, should have beaten Tilton by a month. Later the men
learned that Walker had spent valuable weeks drinking at
Herschel Island.

Chapter 7
Jarvis ... The Cutter *Bear*

Descriptions of the *Bear* and Jarvis were created from photographs and background information (Canney, 1947).

References to the Jarvis family and Jarvis's consternation over leaving his pregnant wife were taken from Kaplan (1972).

The fact that three unnamed ships escaped the Arctic and notified the federal government was, surprisingly, never mentioned in the lengthy congressional report describing the government's emergency response. Mention of these three escaping ships was later found in a magazine article. ("The Rescue of the Whalers," *Harpers New Monthly Magazine*, vol. 99, no. 589, 1899).

Chapter 8: Jarvis ... *Bear* Returns

An inventory of initial supplies carried by Jarvis and the rescue team included:

Tents and poles	30 lbs
Stove and pipe	21 lbs
Oil stove	15 lbs
Oil	15 lbs
Cooking gear and grub box	40 lbs
Two axes	10 lbs
Two rifles	14 lbs
One shotgun	8 lbs
400 rounds rifle ammunition	50 lbs
100 rounds shotgun ammunition	25 lbs
Four clothes bags	140 lbs
Four sleeping bags	200 lbs
Bale of trade tobacco	50 lbs

Sleeping gear and outfit for natives	125 lbs
One ham	12 lbs
Beans	30 lbs
Pork	50 lbs
Bacon	24 lbs
Hard bread	12 lbs
Tea	12 lbs
Flour	50 lbs
One dozen canned meats	48 lbs
Compressed barley soup and condensed coffee	25 lbs
Dog fish	150 lbs
Total	1,294 lbs

For cooking, they brought two frying pans, two camp kettles, two teapots, one large knife, one large spoon, and a small cook stove. The cook stove proved an immediate problem to the inexperienced group:

> The oil stove not being especially constructed for such an expedition, was found of little use, for it had no protection of the surrounding atmosphere, and much of the heat from the burners was lost. It consumed a great deal of oil, and as the article was bulky, heavy and inconvenient to carry on a sled, the stove was finally discarded. (Tuttle, 1899)

The journals state that they generally found driftwood for fires.

The journals never state how cooking fires were started. However, matches were widespread after they had been somewhat perfected in 1826 (unlike today's matches, these contained phosphorus and could be used to poison an enemy). The introduction of matches dramatically expanded the use of tobacco and smoking. Since the rescuers smoked, and the event took place 75 years after the introduction of matches, it was assumed that matches were used.

For dining, each member was issued a knife, fork, spoon, tin plate, cup, and one large hunting knife.

As the trip progressed, the rescue party generally got food from the Eskimos along the way, including fish for the dogs. However, the "white man's food" that they acquired when they could, included hard bread (that term was used interchangeably with crackers), beans, tea, hardtack, bacon, and pork. As supplies ran out, they resorted to tea, crackers, and beans— or just crackers.

Medical supplies described by Dr. Call included:

> 1 pocket surgical case
> 1 hypodermic case
> 1 stethoscope
> 1/2 pound lint
> 1 roll rubber adhesive plaster, 1 inch
> 1 fever thermometer
> 1 dozen assorted surgical bandages
> 1/2 roll isinglass plaster
> 1/2 dozen surgical sponges
> 1/2 dozen pair snow glasses
> 1/3 dozen toothbrushes

The background of Second Lieutenant Bertholf was derived from his biography (Kroll, 2002). It should be noted that the Revenue Cutter Service title Second Lieutenant, was later replaced by the U. S. Coast Guard title of Lieutenant Junior Grade.

The background on Dr. Call was derived indirectly from Cocke (1974).

The Gold Rush of the Klondike began in July 1897 (less than six months before the rescue), following the arrival of the *Excelsior* in San Francisco with $400,000 in Klondike gold. Newspapers spread the word rapidly across the country, and the Gold Rush began. Since the rescue party's initial route took them near traveling miners en route to the Copper River Gold Fields, supplies were sparse and costly because of excessive demand.

Chapter 9
Jarvis . . . The Landing

The descriptions of the landing were derived from the journal of David Jarvis (Tuttle, 1899).

Chapter 10
Jarvis . . . The Split

On one of their arrivals at a strange village, Jarvis reported that

> Our arrival seemed to create some commotion . . . all the women and children ran into their huts . . . it had been the practice of the traders in the old days to steal the women. (Tuttle, 1899)

Like many Americans, Jarvis's grandparents probably didn't celebrate Christmas for much of their lives. It wasn't until Charles Dickens wrote "A Christmas Carol" in 1867 that the holiday made a resurgence. Up until that time, it wasn't even recognized as a day off by most employers. But within a few years that changed. Christmas trees started appearing. They would have seen use first in Jarvis's parents' home, then later in the home of his grandparents.

Chapter 11
Jarvis . . . No Deer

Initial rescue party travels were derived from the Jarvis journal (Tuttle, 1899). Additional background on the people they encountered was created from Oswalt (1979).

Chapter 12
Jim ... *Navarch*

References to the surprise arrival of the *Navarch* with several tons of coal and the later burning of *Navarch* were derived from Charlie Brower's autobiography (Brower, 1942) and *The Journal of the National Archives* (Bockstoce, 1977). It should be noted, however, that the two accounts implied different timeframes for the removal of the coal and how quickly it came to burn after the ship's arrival. The Bockstoce version was much more detailed in its description and research. Therefore, it was the principal source for this book's description of the event.

As to the men who set the fire, Brower noted that:

> The pair were merely garden variety fools . . . suggested punishment ranged from flogging to hanging . . . . . In the end I did nothing at all, merely announcing to the crowd, "Whenever you fellows feel chilly, you can warm up by giving 'em a licking."

Chapter 13
Jarvis ... Tilton

The chance meeting between Jarvis and Tilton was derived from the Jarvis journal (Tuttle, 1899). Additional background information as to the probable reaction of the Eskimo woman they encountered (who notified them of the existence of Tilton) was derived from other historical interactions between whites and Eskimos described in Oswalt (1979).

Chapter 14
Jarvis ... The Herd

The surprise arrival of the small government herd driven by Kettleson was derived from the Jarvis journal (Tuttle, 1899).

Chapter 15
Jim ... The Eskimo Hunt

Hunting was ongoing by whalers, Eskimos, the staff of the Point Barrow Refuge Station, and the three groups in combination. This chapter was created to describe how one such event probably unfolded. The intent was to showcase Eskimo hunting techniques (Oswalt, 1979) and contrast them with traditional whaling techniques (Creighton, 1995).

The three-foot darting gun had been introduced by Captain Ebenezer Pierce three decades earlier, in 1865. News of its effectiveness in delivering a deadly first shot quickly spread, and it was soon adopted by most whalers. If this first shot didn't kill the whale, traditional harpoons were quickly flung to finish the job.

Chapter 17
Jarvis ... Charlie Artisarlook

The weathering of blizzards and interactions with Charlie Artisarlook were derived from the Jarvis journal (Tuttle, 1899).

Chapter 18
Jim ... More Disputes

All accounts indicated that conflict continued as the men fell into general lawlessness. The specific incident regarding the stealing of food from the warehouse was drawn from references in Charlie Brower's autobiography (Brower, 1942). Herein he stated that, " ... men, crowding in for their tobacco ration, managed to steal a lot of other things." In response, Brower instituted new security procedures, wherein "...just inside the door stood Fred and another man, each armed with a pick handle."

In the Congressional report submitted by Captain Tuttle, Jarvis reported that: "...neglect was apparent in the men.... Later, owing to some trouble, the authority used was that of Mr. Brower only."

Chapter 20
Jarvis ... Christians on a Mission

The introduction of Tom Lopp to David Jarvis was primarily created from a compilation of family letters provided by a descendant of Tom Lopp, Kathleen Lopp-Smith. (Smith, Lopp-Smith, 2001). It should be noted that while the Lopps had interaction with the *Bear* and its crew, personal journals implied that only Tom Lopp had met David Jarvis before this occasion.

Jarvis's and Lopp's initial meeting and preparations for the herd were also derived from the Jarvis journal (Tuttle, 1899). Among other things, Jarvis stated that: "Mr. and Mrs. Lopp were much exercised to know what brought an officer of the Government into the country at this time of year...I delivered Mr. Lopp his mail."

The respect that Jarvis had for Lopp was almost unbounded. Jarvis stated in his journal:

> He [Lopp] was indispensable. His capability of handling natives, his knowledge of them and reindeer, was far above that of anyone in the country. While in no way ostentatious, he and Mrs. Lopp had acquired a level of ascendancy and respect among the natives that was productive of the greatest success in bettering the condition of the latter. (Tuttle, 1899)

Chapter 21
Jim . . . The Salvation Army

Two references noted the arrival of bibles from the *Belvedere*, including the Charles Brower autobiography (Brower, 1942) and Bockstoce (1977). The Brower journal implied that the bible delivery was a generally useless endeavor when he stated: " . . . to purify the Station atmosphere would have taken more than a box of Bibles . . . ." Based on that attitude, it was concluded that at least part of the crew held a similar position.

Research on the attitudes of whalers toward Christianity in general indicated that at least half would have probably placed some value on the bibles. It further indicated that while the whalers were generally positive toward Christianity and held some Christian beliefs, they generally disliked missionaries (missionaries were linked to temperance laws in the ports they visited). Attitudes toward an event of this nature were concluded from Creighton (1995).

Chapter 22
Jarvis . . . Perninyuk

The miraculous appearance of Perninyuk, the only guide who could have directed the rescue team through the local terrain of that particular area, was described in the Jarvis journal (Tuttle, 1899).

> The very man we wanted, a native, Perninyuk by name, came tramping over the hill at the back of our camp . . . probably the only man for miles around . . . how he came to strike our camp at the very time we wanted him so badly was inexplicable.

The positive astonishment at this event was at, or near, the top of anything encountered in the expedition.

Chapter 23
Jarvis ... The Crossing

The events of the crossing and the cross-cultural incident involving the possessed Eskimo woman were derived from the Jarvis journal. He specifically noted this incident as an example of general cultural misconceptions they encountered along the journey (Tuttle, 1899). Additional background on the beliefs behind the medical and spiritual practices of the Eskimos was drawn to assign greater reader understanding. This information was taken from Oswalt (1979).

In attempting to get a guide for the crossing, Jarvis noted, "Finally, by bribing, threatening, and offering shiploads of provisions, we managed to reach Toatut at Cape Espenberg." (Tuttle, 1899)

Anna Hunnicutt was sent to Cape Blossom by the Women's Foreign Missionary Society of Long Beach, California.

The Eskimo graveyard for which Perninyuk showed such reverence could have contained bodies buried in the ground, according to Christian traditions, or bodies suspended in the air, according to traditional Eskimo practice. Oswalt (1979) says:

> The word grave refers to bodies contained in the ground, or suspended in the air. Eskimo graves generally involved wooden boxes placed on top of poles, or buried under stones or snow. Some Eskimos followed Christian traditions and buried the body in the ground ... [where weather conditions allowed], while others followed native cultural traditions.

Chapter 24
Jim ... Deprivation

Supplies were taken from Point Barrow to the clusters of outlying ships, including the *Newport, Fearless, Rosario,* and *Jeanie* near Smith Bay to the east; and *Rosario* and *Belvedere* closer to Point Barrow. The ships, likewise, worked in concert to keep each other supplied and in communication through the use of sleds pulled by dogs, or propelled via a rigged sail.

The general deprivation represented in the chapter was drawn from the recorded suffering from scurvy and deaths from dropsy. They were drawn from Dr. Call's journal (Tuttle, 1899) and Charlie Brower's autobiography (Brower, 1942). It should be noted, however, that the Brower autobiography downplayed the poor conditions of the men, implying that he had the situation well in hand. This position led some to question the necessity of the mission. However, later reports by Dr. Call and David Jarvis upon their arrival indicated a grave state of affairs regarding the health and nutrition of the men. These reports further indicated an improvement in the men's health and diet upon the delivery of the deer. Therefore, it was concluded that the mission met its objectives.

Chapter 25
Lopp ... The Boys

By convention, Eskimos had one name, as in the case of the "boys": Tautuk, Ootenna, Kivyearzruk, Sokweena, Keuk, and Ituk. The only exception was Charlie Artisarlook, who adopted two names under European convention.

The events of the chapter including the death of selected deer crashing through the ice on Kotzebue Sound were drawn from both the Jarvis journal (Tuttle, 1899) and Lopp diary (Lopp, 1898).

The dialogue and references to Divine interaction were based on Tom Lopp's other attitudes as indicated in reports written by Lopp for Christian publications (Lopp, 1899) and (Lopp, 1892).

Chapter 26
Jarvis ... Finding Lopp

The events of the chapter were drawn from both the Jarvis journal (Tuttle, 1899) and the Lopp (1898) diary. The Eskimo youth that found Lopp was a former pupil at Cape Prince of Wales.

Chapter 27
Jim ... Scurvy Gets Worse

We don't know the name of the crewman whose death is depicted in this chapter. However, his death was attributed to dropsy. Dropsy symptoms are caused by a gross increase in the production of body fluids due to one or more organs being disturbed by virus, bacteria, or parasites. In this case, the crewman, already malnourished, probably received bad seal oil.

Because most historical references gave only an abbreviated summary of the events involving the whalers, there was no mention of actual funerals. Therefore, funeral traditions of the Eskimos were derived from Oswalt (1979). Given that Christianity was the dominant religion of whalers, a general Christian message was developed for the eulogy and placed within the context that a crewman could understand.

Chapter 29
Jarvis . . . The Reunion

Bertholf was unable to hold the two men, Shukurana and Avulik, accused of the murders he stopped to investigate. "After the killing, the two murderers left this place." His plan was to bring at least one of the accused murderers to the *Bear* without raising his suspicion by stating that they were there so he could collect his pay.

> It had been the custom of the natives to remain at the whaling station until the ships arrive . . . so as to get their pay . . . . I could easily have persuaded him to accompany me on board the *Bear* without raising his suspicion.

Bertholf found that nearly all witnesses to the crime were members of the tribe; unfortunately, they were unwilling to testify. One non-tribal witness, who may have been willing to appear at a trial, was coincidently en route southward. "Mr. Tilton . . . is probably in San Francisco."

It appears that Tilton had an uncanny knack of being in the wrong place at the wrong time. First he was chosen by Brower to risk his life as a messenger to the south, going by the more difficult of two routes, and second, he witnessed a violent crime on the way.

The travels of Lopp to the mountains and the meeting with Jarvis were drawn from Lopp's diary (Lopp, 1898) and the Jarvis journal (Tuttle, 1899).

It should be noted that significant verbal conflict erupted between Lopp and Nelson, the station manager who accompanied Jarvis on this leg of the trip. Their forced confinement in a tent during bad weather exasperated the situation. Lopp was very pro-Eskimo and had an appreciation for their culture. Nelson felt that Eskimos were "deadbeats." Following their discussions, Lopp summarized Nelson as a "jerk."

Chapter 30
Lopp . . . The Mountains

The depiction of Lopp's travels through the mountains was based on his personal journal (Lopp, 1898).

Chapter 31
Jarvis . . . No Help for the Last Miles

Several obstacles were summarized here as Jarvis found great difficulty making the last miles. In relation to the crossing of Kotzebue Sound and the mountains, they were of slightly lesser importance. Therefore, more emphasis was placed on the two major trials.

Chapter 32
Jim . . . Dying Men's Letters

The arrival of Jarvis, followed by Lopp and the herd days later, was met with great astonishment. Many crewmen looked out to sea for a ship, while others looked to the sky for balloons.

Charlie Brower felt that the reindeer weren't needed and that the trip had been made in vain. His joke to that effect caused the only recorded emotional outburst by Jarvis during the entire journey. "It was the first time I ever saw that fine but literal-minded officer really mad," stated Brower in his journal. However, based on the declining health of the crewmen, growing lawlessness, and deaths due to malnutrition-related ailments, the rescue party disagreed with Brower. In either case, the efforts, both at Point Barrow and by the rescue party, will always be regarded as among the greatest of human endeavors.

Miscellaneous

Sunrise and sunset information for background scenes not described in the journals was obtained from the Alaska Climate Research Center, University of Alaska Fairbanks.

Additional information on the Native American tribes encountered was provided by Frank Larson, United States Bureau of Indian Affairs.

The reader may be interested to know that Arthur Conan Doyle served as ship's surgeon on an Arctic whaler prior to this event. Despite being adept with a harpoon and being offered double wages for holding both jobs, he decided to return to England and become the writer we know today. Had he known of Bertholf's investigation into the Eskimo murders, perhaps he would have found material for one of his famous Sherlock Holmes mystery stories.

Bibliography

Belvedere Log (222), p. 39. *San Francisco Call* (1898, April 9).

Bertholf, Ellsworth P. (1899). "The Rescue of the Whalers." *Harpers New Monthly Magazine, 99,* p. 589.

Bockstoce, John. (1977, Spring). "The Arctic Whaling Disaster of 1897." *Prologue: The Journal of the National Archives, 9* (1), pp. 27-42.

Bockstoce, John R. (1986). *Whales, Ice and Men: The History of Whaling in the Western Arctic.* Seattle, Washington: University of Washington Press.

Brower, Charles (1942). *Fifty Years Below Zero. Journal of Charles Brower.* The Long Riders Guild Press.

Canney, Donald L. (1947). *U.S. Coast Guard and Revenue Cutters, 1790-1935.* Annapolis, Maryland: Naval Institute Press.

Cocke, Albert J. (1974). "Dr. Samuel J. Call." *The Alaska Journal, 4* (3).

Creighton, Margaret S. (1995). *Rites and Passages, The Experience of American Whaling, 1830-1870.* New York: Cambridge University Press.

Dana, Richard H. (1946). *Two Years Before the Mast: A Personal Narrative of Life at Sea.* Cleveland, Ohio: The Cleveland Publishing Company.

Jarvis, David. Unpublished Personal Journal.

Kaplan, H. R., & Hunt, James F. (1972). *This is the Coast Guard*. Cambridge, Maryland: Cornell Maritime Press, pp. 265-268.

Kroll, Douglas, C. (2002) *Ellsworth P. Bertholf, First Commandant of the Coast Guard*. Annapolis, Maryland: Naval Institute Press.

Lopp, William Thomas (1892, December). "A Year Alone in Alaska." *The American Missionary, 46,* 12.

Lopp, William Thomas (1898). Unpublished Personal Journal. Seattle, Washington: Property of the Lopp family.

Lopp, William Thomas (1899, July). "A Message from Alaska, Thrilling Experiences of Native Missionaries." *The American Missionary, 53,* (2).

Lopp-Smith, Kathleen (2002). Phone Interview, Seattle, Washington.

McIlhenney E. A. Personal Journal.

Oswalt, Wendell H. (1979). *Eskimos and Explorers*. Lincoln, Nebraska: University of Alaska Press.

Smith, Verbeck & Lopp-Smith, Kathleen (2001). *Ice Window: Letters from a Bering Strait Village 1892-1902*. Fairbanks, Alaska: University of Alaska Press.

Tuttle, Captain Francis (1899). *R.C.S. Report of the cruise of the Revenue Cutter Bear and the overland expedition for the relief of whalers in the Arctic Ocean, from November 27, 1897, to September 13, 1898.* The journals of Lieutenant David Jarvis, Lieutenant Ellsworth Bertholf, and Surgeon Samuel Call. Treasury Department Doc. 2101, Division of Revenue Cutter Service. Washington, D.C.: Government Printing Office.